Breathing While Drowning

One Woman's Quest for Wholeness

Veronica Strachan

Copyright © 2016 Veronica Strachan.

The moral right of the author has been asserted.

All rights reserved.

Excerpts from The Heroine's Journey: Woman's Quest for Wholeness, *Maureen Murdock*, © *1990, Maureen Murdock*. Reprinted by arrangement with The Permissions Company, Inc., on behalf of Shambhala Publications, Inc., www.shambhala.com.

Excerpt from Keele Burgin's blog, "Women", Keele Burgin, © 2013, Keele Burgin. Reprinted with permission. www.keeleburgin.com.

Some names in the journal entries have been altered to protect the privacy of certain individuals.

The views expressed in this work are solely those of the author.

The author of this book does not dispense medical advice or prescribe the use of any technique as a form of treatment for physical, emotional, or medical problems without the advice of a qualified medical or other health professional, either directly or indirectly. The intent of the author is only to offer information of a general nature to help you in your quest for emotional and spiritual well-being. In the event you use any of the information in this book for yourself, which is your right, the author assumes no responsibility for your actions.

Paperback ISBN: 978-0-6485134-0-7
Ebook ISBN: 978-0-6485134-1-4

 A catalogue record for this book is available from the National Library of Australia

To my darling Strack—born at last.

To my beautiful children: Cassi, Angus, and Frazer
— three more reasons to go on breathing and loving life.

To my darling Sweetpea Jacqueline Bree
— seed of my heart,
always loved, always missed.

Praise For Breathing While Drowning

Megan Dalla-Camina, Strategist and Author of Getting Real About Having It All

"Veronica is not only incredibly wise, with great wisdom to share, but she is incredibly brave. The way she shares her journey, in order that it may be of service to others, is courageous as much as it is kind. And it will indeed be of great support to others as they walk their own path."

Rachael Jayne Groover, Inspirational Speaker and Author of Powerful and Feminine

"Veronica is a gifted storyteller with a message of courage and hope that opened my heart. This story will inspire other women to take courage in their own quest to feel, heal and reconnect to themselves."

Sue Howard, Artist

"It is so beautifully, sensitively and honestly written. Lots of tissues, tears and smiles."

Corrinne Armour, Leadership Speaker, Trainer and Author

"Veronica is an amazing woman, just as so many of us are (and don't always realise). This book is an honest and inspiring account of her story. I do hope that it's writing helped her healing, and it's reading will help the healing of others."

Hafizah Ismail, Founder and CEO of Children of Jannah, and High Performance Coach

"*Breathing While Drowning* is an essential companion to anybody who wants to heal from a significant personal loss, reconnect to their dreams and live a joyful life again. By drawing on her own experience of the death of a child, Veronica compassionately guides the reader through their 'ocean of grief' and frustration, to find more vibrancy, passion and enthusiasm, in their time, at their pace. A wonderfully inspiring and uplifting book!"

Contents

Acknowledgements xi

Introduction xvii

Part 1–Defining Moments 1

    Chapter 1:   The Unremarkable Early Years 7
    Chapter 2:   The Unaware Years 21
    Chapter 3:   The Programme Years 73
    Chapter 4:   The Closure and Descent 190
    Chapter 5:   The Years of Guilt, Shame, and Despair 214

Part 2–Finding the Feeling: Do You Remember How It Really Feels to Feel? 295

    Chapter 6:   Is This as Good as It Gets? 297

Part 3–Where Do You Find Healing? 305

    Chapter 7:   The Search Begins 307
    Chapter 8:   Coming Home 348

Part 4–Searching for Connection 359

    Chapter 9:   A Conscious, Purposeful Life 361
    Chapter 10:   And now? 411

Thank you & About the Author 424

Bibliography 425

Acknowledgements

If I thought a heartfelt thank you would suffice, I would wish all the people in my life—past, present, and future—thank you from the bottom of my heart. I would thank you for the colour and texture you have added to the rich tapestry of my memories. I would thank everyone I've met on my quest—allies and ogres alike.

My journals were where I so often poured out my troubles, my angst, and my pain; my journals kept the things I couldn't or wouldn't share. So many happy experiences from the past twenty years are not recorded here; many good friends are not mentioned in these pages. This is, as all books are, only a part of the story. It's the story of me and Jacqui, and it's one that had to be told.

I'm a different person than the one who wrote all those years ago, and I've done a lot of soul-searching about what to leave in and what to leave out. I know if I'd asked for help earlier and more often, many more people would have come to my aid.

The journals don't mention everyone who helped with Jacqui's programme. I will be forever grateful for those fabulous people who turned up week after week and month after month to help with patterning, slides, reading, and games (and those who came when they could from far away or dropped off a meal to help).

I wish to thank the following people (and please excuse me if I forget to mention you by name): Alison Hanniford, Andrea Farrugia, Anne Garvey, Anne-Maree Fitzgerald, Barbara Turner, Barbara Olanda, Barbara Wersching, Beth Donovan, Bronwyn Atkinson, Caroline Patton, Chris McGrath, David Graham, Dolores Stirling, Elaine, Elle Hall, Fran Sullivan, Fred Zeinstra,

Gill Garth, Imelda Dunstan, Jacinta Collins, Jamie Patton, Janet Rickard, Jeanette Walker, Jenny Black, Jenny Garth, Jenny Shaw, Jodie Patton, John Meli, Julie Langtree, Katherine Morrison, Kay Jones, Kirsten Vandenberg, Leanne Haynes, Lisa Davenport, Loretta Conway, Lynn Molloy, Marg Knight, Margot Welsh, Marilyn Harnett, Mary Bretherton, Maryanne Bruce, Nick Patton, Noelene Ward, Nora Bailey, Pauline Graham, Peter Walker, Petra Puschak, Robert Black, Robin Drysdale, Robyn Angarano, Ronnie Zeinstra, Shirley Harry, Stewart Black, Sue Fox, Sue Howard, Sue Meli, Sue Mihailovic, Sue Patton, Sue Porter, Thelma Ronzio, Thelma Yourn, Tim Patton, Wally Vandenberg, and Yves Olanda.

Of course, I also wish to acknowledge my dad, Alan Patton, Jacqui's beloved Grandad, who always got one of her precious smiles no matter how she was feeling.

Some people are born to care for children, and Judy Shapcott is one of those amazing people. She was tireless and compassionate in her care for Jacqui and the rest of the Strachan clan; she has a special place in our hearts and memories.

Our paediatrician was a treasure we were lucky to have close by. She offered great support for Jacqui, Strack, and me. She was available when we needed her, and she was always calm. She supported our use of the Institutes programme, and she always treated Jacqui as an individual deserving of respect and care.

There is a small group of people who always believed that I would write a book and kept the faith for the decades it took to get it done. Sue Howard is my oldest friend; we've been friends since we were small girls playing in neighbouring backyards in Pascoe Vale. Though she lives on the other side of the country at the moment, it feels as though no time has passed whenever we get together. There's no need to explain; Sue knows my life story, and we just pick up the thread and go on knitting the tapestry of our friendship.

Janet Rickard and I started nursing together almost thirty years ago, and she always told me I was full of stories and good at making stuff up. Janet, the next book will be fiction ... maybe.

Veronica (Ronnie) Zeinstra came into my life when Jacqui started her programme more than twenty years ago. And she never left despite all the craziness and grief. She is very persistent, brave, and compassionate, and I love her dearly. Even now, there are some days she can't believe the adventures I get her into. Our latest is the Veronica's Radio Show on our local radio station, 100.7 Highlands FM, where we discuss all things health and well-being.

Lesley Thornton and I were going to write our books for NaNoWriMo a couple of years ago, but neither of us quite got there then. Ever since she waved at a woman she hoped was me from across the intersection at King and Collins Streets many years ago, Lesley has been a guiding force and good friend, always prepared to read a draft or share a glass of wine, to make plans or chat about our fraught health sector.

I need to extend special thanks to Anne Smyth for teaching me to think deeply no matter how much painful unpacking was needed to do so. Yes, Anne, you did help make me who I am.

Dr Cathy Balding is a force of nature, and I've loved being caught in the whirlwind since she persuaded me to take my first job in government. She was also the first person I knew personally who had written a book, and now she's written two. She gave me the shove to get started with my writing and to keep going.

I believe it's rarer to make true and beautiful friends late in life, but I've been lucky.

In one of my brief forays out of the health sector, I met Marguerite Davie, my other evolutionary partner and friend. Over many a late-night phone call, we've laughed and planned and talked about life, the universe, and everything. From our shared love of business, change, and good food and wine, we've made our part of the world a better place. Together, with Veronica Zeinstra, we have had many strange, interesting, and hilarious times. And most of all, we've kept the promise to love and keep each other growing, learning, and living lives that are bold, fun, inspired, and authentic.

When I wrote to Maureen Murdock and thanked her for writing *The Heroine's Journey*, she replied kindly and expressed her sympathy for the loss of Jacqui Bree and her love of the title of my book. Her book went a long way towards helping me find my way through my own quest, and the journey isn't over yet.

Keele Burgin was so gracious in providing her permission to share her blog about women, and I was thrilled that she wanted to chat about writing and escaping the world of business to find ourselves as women.

I've told Rachael Jayne Groover many times what a treasure she is for bringing her *Art of Feminine Presence* into the world. Along with thousands of women around the world, I thank you from my heart and my home for your grace and generosity.

Also, I wish to thank Glen Doman and Carl Delacarto (and all the people from the Institutes for the Achievement of Human Potential). They believed that all of our children deserved a chance to be well, and they have my never-ending gratitude for the difference they have made in so many lives.

Thanks must go to Megan Dalla-Camina for holding my hand while I finished chapter 3. She convinced me that soul writing was hard—and it certainly was—but I made it through.

And I must thank some mentors who don't know how much they've helped with their generosity: Christie Marie Sheldon, who opened me up to spiritual possibilities that could change the story of my life and Brendon Burchard, who showed me the way to find my message and share it with integrity and love.

Thank you for the encouragement and cheering from the Big Girls Pants Mastermind Group. They are our fabulous co-conspirators in The Art of Women's Business. I've learned so much from these amazing and courageous women.

To all the women who have spoken at or attended the Women Who Care Confabs and donated to the Strachan Clan Seil Fund: your time, conversations, and contributions are always welcome.

And thank you to all who are reading these pages as strangers (until now). All profits from every book purchased are donated to the Strachan Clan Seil Fund and the Australian Communities Foundation so we can support other families who have children who need our help.

Words are not enough to thank my darling children, Cassi, Angus, and Frazer, all of whom are the light of my life. They are loving and loved, angels. They know and love their other sister, and they respect the part she plays in our family. They've been patient and supportive while I've been writing and told me how proud they are that I've followed my dream and written this book. They know they have their own journals to read one day soon.

Finally, I must thank my darling Strack. We've been friends and lovers for more than thirty years. I could not have asked for a more loving, kind, and patient witness and partner in my life. It amazes me that our love continues to grow deeper and more beautiful with each year. Thank you for our beautiful Jacqui Bree.

Introduction

It's been a long time since I've thought about breathing as a chore; a long time since I had to tell myself over and over to breathe in and breathe out, get out of bed, take a shower, eat breakfast, go on living.

When did it change? When did the weight of shame, guilt, and responsibility sneak away from my shoulders? What warmed the cold, hard lump deep in my heart? How did that happen?

Breathing While Drowning is my story—a memoir of my life so far. It's my heroine's journey into despair, trials, and tribulations, and it's my quest to heal and return to living.

In so many ways it's Jacqueline Bree's story, written through the filter of her life, from birth to almost five. Without her, I would not be the woman I am: scarred, optimistic, visionary, resilient, impatient, passionate, creative, driven, selfish, mindful, curious, and caring. Without her, I would not have learned how to breathe while drowning in an unending ocean of grief.

This story will offer you hope that, in your most desperate moments, there's a way out. It will give you permission to dream that your life can be better, deeper, and more joyful. I'll share the things I learned that brought me out of the darkness and the desert of grief—and brought me back to my life, heart, and home.

I have three other gorgeous children: Cassi, Angus, and Frazer. They are the joy that I live for. And without the love of my beautiful soulmate, Ian (Strack)—a brilliant and patient husband; my man with a heart, who kept me afloat when, so often, I was drowning—I would not be able to share this part of our lives. But their story is for another day (and theirs to tell). They know how important they are to me; they know they're loved.

Breathing While Drowning is the story of a contemporary woman who is outwardly successful and inwardly lost. She searches for meaning, for feeling, for healing, and for reconnection. She longs for reconnection with the innocent, happy, creative, naive young woman she used to be. A young woman with impossible dreams who wishes for a remarkable life and gets exactly what she wishes for: just delivered in a way she could never have imagined. She experiences a whole new world of hurt, anger, loneliness, joy, triumph, and love.

The writing of *Breathing While Drowning* is me taking my own advice to put myself in the arena (I can hear the howls of laughter and righteous cheers from my friends and clients), to share my vulnerability, to share myself openly, without pretence or defensiveness. It's time to let down the barriers that have held me apart from my family, my friends, and the world; it's time to let myself be held by the experiences of my life without needing to defend against them. Sharing my vulnerability is the way forward, the way to growing my spirituality muscle. I'm learning that I have enough strength to surrender truly to who I am.

Brené Brown wrote, "Vulnerability sounds like truth and feels like courage. Truth and courage aren't always comfortable but they are never weakness."[1] I agree. The writing has not always been comfortable, and I continue to discover truths about myself with every chapter.

My mother was a great storyteller and could remember amazing details about her ancestors, relatives, and children. I didn't see myself as a great storyteller, however, so I kept a separate journal for all my children with the intent to eventually share the exciting moments and stories of their youth. I would pass it on to them when they were ready for their own children.

As Gloria Steinem famously said, "We teach what we need to learn, and write what we need to know."[2] I laughed out loud when I read that recently. I'm a life and leadership coach, teaching people how to find confidence and live the lives of their dreams. So, this job seems like a kind of cosmic karma for a woman who kept her dreams in a back drawer for twenty years! And as for writing what I needed to know, I wrote to Jacqueline Bree regularly throughout her short life (and sporadically for several years after she died). Rereading those moments with tears and smiles twenty years after writing them, I rediscovered a myriad of emotional, physical, and spiritual experiences and choices that shaped me and directed my future.

Now, with hindsight and the wisdom of years, I can look back on that young woman and see how far she's come, and what she and I learned along the way. I can view compassionately the experiences of her birthing a child with a disability; her refusal to accept Western medicine's prognosis; her search for answers, purpose, and direction; and how she and I fell into grief, and for almost twenty years lived as if we could never feel whole again.

Grief is never gone; there are still days when I have to remind myself to breathe, when I can't see the edge of the ocean, and when that drowning feeling threatens to engulf me. But I'm better at recognising the signs these days, and I know where the life buoys and dry land are. I know how to use them and how to ask for help.

I'm more conscious that my life belongs to me; that I don't have to be trapped in the stories; and that what I think, say, do, feel, and believe are what matter.

My last entry in Jacqui's journal, five years after she died—when she'd been gone longer than she'd been with us—I wrote that I was in transition.

'I have something left to give them when I come home.'

I was at a turning point, ready to start over.

> 'My children love me and I them. Life is good, so many things tell me that.
>
> I think I have stories inside. I'm not sure yet what kind but I know they are there, stories to share.
>
> Emotional resilience is what I have, strength inside is what others are drawn to, strength I get from loving you and knowing you. Both of us growing, you helping me see the choices clearly. I have a lot to offer but a lot to learn.'

That entry was fifteen years ago. When I first reread that, I thought, *Bloody hell, I'm still in the same place, freaking transitioning to something with stories left untold*. But then Ronnie Zeinstra, one of my very best friends, reminded me that if we find ourselves saying, "I wish I'd known that years ago," and we are just realising its value now, then this is the perfect time for us to know it, and do it, and be it. We are exactly where we need to be all the time.

Somehow, I keep going and going and going, becoming more passionate and committed to making a difference every day. I'm not content to live quietly; I want to help millions of people rediscover their hopes and dreams and live truly. Yet, on other days, all I want is to hide from the crazy, busy world, to sit at home on the couch with a cuppa and a good book, surrounded by family and love, sharing the small moments of our lives.

For me, it's always a balance between acknowledging and accepting the smallness of my everyday life whilst accepting the magnificence of my human potential.

Bethany Webster wrote, "We all desire to be real, to be seen accurately, to be recognised, and to be loved for who we really are in our full authenticity. This is a human need. The truth is that becoming our real selves involves being messy, big, intense, assertive and complex."³

Why share my full authenticity? What makes my messy life worth being seen accurately? Maybe I'll leave it up to you, the reader, to make a call on that. You know, sometimes I wonder why the hell I'm so freaking optimistic when I've had so much shit happen in my life.

Tara Mohr was recently asked, "What does it mean to you to live a good life?" She responded: "A good life is a life in which your soul learns what it came here to learn."⁴

So this story is me messily exploring the lessons my soul came here to learn. Otherwise, we're born, we live, and we die—and that's it. Where's the fun in that?

In her book, *Letters from Motherless Daughters*, Hope Edelman wrote about the struggle of women who lose their mothers when they're young. It works equally well for mothers losing a daughter. I lost both my mother and my daughter. One of Hope's messages helps describe why I'm writing this book. Some people will ask for help, but some (like me) will search quietly for a book: "A book seemed to be a safe and private way to check my feelings against some kind of standard, and I hoped to find one that would help explain what I was feeling – why, in spite of all my valiant attempts at stoicism, I still missed [Jacqui twenty weeks, twenty months, and twenty years after she died]."⁵

My hope is that this book, my exploration of the emotional and mental see-saw of my life, my search for feeling and healing and reconnection, makes you think differently about yourself and your life. I hope that you find something that inspires you to dust off those dreams, something that gives you some practical tools to help you get to the life that expresses the very best of your true self, and that your soul learns what it came here to learn.

If it's grief that brings you to these pages, I hope that my words encourage you to let go of fortitude and resilience from time to time, to reach out to someone and ask them to listen while you remember with love. There will be a way out of the ocean when you're ready. Take your time.

Women are so good at putting their yearning to the side, at serving and supporting others, that they forget to nourish and nurture themselves, to let themselves really feel.

Women, or at least the feminine part of women, are supposedly the holders of all things emotional. For a long while, I forgot that, discarded it, and disowned it. And my life was poorer for it. Not only poorer, but I was trying to live half a life, one without the innate, genetic, and generational wisdom and skills that are my birthright as a woman. I ranted against the prevailing depiction of women as emotional receivers and the importance of surrender.

I disliked that word—*surrender*—but more on that later.

What can my words do to inspire, instruct, or involve you? There are a growing number of women who are looking for the signposts on the journey, markers that say, "This way to your life's purpose." My suggestion is to stop searching outside for who you are, for meaning in your life. Look inside, take the most dangerous adventure, the journey to you, and start living it every moment. But don't get sucked in by the excitement and hype of the hero's journey because women have their own unique and powerful adventures that are way more fun.

I invite you to come with me on my quest, find a little gem or two that will help you on your own quest, and transform your life the way Jacqui Bree transformed mine.

If I'd not felt despair, would I have discovered that I'm one of the most optimistic people in the world? I believe every cloud has a silver lining—it's just that, occasionally, the clouds are so dark and freaking big that it takes a while for the silver lining to come into view!

Without having to battle complacency and apathy, I may never have discovered the depths of feeling that come with passion, enthusiasm, and commitment. I may never have realised how much I hated being defined by boxes, by other people's values and labels …

nor how easy it was to get out of those boxes once you realise you can. You can surprise yourself constantly with how easy it is.

I may never have discovered resilience, strength, courage, and many other things about myself, relationships, and the world. I'd like to share some of these with you.

Along the way, I discovered some lifelong and evolutionary friends who've made the journey amazing and fun.

I spent decades looking at the world through the filter of Jacqui's life. I was defined by this perspective, but now I'm not. Now I am the sum of all my experiences and the choices I've made.

When I was young, I defined *remarkable* as *extraordinary, exceptional, amazing,* and *wonderful*. My life was changed when I saw a grainy, black-and-white image of Neil Armstrong walking on the moon. I wanted to leave an imprint that would be remembered forever, like Neil's footprints on the moon.

In the opposite basket, among the things I didn't want to be, were the following: *ordinary, commonplace,* and *nice*. My parents said I could be anything I wanted to be, and I believed them ... even though the world was saying under its breath, "well, yes you can, up to a point, as long as you be a good girl, get married, have children, and do what you are told by all the blokes who run the world."

Remarkable is defined as *worthy of attention*. I think my life is exactly that—it's worthy of attention; my attention.

As I began my search for answers, I read a remarkable book, *The Heroine's Journey – Woman's Quest for Wholeness* by Maureen Murdock[6], and realised that I'm not the only one on this journey, nor am I the only who's been in this situation. And maybe by sharing, by honestly putting it out there, someone may find help like Maureen helped me.

"Women do have a quest at this time in our culture. It is the quest to fully embrace their feminine nature, learning how to value themselves as women and to heal the deep wound of the feminine. It is a very important inner journey toward being a fully integrated, balanced and whole human being. Like most journeys the path of the heroine is not easy, it has no well-defined guideposts nor recognisable tour guides. There is no map, no navigational chart, no chronological age when the journey begins. It follows no straight lines".[7]

My quest tracks the stages of the heroine's quest for wholeness through my memories. I share my intimate journal entries written to Jacqui twenty years ago and tell you how I feel about them and myself now. There's a little of my poetry and plenty of words of wisdom from my teachers and mentors. Because I'm a coach to the core, I can't help adding a few helpful tips along the way, things that worked for me, signposts and life buoys that kept me on track and breathing above the water line.

I've realised that I have beliefs, ideas I live by—a wo*manifesto,* if you will. Call me a feminist if you like; I certainly call myself one.

Don't let yourself by defined by other people's rules and expectations. You know the truth of who you are and what you want and can do.

Take time to grieve, all the time that you need.

Treasure every moment as if it will be your last. Show up for every moment with everything you've got.

Love your children.

Love your soulmate.

Love yourself.

Be the friend you would like your friends to be to you.

Be the change you want to see in the world. Go out and get it; don't wait for it to fall in your lap. Get into the arena, get dusty, get sweaty, and get bloody.

Live a curious life.

Live consciously.

Connect to your purpose and pursue it with vigour.

Take time out to breathe quietly.

Meditate.

Exercise.

Eat healthily.

Be healthy, wealthy, and wise.

Share everything you have wherever it's needed.

Sing loudly often, dance whenever you can, and laugh and laugh and laugh.

Say *yes* to every opportunity, even if it scares the hell out of you.

Deal with your stuff and let everyone else deal with theirs. (This doesn't apply to your children—it's your job as a parent to help them deal with their stuff until they are old enough to deal with it on their own.)

Trust your intuition; you know exactly what you need.

Do something creative every day.

Learn something every day.

Practice gratitude.

Always look for the good in people (sometimes its buried deep, but it's always there).

Bring the joy.

Laugh every day.

Follow your bliss and the universe will open doors where before there were walls.

Take time to smell the roses.

Never live with regret.

Get up just one more time.

Take time to dream—it hitches the soul to the stars.

Have conversations with purpose.

Live a life that expresses the very best of who you can be.

Love.

Show up, be present, and let go of the outcomes.

And write ... open a vein and write.

Megan Dalla-Camina wrote, "Our lives become what we think about most".[8]

The thing I thought about most for so many years was Jacqui's death (and the shame and guilt around that). The rest of the time was filled up with the agendas of other people: co-workers, and a little bit left for the rest of the family and friends. There was barely a skerrick left for me.

And I'm here to say that that was just fine. Take all the time you need to grieve—we're not meant to bury our children. When you're ready, the way back will be there, and when you find it, you'll realise it was always there. When the student is ready, the teacher appears. I have had some great teachers—some of them famous, some relatively unknown.

My love of learning and curiosity get me started, and my optimism and resilience keep me there until I have what I need.

I will never forget Jacqui Bree; she's too much a part of who I am, my family, my life. But now I spend my moments living and feeling, and I'm well on the path to healing and reconnection.

So what's the useful truth of my words, my memories, my quest for wholeness?

My wish for you is to have a remarkable life.

Live and grieve on your own terms; your life belongs to you, and everything you think, feel, do, and believe matters. And that's what counts.

Step into your unique and powerful heroine's journey and make the quest your own.

Stop searching outside for who you are, for meaning in your life. Look inside and take the most dangerous adventure: the journey to you.

Let yourself be surprised by life and the potential of you and those around you. Live life consciously, creatively, confidently, and remarkably.

Veronica Strachan

P.S. Since I completed writing Breathing While Drowning, I've created a companion workbook and journal that takes you through a series of exercises to deepen your learning experience and help you on your own quest for wholeness. You can find the workbook at www.veronicastrachan.com.au/the-workbook

Part 1

Defining Moments

When a child dies, the world sheds a tear. When that child is your own, an ocean of grief swallows you whole. You can't imagine how you can still be breathing when your child is not. When that child has had a fragile hold on life from the moment of her birth, and you've used every breath in your body to give her a life full of joy, you want to stop breathing when she does.

In the moment, you scream and wail and die inside. Your heart fills with pain, you plead for just one more minute; to turn the clock back; to make a different choice; to trade places—anything but the reality of the small, still body of your child in your arms. But it's true, your child is gone, and you're still breathing. You begin to drown in that dark, cold ocean. Your world takes on a sense of unreality, and you find yourself just going through the motions. It's the ultimate deception: pretending to live but really drowning.

With years of practice, you get really good at it. It's like life is happening behind a wall, a Perspex layer that keeps you numb, but lets you go on doing all the lifelike things to keep the world from seeing how hurt and broken you are. You're strong, you're courageous. Haven't you done well? Inside, you're pathetic, powerless, afraid to open up, guilty about your failure, and ashamed of your grief.

So how is it that one day you realise that you no longer have to tell yourself to breathe in and breathe out, to get out of bed, to take a shower, to eat breakfast, or to go on living? That, in fact, you're loving life, jumping out of bed, impatient to get the day started. You're going confidently in the direction of your dreams that have been dusted off and put at the top of the to-do list. Although the grief is still there, the ocean is only a small puddle that you unexpectedly step into from time to time. You still never know how deep that puddle is—and sometimes you find yourself in over your head, drowning again, gasping to breathe—but mostly the puddle just brings soft tears and smiles, love and compassion and gratitude for the beautiful gift of her short life.

Breathing While Drowning is me taking you on my own heroine's journey, the hardest of all; it is my journey replete with all my perfect imperfections. My hope is that, in my story, my exploration of feeling, healing and reconnection, you will find some inspiration for your own journey, a way to think differently about yourself and your life. I hope that, in thinking differently, you will find something practical that helps you remember the feeling, helps with your healing and reconnection, and lets you reach for those dreams so that you can live a conscious life that expresses the very best of who you are.

It's taken me almost twenty years, but I've rediscovered my reasons for living. They were right beside me all the time, loving me (broken and flawed as I am). I'm living for myself and for those who are still here and who love me: Strack, Cassi, Angus, and Frazer. I'm living for good friends and family and for people I've yet to meet. I'm living for people I can inspire, instruct, and involve in life, love, and laughter.

The first part of my journey starts out unremarkably, but then it gets dark before it spills back into the light. I've avoided putting these experiences into words for almost twenty years, so please be patient as I stumble around in the shadows for a while and get my bearings.

As Maureen Murdock says: "There are no maps, no signposts and the journey follows no straight lines".[1]

But I have the destination in mind, and I'll get you there eventually. I'm in the arena; there may be tears and tragedy, but there will be laughter and happy endings as well.

A Note on Journaling

I'm a writer and an introvert, so I've always found solace in putting pen to paper. The blank page has frequently been my best friend and the only way I could think and plan or share my thoughts, dreams, pain, and joy. I often found a few minutes to scribble a note about something in the wee hours of the morning, at the end of a long night-shift of nursing. Journal writing is cathartic and forgiving. No one needs to see the words, but putting them on paper does something for the thought—it gives it a voice, a presence that just *thinking about stuff* lacks.

My mum was a great storyteller and could tell you a tale of my great grandmother jumping off the jetty onto the ferry at Queenscliff with the three little pigs just in time to escape the big bad wolf, who fell into the water. She could tell you the special moments for all of her eight children—their milestones and joys. She told them with humour and drama, linking people and places and feelings. I loved her stories, and I still miss her dearly.

When my babies were born, I started a journal for each of them. That way, I could let them read the special moments once they were grown up. It was a way to record more than I could remember off the top of my head or scribble hastily onto the calendar. Of course, the firstborn, Cassandra Kate, has the most written about her. And then comes Jacqueline Bree, and then Angus Peter, and then my youngest, Frazer Douglas. As time went on, I got increasingly busy with living life rather than recording it.

For a while, I lost Jacqui's two volumes because I'd put them away when we moved a few years back. Strack found them just before Christmas this year (2014). He found them just in time for me to turn a new page, to begin again, to read all the memories ... good and bad, funny and sad. Lots of small moments, random thoughts, grand ideas, and momentous occasions.

How very glad I am that I wrote those journals.

Maria Popova, who blogs as *Brain Pickings,* says the following about journaling: "Journaling, writing the words, feeling the pain, opening the vein. What I can't say out loud I can write on the page. I can explore without snap judgement from others".[2]

In the same blog, she tells us that Anaïs Nin wrote: "Journaling is a practice that teaches us better than any other, the elusive art of solitude—to be present in our own selves, bear witness to our experience, and fully inhabit our inner lives."

She also includes this quote from Virginia Woolf: "A diary builds a bridge between our present selves and our future ones, which are notoriously cacophonous in their convictions." I love those last five words: notoriously cacophonous in their convictions.

Words have always held a special power in my life. When I was young, they would take me to another place. They had the power to hurt, but they also had the power to heal.

For many years, words were the only things I had to be honest with. Journaling was what kept me sane, kept me from drowning. So many pages are smeared with tears, and wretched with heartache. So many pages captured tiny, joyous moments that bring smiles and hoots of laughter.

Of books and reading, voraciously, searching for answers, Jo Bradshaw tells us the following about Claire Messud: "We are as much the sum of our lived literary experiences as of our literally lived experiences".[3] Yes, yes, and yes to that. Conversations with purpose—that's what I'm about. Journaling is a conversation with a purpose, a conversation with myself. The act offers a chance for the victim to wail, the fighter to plan, the creator to muse, the observer to reflect.

Breathing While Drowning

In the pages of my journals to Jacqui, I rediscovered a young woman with hopes and dreams, anger and passion, shame and innocence, grief and resilience. I see an unbearably optimistic woman who was destined to lead, to learn, and to love again. So this is my legacy: to share the lessons that helped me keep breathing while drowning.

Where is my writing voice to share with the world? For so many years, I have written in the third person for business—written impersonally from the outside. Now I feel like I'm opening a can of worms, sharing my vulnerability, my optimism, and my hope. My fingers keep bleeding on the sharp edges. What will I find if I dive in? Red Smith said, "There's nothing to writing. All you do is sit down at a typewriter and open a vein."

By the way, I'm also a life and leadership coach, and I can't help adding in a few lessons and tips along the way. Enjoy!

Well, I can't get any younger, so here goes....

Chapter 1

The Unremarkable Early Years

A couple of years ago, I read Maureen Murdock's *The Heroine's Journey – Woman's Quest for Wholeness*[1], and a whole lot of things fell into place for me with a big, fat clunk that must have been heard blocks away. I felt, as many women have, as though Maureen was a witness to my life. So many things she wrote resonated with my experience, my thoughts, and my feelings.

One of the best things to happen as I read was that I realised I wasn't alone. I wasn't even particularly special or unique (not remarkable at all). Many women were confused, lost, searching, yearning for purpose or forgiveness or love.

So as part of this book, I'm lining up my stories with Maureen Murdock's, *The Heroine's Journey*. I will attempt to incorporate the stages described in that text and work through my own journey, my own quest for wholeness. It's not always clean and clear—as Murdock writes, "The journey follows no straight lines"[2]—but stay with me and you might recognise yourself in here somewhere.

My life belongs to me, and what I think, feel, do, and believe matters—and that's what counts. It's taken me until now, at fifty-four years of age, to recognise those words in a way that my whole body and mind know it and know that it's right and true.

As Murdock points out, "Our society is androcentric: it sees the world from a male point of view".[3]

So is it any wonder that the first stage in *The Heroine's Journey* is to reject the feminine, to see it as something that's holding us back, that's not enough? "Men are rewarded for intelligence, drive, and dependability through position, prestige, and financial gain in the world".[4]

Women who try to be like men or see themselves through the male-centric lens in the world of work are not equally rewarded. As women, we will always find ourselves lacking if we look through the male-centric world value lens because we are not men. As women, we have our own world value lens, and we are enough in our own right. Both men and women are challenging the patriarchal forms and norms, but there is a personal journey to be taken, too. Murdock says, "The heroine's first task toward individuation is to separate from [the mother, the feminine]".[5] The devalued feminine seems insufficient, and the struggle with the separation can take your whole life. Initially, this separation is usually aimed at mothers. They, like their mothers for generations before them, are steeped in the low self-esteem experienced as part of living in a "culture that glorifies the masculine".[6]

Separation from the Feminine

So what about me? How do I see my separation from the feminine? For me, it isn't in one particular moment or year. I feel there are moments that fall under this part of the journey that happen over and over throughout my life.

I'll start at the beginning and then work the journey stuff in as it comes up.

Born the third child of eight to working-class parents in Melbourne's northern suburbs, I was as loved as all the other children who were squeezed into our small, suburban home. My parents worked hard to support the family, to help us become healthy adults capable of learning and loving. Though we didn't have a great deal of material wealth, there was always someone to play with or look after, and there were always chores to do.

I had the usual struggles growing up and finding myself in the middle of a large family. I watched the older ones do everything first and the younger ones get away with way more than I did. It was easy to stay under the radar and find a quiet corner to play or read.

Strack's childhood home was a little quieter, but it was just as loving. His parents emigrated from the United Kingdom when his older and only sister was two. Both his parents worked, and he learned independence early.

All our siblings were healthy and bright, and both sets of parents remained happily married all their lives.

When I reflect now, though I was happy and loved, childhood was also the beginning of feeling powerless and being guided by people who knew better: parents, older siblings, teachers, adults, men. I often think of the scene in the movie *Matilda* where the mean teacher says to Matilda: "I'm big, you're small, I'm right, you're wrong." She dismisses her as a girl of no consequence. No consequence, just one of the crowd; it's hard to have an identity when there are so many—so many that it was easy to forget one. At least that's what I remember. I was once left behind after a visit to my grandparents. I came out of the toilet to see my grandfather closing the door. The rest of the family had driven off without me.

Primary school was my introduction to the world of words and learning. I learned quickly and was happiest with my nose stuck in a book or writing stories (which was also a good way to get out of chores). I was quiet and shy, never quite one of the members of the popular crowd, but I had my best friend and a few others to play and grow with. I played netball and did well at athletics; I enjoyed the camaraderie of teams. Looking back now, though, I can see I often avoided crowds and more public events, content with my own company or close to home.

I spent many hours reading and learning about this world and others, even pretending to be asleep for the parental check and then turning the bedside lamp back on to read into the wee hours of the morning.

I wrote stories, mostly fairy tales or tales where I was secretly discovered as having magic power. And in those stories, I rarely belonged to the family I was living with. Wishful thinking, perhaps.

The thing I most remember at high school was being bullied for four years for being bright—the Australian tall poppy syndrome. (This is our national tendency to eagerly cut down anyone we see as successful in a given field, particularly if that person shows the slightest imperfection.) Up to that point, I'd been encouraged to learn. Now it was unpopular, and smart children were seen as arrogant or nerdy. Though the bullying was blatant, from my view the teachers and nuns did nothing to help or address the culture in the school, leaving me leery of religions that preached kindness, tolerance, and love but practiced meanness, intolerance, and fear.

In my penultimate year, I changed to a mixed-gender high school with far less focus on religion. And I found that boys were much easier to deal with than girls. In my experience, girls were often mean, and boys were mostly fun. They still teased me, (like brothers, and I had plenty of those) but they didn't hold grudges. The best thing was that some of the boys and girls were smarter than I was—and proud of it—and I wasn't seen as quite such an anomaly. Learning and striving to achieve were okay, especially if you happened to be male. Balance was restored. I re-established friendships I'd lost in primary school and made some good, new friends.

In retrospect, I was learning lessons about the patriarchy. Girls were apparently equal, allowed into the science and maths class, but we were still a minority and not quite in the club.

My mum was a traditional mother and housewife for most of my childhood. And although I didn't consciously try to distance myself from her way of life, I was encouraged to make the most of the opportunities she and Dad had given us through education and a loving home. Get a job, get married, have children—that was the unsaid message. What was not spoken about was making a difference, making a contribution to the world. My family didn't have a particular political or social passion. In fact, my dad would not even tell me who he voted for in elections. No, social passion doesn't ring quite true. A quiet achiever, my dad was always a part of his church groups, counting the donations, helping at the homeless men's centre, and transporting second-hand goods to those in need. Mum was involved as well, but with eight children, most of her energy was spent on us. In later years, when some of us had left home, Mum followed her dream and went back to school to earn her Higher School Certificate. She came home full of stories of injustice in Australian history and the beauty of English literature.

After high school, I followed my older siblings to university. I intended to do a biochemistry degree, but I found the lessons repeated much of what I learned in high school, and the disrespectful and spoilt eastern suburbs kids who ran rampant in the classes were too much to swallow. These kids seemed to have an expectation of privilege that stuck in my throat and made me angry. I was here to learn; they were here to mess around and disrupt. There was no adult intervention or discipline to curtail the riotous behaviour. University life was not quite what I wanted.

On reflection, the feeling that I was not quite good enough—I came from the wrong side of the Yarra, I was Catholic, and I was female—were all pretty heavy marks in the wrong column. But it was also the chance to do something on my own, unlike my older siblings. I left university to work as an office assistant in a frozen food factory where I grew up really fast among the truck drivers and storemen who embraced life with gusto and colourful language.

I applied to nursing school at the same time because one of my best friends who had always wanted to be a nurse was there and getting paid to learn, work, and have a great time. It sounded way more fun than university. Three months later, I was in my starched white uniform, my cap, my black shoes, and my red cape. I was all shiny and ready to begin.

Identification with the Masculine

The health sector has been my home for more than thirty-five years, and I still find it one of the best places to be. On my very first shift that I worked in a hospital, an elderly woman with chronic lung disease who'd been resuscitated the night before stated that she didn't want to be resuscitated again. In short, she wanted to die. That was my raw introduction to life-and-death struggles and people's frailties in the face of disease and a finite existence.

Working in health is tough, and it takes a certain practice to manage the see-saw balance in yourself to care for others but still function individually in the life-and-death struggles you see almost every day. Healthcare is often seeing people at their worst or lowest, at the most vulnerable and challenging times of their lives.

After almost four years, I couldn't wait to get out of my training hospital and see the world—free from the shackles of studying and the meanness of small-minded charge sisters and arrogant surgeons. Talk about separation from the feminine! Most of these women were tough as old boots and loved nothing more than forcefully pulling young nurses into line. You learned to take whatever was dished out and get on with it. If you got on the wrong side of anyone in power, you were history—they made life miserable.

Even though it'd been tough, I had lots of happy memories of that time and lots of firsts: living away from home, flying in an aeroplane, visiting another country, driving across Australia, dancing with strangers, getting drunk, and losing my virginity.

I worked in all sorts of places and locations in health. The pattern of my life was to move around, learn new things, meet new people, but never stay in one place too long. I kept things light and breezy, always competent and quietly building on my perfectionist proclivities. I also learned some hard lessons in responsibility, loyalty, deceit, power, politics, and life. There were many bullies in hospitals. Based on decades of military hierarchy, it was a culture where it was easy for bullying and misogyny to be disguised as discipline and order. I learned to do things well the first time, to put everyone else's needs ahead of my own, and to keep my head down and stay out of the spotlight. I was not a fighter or a rebel; rather, I was a survivor.

More lessons! People in leadership roles can be mean, selfish, and wrong. Just because they're in charge of the ward or the shift or the hospital, it doesn't mean they're in charge of your life or your career.

But like so many generations of women before me, I was not taught that my life belonged to me, that I was worthy of attention, that what I thought mattered.

Even when I moved into management—because that's what you did when you were smart—I didn't believe what I said mattered. My opinions were not my own, not really worth listening to most of the time. This was at odds with my natural inclination to be creative and innovative.

I had a highly analytical and strategic mind; I could see patterns and opportunities for improving things. Sometimes people listened, sometimes they took my idea as their own, and sometimes I was ignored. I learned mostly about the kind of leader I didn't want to be and, occasionally, I worked with the kind of leader I did want to be. These leaders, mostly women, were smart, compassionate, and capable. They inspired, they instructed, and they involved people in their vision. They never expected more of people than they offered themselves. They made me feel like I was part of something bigger, something important. And they made me believe I had what it took to get the job done.

I moved interstate to Tasmania, ostensibly to do an intensive care course, but in reality to find myself, my own identity—who I was and what I was supposed to do with my life once away from the loudness and intensity of my family. I guess I did find myself somewhat. The few experiments I made in trying to be different, to be more confident, had mixed success. But while I was there, the love of my life found me and enticed me back to Melbourne rather than me heading off to Europe solo (as I'd planned).

I stayed in Melbourne and did midwifery instead. Strack and I got engaged, found an acre of land an hour out of the city, got married, and moved into our semi-complete, mud-brick house. (Warning for any owner–builders out there: your house is never done. Even after thirty years, we still have bits and pieces unfinished.) The trouble with moving in before it's finished is that you stop seeing what needs to be done. And of course, now that it's thirty years old, there are things that need fixing and replacing to add to the list of things that never got done in the first place.

But on the plus side, our house is a home, lived in and loved, full of happy memories. The flotsam and jetsam of family life lived fully litter the hallways and grooves—there's not much time for housekeeping. Let's face it, mud bricks and exposed, unfinished timber make for great cobweb and dust gatherers. It all adds to the ambience. And this suits me because I am so not a housekeeper … a once-in-a-while neatness is fine by me. There's comfort in disorder, which is different from how I feel at work. At work, all must be in order, tidy, a place for everything. Maybe that's the masculine keeping me on the path. At home, I surrender to feminine, spontaneous, flowing reality.

I created a strange reality when I started my own business and started working from home. I have a corner of the house—it's an open-plan space and, in the beginning, I often struggled to get my head into business because I was easily distracted.

Life rearranging itself, something new, never standing still, never content, always searching—this is the map of my life. My searching began as a child: I had an insatiable curiosity … Why do things work? How do they work? I always liked to get in to the nitty gritty, right down to the microscopic and quantum level.

Becoming a wife was joyful and wonderful and hard. The joyful bit was finding my man with heart who loved me and wanted to share his life with me, witnessing through sickness and health, richer and poorer. Mind you, when you're young, it's hard to imagine the sickness and the poorer bit because it all seems so theoretical.

The hard bit was that, for a while there, I lost my independence because this person loved me. I got caught up in the story of being in a relationship and forgot that my life belonged to me. I forgot that what I think, feel, do, and believe matters. I caught the fairy tale and lost some of the independence I had been nurturing. I'd been totally independent as I travelled, worked and thought as an individual.

There's one memory that stands out around that time. I was living in East Melbourne and often shopped in Collingwood. I had a good radar for trouble and could keep myself safe. Strack and I were on our way out somewhere, and I needed to stop and get cash from the ATM. I got out on my own and was almost finished when Strack got out and stood beside me. As I looked up, a young man of dubious character was stumbling past. Strack felt the need to protect me. In that moment, I remember feeling cherished. How wonderful it was to be protected by this man who loved me.

And almost without realising, I handed over some of my self to our relationship. It wasn't something that Strack asked for; rather, it was something I gave. And it took me a long time to realise that I needed it back. What I gave was too much of my independence, my sense of being whole and complete as just me. I put the centre of my being outside my body and into the relationship. Talk about separation from the feminine!

This realisation takes nothing from our love and relationship. I've known this wonderful man since he was sixteen, almost forty years, and we've been married for more than thirty of those years.

Two years later, baby number one was born. Cassandra Kate. She was a delightfully easy child, all blonde and pink. Although I came to love her dearly, I didn't enjoy being a full-time mother at home. I was lonely (even introverts need other people sometimes). We needed money though, so I went back to part-time work twelve weeks after Cassi's birth. I shared the childcare with Strack.

Becoming a mother was much harder than I could possibly have imagined even though I'd been a midwife for five years. The first six weeks was fine because I knew all the things I had to do. What I didn't realise was that you fall in love with your children. Sometimes it doesn't happen immediately—at least it didn't with me. It took a few weeks, and as Cassi became aware of me, started to look into my eyes and smile, I found myself sitting with her in my arms for hours, just watching her sleep, looking at this amazing creature that I had created and nurtured in my body, given life to. She was so perfect, so beautiful.

Nothing prepares you for motherhood except motherhood. You begin to understand your own mother more, and it's a time of growing up, separating from your own mother.

Being Cassi's mother was a slow awakening to joy, but it was tough, too. I quickly realised I didn't want to be a stay-at-home mother. I wanted adult conversations and had dreams of bigger things. I wanted to make my mark on the world, to live a remarkable life. Cassi was incredibly bright and beautiful, and she was full of life and energy and words. Neither of us enjoyed long stretches of days on our own at home. We would search out any excuse to jump in the car and go elsewhere.

I really struggled with motherhood and probably had some degree of post-natal depression—or it could have just been adjusting to a new stage of life. I lived only fifty kilometres out of the city, but I may as well have been on the moon. It was a small town with only a few first-time mothers around. Cassi was six months older than most, and she was way ahead on her growing milestones. Most of the mothers were local and had good support networks. I didn't know anyone locally, and my mother lived forty-five minutes away and had breast cancer.

I grew up in a world where women were beginning to step out from the yoke of paternalism and demand equal rights. I was a child of the sixties, so my choice was to rail and rant and push against what I saw as the constraints—shackles, if you like—of the traditional motherhood role. It felt like I was drowning in isolation, I had to get out. I had to have adult conversations that were about things other than babies and houses and husbands.

I've always wanted to do things differently, sometimes I've been able to achieve that, sometimes I've buckled under pressure. My life in a series of moments is kind of funny when I think about it. And the greatest learning I've accomplished has occurred when looking back, looking within, and being here and now.

I like Fairchild's quote: "To accept the smallness of your everyday life whilst admitting to the magnificence of your being, to open up to the divine light that pours through you into a myriad of forms, endlessly creating, destroying, creating again – this is your sacred task".[7]

When Cassi was born, life was rosy. Strack and I were a young couple with a half-finished house. We were both from working-class families. We were doing the usual thing with some individuality thrown in for good measure. Basically, however, we were middle-of-the road folks.

I'd never been a particularly maternal person despite being a midwife for twenty years and, luckily for her, my first daughter was a perfect child who followed all the rules. With blonde hair, blue eyes—the image of her dad—and a bright mind, she reached all her milestones early and slipped into our family with little fuss and lots of joy. My sheltered, perfect life continued with her arrival. I was distantly but clinically aware of such things as disability and imperfect children, but these were not things that had crossed my mind.

The lessons I learned about myself and the world that I realised then—and that I realise now—mean a lot of different things.

The lessons I learned the most from tended to be the tough ones. So even though there was much joy in these years, I've included some of the challenging lessons here.

So many rules, so many judgements, so many perceptions, so many realities created in childhood and early adulthood.

Lesson: love your kids, give them space, help them learn resilience, and give them your presence not your presents. Live the life that expresses the very best of who you can be, and show them that it's worth it and can be done.

My unconscious disconnection from the feminine began early with being smart; girls aren't rewarded for being smart. The messages were mixed—it's great that you're smart, but don't be too smart because you might embarrass a boy somewhere. Girls can be smart at feminine things, but girls can't do science.

Generations of subservience for women. You need to put everybody else first. You can dream, but get a real job. But you'll only need that job until you have babies, then give it all up.

Lesson: girls can do anything they want to do. So can boys. Let it go and let people be what they want. Women are saving the world because we value love above competing with each other to win. We want to be happy and have lives full of joy.

I learned how to fly under the radar. It doesn't pay to be smart—don't shine too brightly because someone will want to put out your light or dim it so they can shine brighter or keep everyone else in the dark.

Lesson: you owe it to yourself and the rest of the world to shine because you shining brightly gives others permission to do the same (thanks, Marianne Williamson). Can you imagine a world in which everyone was shining?

Don't get above your station, stay in your box with your label firmly around your neck. Stay in control; don't express your emotion.

Breathing While Drowning

Lesson: they can only put you in a box if you're willing to stay there. Take the lid off, step out, and move on. Listen to your own music and dance down that road.

Adults don't always do the right thing. Adults can be cruel and dumb and make you feel guilt and shame when you don't deserve such emotions. —Also, girls are mean.

Lesson: yep, that's all true. Get over it, get your act together, and show the world you can do better. The best revenge is success. Raise your vibrations, learn gratitude and joy, share kindness, and practice compassion. Find your inner mean girl and love her even more.

I learned that I hate conflict. I've avoided it as much as possible because it makes me feel frightened, afraid that I or someone I love will be hurt, afraid I won't be loved. I worry I'll end up alone.

Lesson: conflict happens. The best ways to avoid conflict include living with love and compassion, getting clarity about your purpose, and living lovingly. There will still be conflict, but you will have given it your best shot. And the aftermath is that you will let it go, you will learn something, and you'll get over it. You'll keep on breathing. And you won't be alone. You will have you, and you are enough.

You have to pay your dues. You have to work hard for what you want.

Lesson: the pay your dues part is such a crock. If you want access to a community, spend time learning, watching, reflecting, and progressing. But the work hard part is true, work hard for what you want; nobody else is going to do it for you. They're your dreams, and it's your purpose. Just remember to give yourself some slack (self-compassion) every now and again.

Despite the ups and downs of childhood, I am an optimist. I can see the good in almost anything, and I get more optimistic as I get older. I'm a futurist, always plotting and strategising, which is great for my clients. My greatest personal challenge is to stay in this moment, savour the joy and sadness, the love and fear, and the act of learning. Don't let the emotion pass you by, and don't focus on the good stuff exclusively—it's all there to give us food for thought, to help us learn.

Chapter 2

The Unaware Years

Two years later and baby number two was on the way. I could see my life unfolding down a traditional path, and I wanted to get off that path so badly. I found the routine of my life constraining, and I wanted to do things out in the world, remarkable things, I could see my dreams drifting further and further away.

Jacqueline Bree slipped quietly into the world on 28 October 1990. She had a flock of dark hair, and we had no idea what she was bringing into our lives by her very existence.

Her birth was easy, but from the beginning, things were not perfect. She had a mildly twisted foot and, a few hours after her birth, I was bundled into a taxi with her and sent off to get a plaster applied to her leg from toes to thigh. When I took her home, she was a very sleepy, very floppy baby. To top it all off, she didn't grow well.

The Road of Trials

Murdock suggests that the road of trials can be seen and felt each time we cross a threshold or leave the safety of home and what we know to go into the unknown (including going to school, starting a new job, or embracing a new relationship). The road allows us to discover our strengths and abilities and uncover and overcome our weaknesses. It also gives the heroine lots of opportunities to "look at and experience her positive qualities as well as the negative aspects of herself that she projects onto others".[1]

And then Murdock goes on to explain *why* the road of trials is important. Once on the road and away from home, separated from the feminine, the heroine can't blame anyone else for the outcome of her life. Instead, she has to look to herself, look within herself—"Her task is to take the sword of her truth, find the sound of her voice, and choose the path of her destiny. Thus she will find the treasure of her seeking".[2]

With Jacqueline Bree's arrival, my life left the traditional track—any track, really. In fact, it was more like an express train leaping over the rails in a Bruce Willis movie. I had planted my feet firmly on the road of trials, and I was beset by dragons and ogres … lots and lots of them. At that stage, I thought I had only just begun; I had no idea of the journey ahead and the treasures I would uncover.

Saturday 19th January 1991

Jacqui, I finally feel I can begin to put pen to paper for you. You will be 12 weeks old tomorrow. 2 days late and after 1 false alarm you made your way into the world. It was the night Summer Daylight Saving commenced so you were born at 0300 Winter Time and 0400 Summer Time.

I can't say you haven't worried us, almost from the word go. You have a left talipes equinovarus which was in a plaster cast toe to thigh the day after you were born. I think I fell in love with you that first day. Sitting in the doctor's waiting room you were so tiny and helpless and mine.

Breathing While Drowning

Your face was so serene, with only 5 milia spots over your left cheek. And dark hair! Wonderful. Everybody kept saying how much like Cassie[1] you were but all I could see was this beautiful petite face framed by a crop of dark hair.

When we got home you promptly went to sleep. It has taken you almost 12 weeks to wake up again. We can't decide whether it is just you, or if there is actually something wrong. We are taking you back to see the paediatrician on Monday. I've shed quite a few tears for you already. Anxious mostly about what the future holds for you. You are so precious to me and to your Dad.

I guess I finally feel you may be okay because today you've given me the most beautiful smiles. At last! You were sitting up in the little Frazer Seat watching us do the dishes and get ready for lunch.

You are on the blanket on the floor at the moment and starting to get hungry. Little bird cries and arms swimming.

An anxious few weeks coming up. Have to see the paed on Monday, then the following week for surgery on your foot. The less said and thought the better. My little babe under the knife. It will be a hard few days.

---

[1] Cassi dropped the 'e' from her name in 1999 when she switched allegiance from favouring even numbers to odd, most journal entries pre-date this decision.

Reading that first entry almost twenty-four years later, I can remember the worry, the hope, and the unknowing surrounding Jacqui Bree's birth. We were so naive, so raw. Our parenthood blank slates were waiting to be filled with colour and movement. Little did we know that those first few (hard) days I wrote about were just the beginning, that things were going to get much harder. We would have to find uncharted depths and breadths in ourselves, and the road would be years long.

Monday 21st January 1991

12 week check up with the Paed.

Devastation, there may be a problem. How do we deal with a maybe? Try not to think too much. Mum looks faded and dreadful. Dad worn out. So we play it down a bit. I feel like unloading but I can't. Ian talks a bit about how he's coping. We are hanging on to each other. The love is there, strong and silent. Cheerful too.

When Jacqui Bree missed each growth milestone, we searched for answers and help from Western medicine. This was when my powerlessness story started to get some real ammunition. I knew the health system and worked in the medical patriarchy. I'd been a good soldier, done all the right things, paid my dues, taken my medicine. So why didn't they have the answers? Why couldn't they help? Why did I feel like such an outsider? Why did I feel like I'd somehow rocked the boat? I made a whole lot of people really uncomfortable with my searching for answers other than the one's they wanted us to believe.

And Jacqui kept us focused on the moment. We began to realise how precious each moment was, how each breath or smile was precious—not just for her, but for all of us. This is a lesson I keep encountering: live this moment fully.

Breathing While Drowning

Saturday 23rd February 1991

Jacqui, we nearly lost you. It's hard to talk about it but I guess it will get easier with time. We got a call to take you to the hospital on Thursday 31st Jan 1991. So off we chooff, you & I & Cass. Cassie got dropped at Nana's place for a holiday & you & I were admitted for a routine operation. One night in hospital, possibly two! Your Dad & I handed you over to the anaesthetist about 9 o'clock. We went back to the ward to wait. We received a call at 1030 that basically said they had trouble after the operation with your breathing. They had to reinsert the endotracheal tube because you wouldn't breathe on your own.

By the time the anaesthetist came and got us we were nearly demented thinking we were going to lose you. But you were okay. So we came to Recovery & saw
you, so tiny, with one arm splinted with an I.V. an enormous plaster on your left leg. The operation had gone well. Then you stopped breathing again. They asked us to go out. Your Dad grabbed my hand & said "What did you have to do that for Jacq?" A few minutes later we went back in & you were okay. For the next 2½ hours you were basically out cold. We tried to wake you up a few times with no success.

Then while only I was sitting with you, you stopped breathing again & your heart started to slow down. I screamed for help & a nurse came running. Luckily another anaesthetist had just come out & started ventilating you. You also needed adrenaline. He said "You don't want to get any closer than that!" I don't even know his name but I'll never forget him. The sight of my darling daughter going blue and apnoeic in front of me is an image I'll find hard to forget.

If I hadn't been there you would in all probability be dead. It's as plain as that. If I do nothing else in my life, hopefully you'll be grateful to me for this. I still have a kind of numbness around my heart when I think of those moments. Someone is watching you. You spent the next 18 hours in ICU with a naloxone infusion. Not much fun. Then back to 3W where you proceeded to go dusky on me again. Mucous was obstructing your airways, but you were still very sleepy. Another dose of Narcain & you slept for another 4 hours.

Finally, at 4 o'clock Saturday afternoon, you woke for a feed and were almost your normal self.

The experience doesn't seem to have done you any harm. We saw the orthopod yesterday & got good news. Your plaster will come off in 2-3 weeks for good. Then you'll be able to have baths with Cassie.

> We still have to get your eyes checked on 8th March. I'm happy that you're developing better & catching up a bit. You look around much more & seem to be aware of your surroundings. When you are on the floor you are rocking side to side to try & get things and you are looking further afield. Your smiles are getting very cheeky and sometimes you cry until you are picked up then you smile & carry on. Very bold! But very, very precious. Also, your hair is growing. It's starting to get fluffy.

In my world, children don't have brushes with death; that's for adults, the elderly, the infirm, and the fearless. Children are loved, and they grow and play and learn and fill the world with imaginative ideas. But life is not a storybook; it doesn't always go to plan.

Every moment we had Jacqui taught us to treasure what we had, the real things in our hands. Take joy in the small things. When the changes are so small, you have to watch closely or you'll miss it. Be there.

Tuesday 23rd April 1991

> Your first tooth appeared today, bottom left front. Another big day tomorrow Jacqui. A visit to the neurologist. He is going to suggest we give you an MRI scan of your brain which requires a 45 minute anaesthetic. Naturally we are reluctant, unless he can convince us it will be able to do something positive for you. We don't want to put you through

unnecessary risks. You are improving well with physiotherapy. I still think you are a very solemn soul.

Sometimes, downright grouchy, especially first thing in the morning it is impossible to get a smile. All you want is food, right then & there. Even after 1 side it's still hard to get a smile.

After lunch you're better. You start to brighten up and get active & happy. You are starting to get to your toys too. Cookie & Big Bird get a bit of a bashing. You have also started to give yourself squeezes. Eyes shut, face screwed up, hands & legs tucked up, very cute.

Solids are going well, when you're awake enough to eat them. I'm trying to get you to have extra drinks as your bowels are a bit slow but most days it's pretty difficult. By the time you've had milk & a play you're ready to sleep again.

We are counting down the weeks till your Dad is finished at work. I hope I can still manage to feed you. You are still such a precious little bundle, I'm sure it helps you to be steady after you've had a feed. Jacqui Bree I love you dearly, even if you give most of your smiles to your Dad.

Your hair is growing and sticks up a bit on top. It's staying dark which is wonderful. I have to have someone look like me. Sorry it has to be you.

Breathing While Drowning

> I wonder how much of you and Cassie will be recognisable as me & how much as your Dad.
>
> Cassie seems to be a dynamo with her own personality way out in front. But gorgeous.

We found out later that the squeezes Jacqui was giving herself were epileptic seizures.

We spent a lot of time with doctors and in hospitals as inpatients and outpatients. All they wanted to do was put Jacqui Bree in a box, find a label, and give her drugs. Several of them told us to go home and let her die. All we wanted to do was the complete opposite: find answers and help her live. The Grow Foundation expresses it beautifully: "The only thing worse than being told that your child has a disability is being told that nothing can be done".[3]

The realisation gradually dawned on us: if we didn't do anything, the world was prepared to let Jacqui die with a life unrealised. We did not let that happen. We became parents of a child with a disability and adjusted our present and our future to match. I had to become a warrior, fighting for Jacqui's right to a life lived fully. I had to leave any soft, feminine mothering to someone else.

And all through this, I maintained my optimism—if we just did certain things, everything would be better; if Jacqui just managed one particular thing, everything would be better. I learned resilience.

I felt badly let down, and I'd learned that Western medicine, my Western medicine, did not have all the answers. The arrogance of the system was that they were right, I was wrong; they were big, I was small. They thought I should accept my lot and stay out of the way—I was embarrassing, an anomaly. I was not one of the club and didn't belong. I wasn't enough. I'd done something wrong and made an imperfect child. I tucked that away because there was no time to look at that. This beautiful and perfectly imperfect child I loved and wanted so much more for. I was prepared to fight for her right to live, to fight more for her than for myself.

We started a programme of physiotherapy and speech therapy, which meant lots of trips to the city for the whole crew.

Thursday 30th May 1991

Jacqui, I think the pressure & pace are starting to get to your Dad & I. Even though we try to be positive and encouraging it's hard to maintain. Your progress seems to have slowed a bit at the moment, though I can still see improvement every day. You can now look at me for 2 or 3 seconds before your eyes flick away. You are beginning to hold your head under control a bit more also. But you are still a "night owl". 1 o'clock yesterday morning. I had worked till 11 and when I got home you were supposed to be in bed asleep. No way, bright-eyed and bushy-tailed! I hate to let you cry at that stage because you are so alert & happy. I wish you would be like that in the morning. You are a different person grouchy & antisocial.

You get bored if we try too many exercises or use the same toys too much. We have to start giving you some weight through your arms & legs now in an effort to work towards sitting Unfortunately the current physio is leaving in a month to have a baby, so I hope we get a nice one to replace her. We've also seen a speech therapist who has given us a few things to do to encourage your "pre-communication skills".

Your day is so full, between exercises, nappy changes, milk drinks, solids 3X and sleep, there is not much time for playing, for neither you or I. Nana is still very sick, she held you in her arms today, singing her tuneless song in her flat Patton voice, you loved it, giving her smiles and cuddling in. I wonder if she was thinking whether or not she would see you grow up? You were responding to her beautifully, smiling all through your banana yoghurt dessert!

We have to keep giving you as much time as we can. These early years are so important. We will never get the chance again to help you start out right. I think of you a lot, even if you're asleep. I wonder what you'll do next & what next year or two will hold.

It will be much easier when your Dad is home. I get so lonely some days, even though I have you & Cassie, I often yearn for an adult to talk to & discuss things with. I want to spend every minute with you, yet after a couple of days at home I'm nearly demented. You just can't win!

My own mother, who would have been a great source of love and support, was dying of a particularly aggressive form of breast cancer when Jacqui was born. The cancer was a result of being given hormone treatments following a hysterectomy. Bloody Western medicine.

Although Mum knew Jacqui had something happening, it was all she could do to keep herself going. She told me Jacqui was a gift, a blessing from God, and that I'd have to be strong for everyone. I couldn't see how Mum's merciful God would give an innocent child so much to bear. What had Jacqui done to deserve this? Why pick me? What had I done? What had Strack and I done to deserve this? Mum was a beautiful, generous, and loving soul—what had she done to deserve cancer?

I felt so alone. I'd failed at motherhood and couldn't talk about it to anyone. I didn't know how to express my horror and loneliness; friends didn't know how to approach the subject. Some tried to skirt around it, but it was like a raw wound; all I wanted was the scab to stay on and my life to go back to being predictable. I wanted to be normal, to belong.

I continued to pour out my thoughts and feelings onto the pages of my journals, finding a willing and sympathetic ear in myself. This is a practice that has helped me for years, but it has its shortcomings. Too much writing about emotion to myself and not enough experiencing and sharing openly left me a bit barren on the emotional side, a bit of a novice when it came to being whole. In later years, I tended to shy away from people who expressed their emotions readily and easily. It took me years of work to get the lid off and learn to leave it off. In the meantime, it was all I could do not to scald everyone in the immediate vicinity when I let off emotional steam.

Breathing While Drowning

<u>Wednesday 10th July 1991</u>

> *Jacqui, your Dad and I are gradually coming to terms with your problems. They aren't going away and may be with you forever. We will do everything in our power to help you reach your greatest potential.*

This is one of the first times I wrote this, and I kept writing it over and over again. My baby girl was almost nine months old.

This is where my passion and purpose come from for my second life, my reincarnated career. I help people open the door to their potential, to live the life that expresses the very best of who they can be. I start where they are and go for progress, not perfection.

> *You are getting stronger by the day but your head is still too heavy sometimes. You can't hold on to your toys yet, but you can give them a good bash. They are getting more & more controlled movement. The new physio is so-so at the moment. I hope she improves quickly. Your time is so precious. Your Dad & I took you shopping the other day & you decided to laugh. It made me cry, it was so wonderful to hear the joyful sound coming from you.*
>
> *Your Dad hadn't heard you laugh for months so he was rapt.*

When Jacqui laughed, we all stopped because it was so precious. Our faces would crack, and overwhelming joy would burst from every pore. Life would be worth living again. It would give us hope. Surely, we thought, *if she is capable of such joy, she is capable of anything.*

He has finished work now & is home full time. I'm still not sure how he is going to manage. I think he'll be physically more organised than I am but emotionally it's going to be a strain, especially with you. I think he may find the realities of your condition hard to cope with, as I do myself.

We are going to try a playgroup for children with "special needs". I hate it when you get called a "special" baby. Both my girls are very special to me, but "special" in that it implies "abnormal". You may still be able to catch up physically to your peers.

We'll have to go & see the neurologist soon for a check-up. I'm not happy with a couple of things. One is your startle reflex, which persists & sometimes seems to happen for no reason, it's almost like all your muscles spasm & your head turns to one side. You seem to smile after you've done it and don't seem to lose consciousness. It is becoming more definite though. I'll have to start counting & try & observe when & why you do it.

The other point to note is when you seem to shut down for a few seconds. Eyes half closed, staring at nothing, lying still. It's probably just that you're tired & need 40 winks. I know I'm starting to sound paranoid. I worry about you so much.

Breathing While Drowning

Both of these movements were epileptic seizures. I had a right to worry.

> You are not going to remember your Nana, my Mum. She is dying a slow & painful death from breast cancer at the moment. It's hard to look at her & not cry. Her hair has fallen out, her face is gaunt with no light or life due to large doses of morphine for pain.
>
> She was always such an active happy person, it's cruel to see her like this. She is in hospital at present while they try to kill the pain without killing her with nausea & vomiting. I'm beginning to wish she'd die quickly & not suffer any more. Even if this chemotherapy holds off the inevitable, what sort of days & nights will she have?
>
> She asked me the other day to discuss with Mary & Imelda which of her rings we would like. I think she's becoming a bit frightened that the end is near.
>
> I am going to miss her so much. There is so much I want to say. She has always been such a loving & giving person it doesn't seem fair that she is not going to enjoy her old age watching children & grandchildren growing up.
>
> If I could be half the mother & friend she has been, I'd be happy.

I was about to enter the long, dark night of becoming a motherless daughter.

> *You have a new tooth, left front top & right front top looming down soon.*
>
> *I hope you didn't stay up too late last night & run your Dad ragged. You get such a cheeky grin on your face when you are awake late, I swear you know it's nearly midnight. You chewed your first biscuit yesterday & had a drink from a cup too. Big day!*

I was not paranoid, just an observant and intuitive mother who loved her daughter. I got so used to watching her, watching over her.

I chose to go back to a full-time job. Ian chose to stay home with our girls. That was a tough gig for a bloke in those days—especially given our home in a small country town with few babies. He did and still does an amazing job parenting our beautiful offspring.

Our life was an emotional roller coaster. The highs were so high but so brief, and the lows were so low and so long.

Wednesday 24th July 1991

> *Another emotional day. You had an E.E.G. today to check whether you are having seizures. I don't think you are, but at least it will be one thing ruled out.*
>
> *Your Dad has put all your photos in an album and a multi-frame. There was a cute one of you a few days old "whistling". I'd almost forgotten that you did that. A cute little rosebud mouth, pursed like a cat's behind. Ian says the physio is improving, it sounds like she's a bit more interested this week.*

Breathing While Drowning

You haven't done enough physio this week though. You seemed to be forever in the car. We'll just have to make time for you. If only we could squeeze more hours into the day. You and Cassie have both have colds this week as has your Dad. I've just started it. Runny nose, aching head!

I don't think I realised how much I would miss my girls when I went back to work. I worked a late then early & couldn't believe how much you had grown & matured in that time. I just want to hug both of you as soon as I see you. Cassie is getting a big girl now, 3 years old!

She goes to kinder at crèche on Tuesday mornings. She seems to love it. As for you, you seem to love her when she's around.

She is trying to give me a hard time again, we've had to step up the discipline. I'm sure if she wasn't so cute it would be easier.

Jacqui, it's hard to figure. Why? What happened along the way? Sometimes you seem to be doing things really well and sometimes it is so hard for you. Then you show me your beautiful smile & it's okay. Cassie tells me you are saying Mum! I'd like to believe it.

I can't wait for the day you can give me a cuddle & say "I love you Mum". For the moment I'll just give you cuddles and kisses. I love you very much.

I never had that moment.

Now, working a full-time job seems like something I've always done. I mostly forget the guilt of wanting to work and having Ian be the primary caregiver. Still, I can recall the startled looks, the insincere comments about working mothers. I felt like I was not good enough. What was wrong with me that I needed and wanted to be out in the world more than I wanted to be home with my daughters all the time?

I was a better mother when I was working. Ian is a brilliant parent and, together, we're what they got, what they chose. We did our best, the best we knew how to do at the time. And it gave us a different perspective on our own parents. They all did the best job they could.

Wednesday 7th August 1991

Well Jacqui, how do I feel? I think I've got over the shock & despair & am now ready to move on. Thursday 25th of July we received the call from the neurologist. You have myoclonic epilepsy. We went straight down to see him the next day. He said you showed on the EEG almost constant epileptic activity. You started on medication that night. We've slowly increased it with not much success at present. Following some reading we think you have several types of seizures.

I hear Jacqui's diagnosis and, thirteen days later, I'm ready to move on! I think it was more like move *forward,* but at the time, it was easier to shove all the feelings of helplessness down and plan for action, lots of action.

Breathing While Drowning

Wednesday 14th August 1991

Jacqui, sorry for the disjointed memories. I'm sitting by Mum's bed at the hospital. She is dying. Slowly, often painfully. Cancer has eaten away at her over the last 12 months. It began as breast cancer and despite chemotherapy & radiotherapy has progressed quickly. She is on very high doses of clonazepam and chlorpromazine. Despite all of that she still calls out sometimes. Finally, after a couple of hours of discomfort she seems more relaxed, her breathing is easier and the frown is gone from her face.

My head is pounding with tension. Yet it is insignificant to the pain she must be feeling. We carry on, almost normally, eating, sleeping and talking, all the while hoping that each breath is her last.

And so to you my darling. Your medication doesn't seem to be helping very much. We've got two increases to go before we'll have to try something else. I hardly see you at all these days. I miss you heaps. Between sitting with Mum and working there isn't much time left. It's mostly up to your Dad to help you and feed you and play with you. Both you and Cassie are missing out on a lot at the moment. We are staying at Nana's house and you both realise that it's just not home.

Each time I hold you and talk to you it takes so long to establish that bridge of communication.

> I haven't seen you smile for so long. The medication you are on is quite sedating. You are asleep even more than you were before. Just after we started you on medication you had a beautiful episode of laughing. It was absolutely delightful. I was holding you and then cuddling you close & tickling you under the arm. It seemed to go on for ages, the sound of it brought tears to my eyes and your Dad's. You had another couple of short laughing times that week. 3 laughs in 1 week instead of 1 laugh every 3 weeks. It was amazing!!
>
> You've had a CT scan on your brain which shows that the ventricles are enlarged. This means that there was some interference with the brain's development at some stage during the pregnancy. They don't have any pointers to say exactly when. I wish I knew. Not that it's going to help you, or me for that matter. We have to put that behind us and go on.

That guilt meter just keeps adding up, and I learned to put that deep down and keep it away, mostly. There is no time when every precious moment of your child's life entails you doing something for her. Every moment you waste on unnecessary, self-indulgent emotions is a moment you could be doing something for her. So get busy and get on with it!

Breathing While Drowning

There is still no firm prediction or even a faint one about what your future will hold. The books we were given to read seem a bit depressing. So many facts & figures, so few faces behind them.

By those accounts you have only a 30% chance of being physically & mentally normal. That's if you only have epilepsy. We know you have more than that already.

Can you imagine the fear that settled into my heart when I read that? And yet I am hopeful. Look at what you have achieved to now, despite your problems. Who knows what you may achieve if we get the seizures under control?

I see in your eyes, a knowing look, a little smirk on your lips as if you understand when we talk to you. You look for your Dad or I when we talk to you. And Cassie. She always gets a bit of recognition. Sometimes it's an exasperated sigh but you know it's her.

You haven't had enough time of late to enjoy yourself so it's no wonder I haven't seem you smile.

The medication makes you produce more saliva and you sound like you need to cough to clear your throat all the time.

Each time I see a shooting star or any lucky omen it's you I think of. I wish you a "good life". Maybe I should wish a "happy life". But good seems to embody the soul as well as the physical being. Maybe I should make the wish "fantastic" or "remarkable"

> or "wonderful; or "great". I just want you to be happy and to have every opportunity to reach as high as you are able.
>
> To be honest I still have many times when I ask "why"? I look at family & friends with children and feel jealous. Jealous that their children don't have your problems that they can laugh and play and move as they wish. They can return their parents love with obvious affection. I guess it's something that will fade a bit in time, or become less painful.

Is it wrong to have wished for normal? To have wished for her to be other than what she was? Where is the natural order of surrender and ambition? This is something I've always struggled with. If we're meant to surrender to a higher power, there is no choice in our lives because everything is already decided for us. I can't see that. I believe I have the power to change my life, to make different choices, to experience things differently.

I struggled with the word *surrender* for a long time. I have such a problem with that word. Every bloody thing you read about feminine power talks about surrender. It's such a male word—it refers to war and giving up control and being a victim, all of which are male concepts. Give up everything and subjugate yourself to the rules and wishes of some bloke who thinks he should rule the world.

And the same goes for spiritual surrender. I'm not a devotee of organised religion. No thanks—rules and mostly men in control again … and not many with a great track record of doing only good in the world or looking after the best interests of their female communities.

Surrender, in spiritual terms, means to give up your will, thoughts, ideas, and deeds to the will and teachings of a higher power. Surrender is a wilful acceptance and yielding to a dominating force and its will.

Why would I do that? I've worked hard to get where I am, to have control of my life, my beliefs, my experience. Why would I hand that over to someone else? What if the higher power is myself?

Wednesday 4th September 1991

> My Mum died finally around mid-day 15th August 1991. Dad & I had spent the previous night with her, she was quite peaceful. Mary & Imelda were with her when she died. My overwhelming emotion has been relief. She was suffering so much, yet she was so strong & held on to life for so long.
>
> We are all very sad. The funeral service was beautiful. There were so many people there. Your Dad & I bought a beautiful wreath of native flowers to leave by her grave.

My mum died not long after we got an initial diagnosis that, among other things, Jacqui had athetoid cerebral palsy and myoclonic epilepsy. I was mourning the loss of two lives: my darling mum and my daughter's perfect life.

Saturday 7th September 1991

Nana Brethie decided to have all the grandchildren carry a white rosebud down the aisle of the church and put them on the coffin. It was beautiful. There was one for each grandchild & one for herself, 12 in all. That broke me up. I had been okay till then. The party back at the house was pretty torrid going too. I guess that's the worst gone although there are some sad times ahead.

I miss her heaps. I go to ring her up and tell her something that you girls have done & I have to stop myself.

I don't feel I have anyone I can chat to about you & how I feel. You had another EEG last Tuesday which showed no improvement since the medication, so, thank goodness, you are off it. You've started on prednisolone orally, a 4 week trial.

You have to see the general paediatrician every week to have your blood pressure checked. But the most amazing thing is that we have our baby back.

Smiling, eyes open & delightful. Your eyes are steadier too. They don't shake as much as they did before the Rivotril. You are like a new person. You watch everything & get really excited.

Last night I gave you a fright by accident and your reaction was gorgeous. Your eyes wide at first then a big trembling bottom lip & then your eyes started to fill with tears. I know it sounds crazy but it was great to see that reaction.

Breathing While Drowning

Life became about small things—things I had taken for granted with the gorgeous and gifted Cassi Kate. And the taking for granted started to feel like a punishment, but Jacqui was the one who suffered the punishment, not me. I just had a head full of recriminations and a heart full of anguish and hope. I had been so unconscious, so blithely arrogant about my life and my right to perfection, to normal. I had belonged, but now I didn't. I was different, I was remarkable—be careful what you wish for!

Sunday 15th September 1991

Jacqui, a good day. Last night you had a big pooh! Today you spent nearly the whole time awake. You've been feeling grouchy because you're constipated. But today, all smiles & a few giggles. Kicking, waving and yelling. Generally having a good time. You were actually enjoying yourself, responding to playing. No. 5 tooth is on the way.

The cycle of Jacqui's moods and well-being followed how much shit she was holding on to. It was a mirror of life. It's like there's a crap filter over everything, and if you're holding on to too much shit, you can't see the joy in anything, let alone do something brilliant. So let go of the shit and live in the sunshine.

Wednesday 18th September 1991

No poo since Saturday! We keep pouring stuff in but nothing comes out. You are still eating but I wonder when you are going to clog up completely. We'll give the paed a call this morning & see what the story is. Good news, no seizures for a week! Amazing and wonderful.

You have a lot more awake time now. It makes me even more reluctant to leave you, even to play with Cassie, than ever. Cassie seems to miss out a fair bit. She is learning to compromise a fair bit.

The mental, emotional, and physical roller coaster continues. I'm watching every moment, every in and out. I'm understanding the processes and how everything is connected. No wonder I make a great project and change managers. I sense things before they happen; I am a great watcher and listener—skills honed in the fiery crucible of Jacqui's life.

And then, sometimes, there was joy.

Wednesday 2nd October 1991

Well Jacq, LAUGHTER!!!

Once last week & then on Sunday 30th, more laughs than we've ever had put together. You were so happy & responsive. Cassie & I rushed over to where you were with your Dad. We couldn't help

Breathing While Drowning

all laughing with you. It was a wonderful morning. In the afternoon you clogged up and needed an enema but the joy of the morning is still with me.

Prior to the laugh last week, it was 2 months since we'd had a chuckle. It's been a long 2 months. At the moment you seem to be coming out of the dark. Apart from a couple of mild seizures you've been free of them for about 3 weeks. The only thing to put a damper on this is that your head isn't growing. It's been measured the same for a couple of months now. I hope that now you are more alert & active that this will stimulate the brain to grow and your head.

I guess your Dad & I are feeling the strain a bit at the moment. I haven't got anyone to let off steam at so he gets all the flack. He is trying to work out his changed role and finish the house and care for you and Cassie. It's not easy.

I had a beautiful card from Jenny last Saturday, no Monday. She is trying to be a support to us all, which is great. It's hard to unburden myself to her though, especially with Sophie. How can I tell her about the pain I carry in my heart for you when every time I see Sophie it hurts a little more deeply? There were so many babies born near your time that I'm getting constantly bombarded with reminders that that could have been you or I. You would probably be walking by now, certainly saying "Mama"!

Jacqui, it's not that I wish we didn't have you, it's just that I wish for more for you, and Cassie & your Dad.

I made a query about home help from the council today. It wasn't easy but life is becoming increasingly difficult. We aren't even managing the bare necessities any more, let alone all your care. We must persist though.

Your arms are making big progress. Rather than remain flopped by your side they are more often bent at the elbows, hands on your tummy, grasping & clasping.

Your eyes, although still difficult to control are much steadier. They no longer quiver when you're trying to look at something.

We've got you in the high chair for meals with some support from the hospital orthotics dept. You look so cute sitting in there. You are able to hold your head quite well while you're there.

I hope you didn't keep your Dad up too late last night. When I left for work you were pretty happy & bright, having just had an enormous result from your enema.

What does your future hold? You are getting heavier & harder to hold at the moment. I hope the early intervention group can be helpful. I want you to walk & talk and be happy. I don't know if it will come or not. I hope so. I'll try to do everything in my power to achieve that for you. I just hope I don't lose your Dad & Cassie in the process. Love you Jacqui.

Breathing While Drowning

How much did I push people away because I didn't know how to share what I was feeling? How hard did I try? Many of my friends dropped off the radar. They, as well as I, found the reality of Jacqui too hard to share. But new friends came too—great friends with enormous hearts and unending patience.

How many years did I push down how I felt as well as any sense of fear or panic? My role was to get out there and make it happen for my family no matter what. And I did. How else could I go back to work as a midwife only two weeks after Jacqui died? Back to the birthing suite to help a family bring their own child into the world; my world of pain, their world of joy. Many people called me courageous, but what else could I do? The choice was made: do everything in your power to get Jacqui well and to let Cassi know she is loved just as much.

I put Jacqui first, I put myself last. I wished it and lived it with all my might. I still put myself last unless I consciously think about it. And that's okay. I'm a kind and generous person, that's who I am.

I ran into strife when my dreams were just dreams. There came a point when I knew it was time to make the thought words and the words action and the action reality. I owed it to myself.

Even now, I put a lid on my feelings. I'm slowly learning to share my vulnerabilities. Reading Brené Brown's book, *Daring Greatly: How the Courage to Be Vulnerable Transforms the Way We Live, Love, Parent and Lead,* was an inspiration.[4]

One of the biggest aha moments was that I wasn't the only one to switch immediately from moments of incredible joy to moments of sheer terror about it all crashing down. And it was steeped in I-don't-deserve-this nonsense.

Now I practice feeling. When emotions come up, any emotions, I tend to and still do move past them quickly. Now I try to let them be and observe them without judgement or analysis. I think, *That's interesting,* and then I let them go.

There is a physiological phenomenon of six seconds that emotions produce in our body. After that, it's all pretty much in your head.

It's been termed the *amygdala hijack* because that's the place in your brain where it all happens. Luckily for us humans, we can rewire the response. Taking one long, slow, deep breath will get you past the six seconds, and the chemicals will dissipate. For emotions that you want less of, think about what triggered the emotion and set a goal to respond differently next time. Your amygdala learns from experience, so you can change the way you respond.

For emotions that you want more of, take your long, slow, deep breath and, at the same time, feel where that emotion is in your body and sit with it. Let it be, enjoy it, and remember it so you can call it up whenever and wherever you need it.

Starting up Women Who Care[5] and saying out loud how Jacqui's life and death was so much a part of mine was a big step for me. Sometimes, I can express it with barely a hiccup, and sometimes my voice cracks and the tears come. Either way, it's okay. I am who I am, the sum total of all of me up to this point. This is now.

The separation from the feminine continues here. I had to protect and provide for my family—not my physiological role. So I shut down the mother, shut down the softness and vulnerability, and began chasing the masculine version of success and happiness quite seriously. I got suckered like so many people, men and women. There is no one version of success—it means different things to different people.

My version is joyful. That's it: bring the joy; be the joy. I am joy.

Monday 28th October 1991

Jacqui, my beautiful baby girl, you are 1 today. It's just past midnight and you are sound asleep in your cot. You had only 1 false start last night. Just after you'd gone to bed you grizzled to get picked up. Two burps later you were happy to get put back to bed.

Breathing While Drowning

I've spent the last hour or so crying. Crying for you and for Cassie and for your Dad & I. How can I describe the pain that I feel inside? Every time I look at you or at Cassie, the knife twists a little deeper. Cassie has so much, and I wouldn't wish anything less for her. She is so active at present and bright and inquisitive and like a sponge soaking up facts and activities as quickly as you can think of them. On the other hand, a high point in your day might be that you managed to have a poo by yourself. No, that's not true.

You smile and give us laughs sometimes, all our faces have smiles so big we feel they will crack. Your laugh is so infectious, so unique and wonderful.

Jenny came up [with] Sophie today. She is trying so hard to be a friend to all of us.

I was holding you in your usual state, floppy and half asleep. Cassie was playing with Sophie who was smiling and "looking" and laughing at her. Cassie's face was full of wonder and delight. I wanted to curl up and die. Why should you have epilepsy? Why should Cassie not have a little sister with no problems? It's not until we see other little babies that we realise how much behind you are in your development.

I guess with your birthday it brought it close to home.

On her first birthday Cassie was walking, no - running around at Mum's. Eating cake & playing with the other kids. She barely had time to stop and say "hi" to boring old Mum.

We had her party at Mum's because our carpet was all up getting blow dried as it had been flooded.

Jacq, we're weaning you off the prednisolone at the moment. Your Dad & I wonder if you had the seizures return today or whether it was to do with your big poo that you did all by yourself. We'll see tomorrow.

You are no longer being breastfed. I didn't have enough to feed you what you needed. You would still suck although somewhat reluctantly. So now it's a big drink of cow's milk. That was a tough decision to make. Your Dad helped me make up my mind. I don't think men understand how that churns your emotions up.

While you're feeding you're totally dependent on me. I nourish you and nurture you. Anyone can give you the bottle. However, I prefer if it's me or your Dad.

I'd better go. Cassie will be up in a few hours.

See you next time my love. Have a magnificent birthday.

Love Mum XXXOOOXXX

Milestones were always hard; I could convince myself that things were progressing until the milestone showed that that wasn't really true. But milestones are what you pin your hopes on; they are something to strive for, to work towards. To capture the sense of overwhelm and give it a container, a shape, a path to follow.

Breathing While Drowning

Wednesday 11th December 1991

Jacqui, I don't know who is the hardest to write to, you or your sister. Anyway I'll start with you. Have you done anything cute of late? Well as we've just been down to the beach I can relate the screaming and yelling that went on when your Dad tried to introduce you to the ocean. You left us in no doubt that you thought it was cold and you didn't like it. It was your first trip to the beach.

We took Dad's (Grandad's) caravan and him away to Lorne for a few days. It was a hectic but good break. Mind you the washing machine has broken down again which makes it a bit of a hassle.

Anyway, as I was getting around to saying. On the way home from the beach you decided you were going to hit your rattle that was stuck in the window beside you. You spent a good hour perfecting the motion. It was deliberate and delightful. You are getting stronger with your movements all the time. Your head is steadier and eyes are looking better. You still love to watch Cassie, although she is pretty hard to keep up with.

You have started swimming at South Gisborne. So far you have really enjoyed it. You do these little dolphin kicks that are pretty amazing. Your togs are very small but you still need to grow a bit to fit them.

Life seems to have taken on a bit more meaning for you at the moment. You smile more often and seem to be seeing what goes on around you more.

> I have to admit I'm a bit jealous though. You seem to save all the best smiles for your Dad. When you hear his voice, even if I'm holding you, you start looking for him, a big grin on your face, eyes wide & searching. It is something that should be reserved for mothers. I s'pose it's something I gave up when I wanted to return to work full time.

Okay, let's see if I can beat myself up a little more. Poor me—ugh! Pile on the guilt. No wonder my back is bent and my shoulders stooped; I've been carrying this crap around for decades. It makes me cringe reading it, and then I remember how it felt, and all I feel is compassion for the younger me, learning this lesson for us.

> It is good for your Dad though. I worry about how he is managing. Being a househusband is not an easy job. There aren't enough of them around to make it relaxed and supportive.
>
> And yet, he copes with it all in his own special way. Some days I don't know how he puts up with me. I can be so grouchy and horrible. He seems to take it in his stride. He knows when to ignore me and when to be patient or gentle.
>
> He is really good with you, always patient, always tolerant. I worry about Cassie though. She tends to get short shrift a lot of the time. She is at a frustrating age at present. Just trying us out. And trying to get our attention especially when we're working with you.

Breathing While Drowning

It's 4 o'clock. My worst time at night. Mind you, if I've been reading magazines it's worse. Then I see all these children that aren't mine, doing all sorts of things you may never do. I think your Dad was a bit down tonight. You had a pretty ordinary session on the ball and I'm sure he's tired. I was saying that I'd like you to walk by 5 years of age. He jumped in quickly with 3. We both look at you and can't help smiling. You are so beautiful. We enjoy having you, baby or not.

Hope you have a wonderful Christmas beautiful baby.

Is it fair that mothers have to give stuff up to work? Here's another nail in the coffin of my feminine essence that is so connected to motherhood. And I gave it up—at least that is what it felt like, that I had to choose. In fact, I could've chosen to believe that motherhood is motherhood, an individual journey for each woman. Society suggests you can have one or the other, not both together at the same time. Looking back, if I'd had the presence and energy, I could've lived those moments as exactly that.

Talk about the lean-in circles and the controversy around *yes* or *no*. I used to believe that one could have it all, just not all at once. Now I believe you can have it all—full stop. If you're present and mindful and live in the now, this is it. It's everything.

If we're present, we can have it all because that's what it is. Be conscious of what you want—thought, words, and action. Enjoy the small stuff, share the little moments, and keep your eyes on the prize at the end. Just put that out there and let the universe take care of it. The prize for me is a joyful life, a life that expresses the very best of who I am. "Life is meant to be a vibrant, deeply felt, growing mosaic of long, meaningful moments".[6]

How lucky am I to have a man with heart who loves and cares for me? How lucky am I to have a man who is willing to be a witness in my life and make his life with me? Strack is the kindest most compassionate bloke I know. And he is such a strong, masculine person that I often followed his lead.

I let go of my feminine to pursue the ferocious protectiveness of the masculine. Along the way, I found an easy alignment with striving, power, control, and leading. It helped that the world works that way.

Wednesday 25th December 1991

Christmas Day. I hope you are sound asleep like your Big Sister. Amazingly you went to bed at ¼ to 10 last night. Perhaps you were just giving us a Christmas treat. Or you may have been saving it for 3 o'clock. I hope you don't wake your sister.

You have done a lot in the lot couple of weeks. Firstly, you can now grind your teeth. They must be hurting you a bit. You've had quite a few unsettled patches & rubbing your gums seems to help. That lovely grinding noise is becoming more frequent though as you discover how to do it better. At first it seemed like an achievement, then I began to wonder if it was another type of seizure & whether I should be sorry to see it appear. You also seem to have started a type of seizure involving blinking. You blink a few times in quick succession. Who knows? Maybe I read too much into them. Maybe I should do some more research. I know I will. After the holiday season is over. We can't fit another thing in at the moment. We are going to be busy with Cassie going to kinder next year. You will both be going to swimming and playgroup too.

Your muscle strength is improving. When we change your nappy we do leg exercises to help move the bowel. At first we could push your legs all over the place but now you offer a lot of resistance to it. Even when you are playing, your arms & legs are doing a lot more. You seem to be so much more interested in what is going on around you these days. You must be able to see things further away too. You are watching Cassie do things at some distance.

Today your Dad got a giggle. I haven't heard one in such a long time. I hope tomorrow brings a few. I hope you enjoy opening all the presents too. I know Santa has been good to you.

I wonder what the next 12 months will bring. What will we all be doing then? Will you be mobile? I hope so.

We must take you swimming in the next week. That does seem to have helped, plus you enjoy it & so does Cassie.

Bye for now, love Mum

The always looking forward and always wishing. I'm never happy with where I am. I'm not present. Looking back, it was too much thinking and not enough being. But it was what it was. I did the best I could at the time and used the tools and skills I had.

I also learned that having the wish and the intent is powerful, but it's the action that makes the difference. Don't just dream it, get direction and do it.

My dreams are my own, and no one else will own and love them for me. If I let them slide by, living in the past or the future and doing nothing about them now, the only person who will care will be me.

Thursday 2nd January 1992

Another long night at work. We've left Cassie down at Balnarring with Mary & the children. She is having a wonderful time at the Beach. You had a lovely paddle in the ocean yesterday, no day before.

Yesterday you had the most brilliant day. You woke at about 10am & started with smiles. You didn't go to sleep until 1015pm, 12 hours awake. Most of that time was spent, smiling & kicking. You looked like you were on fire.

You had an enormous clean out of the bowel in the morning and that must have helped you feel good too.

I s'pose you'll have a sleepy day to catch up today.

You're off to the hospital to have an audiometry test done. I'll be sleeping so your Dad will take you.

The start of a New Year. New hopes and dreams. How much will be achieved?

If today is any indicator you will have a fantastic year ahead. You had a good day Christmas Day. Cassie helped you open all the presents in

> your stocking and the others. You enjoyed ripping all the paper off (with a little help).
>
> We took Dad (Grandad) down to the beach too. He drove me down after I'd been working. It was sad at midnight when we ushered the New Year in. I got up to kiss Ian & Mary got up to kiss Les. Dad was alone. We drank a toast to Mum.
>
> Ian helped keep the mood light & enthusiastic. We were playing Scattergories and Pass the Pigs! Interesting!

The cycle of life, farewells and hellos. New Year's Eve is such an arbitrary way to forge intentions. The best intention I had was *bigger and better*. I have always been an optimist and believed that things could only get better. That belief has been tested over and over; somehow, optimism and resilience keep winning.

And I had to be resilient so often.

Wednesday 5th February 1992

> Jacq, after a slow few weeks you've had a great couple of days at last. Your Dad & I were really down, you seemed to have slumped a bit, hit a plateau. Anyway, the night we had finally voiced these opinions, you decided to wake up, and laugh. I mean really good belly chuckles from 0030 till 0430. Cute, but the timing was off.

You were actually lying in the dark, on your own, laughing. I got you up and tried to give you a drink. No way! It was all just too funny for words. It was beautiful to hear though. The next day you slept, of course. But you seem to be sorting yourself out a little, with one awake day, then one asleep day.

You've started back at swimming again and seemed to enjoy it immensely. I feel swimming will be of great benefit to you.

I took you to physio today. You performed well. The physio was quite pleased with what you achieved. She spoke of the standing frame again. We talked about your cognitive function and I was pleased she agreed, without prompting, that you had a lot of potential and showed significant signs of developing well.

Your right side seems to be emerging as your dominant side. While lying flat you insist on turning your head to the right 9 times out of ten. We're working on it.

The other day I changed your nappy and I had you in my arms by the laundry sink. I turned on the tap and you looked straight at the sound. So I washed your hands too. You smiled, a simple pleasure.

Keep at it Jacqui. I know you can do it.

Where does belief come from? Our beliefs are our whys—why we exist. I so needed to believe that Jacqui Bree could have a chance to live a joyful life. But there were more trials ahead.

Breathing While Drowning

Wednesday 18th March 1992

Jacqui, you've done it again.

Discharged from hospital at 1100hrs yesterday.

In with? Sixth nerve palsy due to a viral illness you picked up from your sister.

Cassie had croup last Monday & Tuesday & was really sick Wed & Thurs. We had her to the doc's on Tuesday & Saturday. Then you decided to come into the act. Cassie's temp was 40.2 Friday night. You peaked at 39.5 on Saturday morning. We brought you over to the paed's on Saturday and she decided it was just a viral illness, no focus. You started vomiting almost before she got out the door. You kept that up till lunch time the next day. I rang Anne back to tell her you were a little better & told her, by the by, that your left eye was turned in, since that a.m. Well, the short story is, you were admitted to hospital to investigate the eye & illness.

The eye resolved by that evening, so no CT scan thank goodness! However, you were left with a fever and you wouldn't drink for us. So we had to stay another day & keep topping you up with fluids or they were going to put a nasogastric tube down. Well, you just managed to escape all of that.

Your Dad & I stayed up with you & gave you drinks. Because I didn't want to leave your bedside we both stayed and took it in turns to sleep. Your big sister stayed at Grandad's, much to her delight. She helped him pick the kids up from school. She was so pleased to see you this afternoon, it was beautiful.

Your temperature was still up this afternoon when we bought you home but it's down this evening.

Your tongue is really revolting and coated. A job for the toothbrush tomorrow. The fluids are going down better, but the solids are a bit of a worry as yet. I hope you are having a good sleep in your own bed. I hope your Dad is too. I'm sure Cassie will be. She slept for 2 hours this p.m. when we got home, unheard of for her. But at least she had her favourite tea — fish & chips!!

I don't know if I can stay awake to talk about how I feel. It's hard enough to document the facts tonight. I also went for my interview at Kyneton Hospital. I don't know how I fared until Friday. I wasn't at all prepared. My hair was still wet too.

While we were in hospital with you there was a 6 month old boy who had a seizure, his first and only one. He was definitely a funny-looking-kid. He was a bit behind developmentally and didn't focus with his eyes. His mother kept saying things to compare him to you and then she'd say but he's not that bad. Meaning, not as bad as you. Then she asks outright "Is she retarded?" I said "No" immediately. People like to classify others into various acceptable boxes & sometimes it just doesn't work.

Breathing While Drowning

> *Needless to say that hurt.*
> *It was difficult to sit and watch you lying there doing your best to frighten me to death.*

As I read through the journal entries, I am amazed at how much I've forgotten. How many times Jacqui scared us to death, thinking we would lose her … the emotional roller coaster of health and life. No wonder I developed resilience, no wonder I shoved the emotions down deep, clapped the lid on, and let them fester.

We like to label people, find a box that explains the differences rather than the things we have in common. Why is that? What frightens us about difference? I can read in my words that my judgement of the little boy was just as immediate as his mother's judgement of Jacqui. Resist, resist, resist.

Some people have no social filter; at the time, I was one such person. Nowadays, compassion and the shared human experience are how I aim to live.

It's so much better to focus on strengths, how you do well, and how positive you are. Where the focus goes, attention flows. If you focus on the positive and strengths, that's what you'll find. If you focus on the weaknesses and the negative, that dark cloud will follow you around. The doom and gloom prophecies become self-fulfilling ones.

I'm living proof that focusing on the positive works. I've so much more positive in my life now, and I'm surrounded by so many more positive people. I really notice when I go into a room or situation where people are stuck or negative.

I started with the Silva method. The science of it got me going; the evidence seemed much less namby-pamby than other things. It gave me a framework and practical exercises to switch me out of the old way, and that's what I needed at the time.

As you can tell from the last entry I was pretty tired. I kept dropping off to sleep. After that day your Dad came down with the same bug and diarrhoea too. He's mostly over it, but really washed out and he has no energy. It gives us some understanding of how you must feel. You seem totally exhausted. Last night there was a sparkle of your former self returning. Unfortunately, it started at 2100hrs & went to the wee small hours. Dad said you were as bright as a button this a.m.

At least at the moment your seizures have decreased back to very few. While you had a temperature you were having them quite frequently. Ian & I feared you would have to go back on medication. We were dreading that. You've made so much progress lately that doping you out on medication would have seemed a really backward step.

We have to see the neurologist this week so hopefully you'll stay well & relatively seizure free.

I should find out today if I got the job at Kyneton. If so, it will mean a bit of messing around until we get a routine going.

It's going to mean a few trips up & down the highway but at present it's necessary. I don't really want to go; I'd prefer to stay at Sunbury but I don't have enough guaranteed work at present.

It may mean getting Judy in more often to help your Dad with physio for you. I know if we just persist you will achieve major things.

We can't help loving you so much. I speak for your Dad 'cos his love for you is obvious in everything he does for you. He gets an excellent response from you too. When I hold you, you are so beautiful and endearing I can't help squeezing you in close. Your hair is getting long but not quite long enough to not stick up. I'll have to start putting a fountain in. Not that I think you could look any cuter at present. Your molars are a bit slow to come down properly, I hope it helps with chewing when they do. Your eyelashes are as long as Cassie's. It doesn't seem fair for you both to have them. Usually only little boys have the long eyelashes. Your eyes seem greener than usual at present because you are so pale. You've lost a stack of weight too. I'll have to take you to the health centre soon to check.

Life goes on in a series of days and nights, of dreams and practicalities.

Wednesday 8th April 1992

Jacqui, I just have to record a small event today.

I was hanging out the washing on the line. You were in your pusher with 2 dolls in front of you & feeling good. As I watched, you tilted your head down slowly to look at your right hand. You watched it for a moment then began to move it up to your mouth. It took a few tries but you made it. Then a few delicious sucks took place followed by a delighted smile of achievement!

I couldn't help but be proud of you. More & more we can notice improvement in your powers of concentration and interest in things happening around you. You are not yet ready for the standing frame but we're working on it. We need to try & do more physio but we seem to run out of time. Cassie & kinder keep us busy. Swimming lessons for both of you, playgroup to name a few. Each day of your life is different. How long & when you will sleep changes constantly. So we find it difficult to work a physio session around when I'm working. I will be working more too, very soon. We need the financial support but we could do with some extra time somewhere along the line.

We are all having 10 days off, up till Easter. Boy! Do we need it!

You've been up at night with new molars coming through. You seem to be having more trouble than Cassie did. It may also be that I've just forgotten. It's difficult for you as you are unable to put something in your mouth to grind your gums on. You have to rely on yelling at us to do something about it. Sometimes we're a bit slow!

Breathing While Drowning

> *Hope you're more settled when I get home. Your Dad said were pretty grouchy when I rang. Keep working at it Jacq.*

There is this constant need to keep working, to not accept anything less than total commitment, regardless of what is going on. The drive to get things done and work hard to get results comes from my working-class background. Things were a struggle, and getting stuff was the reward.

Brendon Burchard, one of my favourite people, asked, "Isn't a better life worth the struggle?" Hell yes.

Reading and thinking about the younger me, I was broken and trying so hard to do it all on my own with just Strack. The single-minded focus kept me going, but the drive to do threw me off track for living in the moment. My head was down and buried in work, which meant I had no idea where I was going.

Now I'm more mindful, practising the joy of the moment, practising to live as I mean to, expressing the very best of who I can be: creative, bold, and mindful. Practising my interactions with others; being caring, connected, and inspiring; staying curious, authentic, and thorough—all this because these traits were part of my success. And always learning. That makes me sound like an enlightened paragon of virtue, which I am not (though I am working on that!).

Thursday April 23rd 1992

> *Jacqui, 5 new teeth in one week, naturally that week had to be our holiday. What a disaster from go to whoa. After a 10 hour trip we arrived at 10pm. 2*

days of getting you back on track & one of the other kids got a virus, a very nasty one with potentially fatal problems for you so we packed up on day 3 & left. You vomited all the way to Wodonga. Christened the new car beautifully! You had a few bad days & a few good days. It is very restricting. Cassie seemed to have a good time. She probably enjoyed the holiday the most. But as long as she isn't at home she's happy.

Surprisingly, she was glad to get home finally and told us so in no uncertain terms. Some days I feel like telling her to just stop talking, she wears me out with her constant questions and chatter. She is so interested and involved in the world around her.

I was in bed today after night duty. Cassie had woken me up a half hour earlier to tell me to get up for lunch. I explained I was sleeping. Anyway I listening to the muted sounds of Cassie. Now there is contradiction in terms! She was laughing and talking or should I say shouting, sixteen to the dozen, and that was through 2 closed doors. It was a beautiful, joyous moment, life and carefree seem appropriate. Yet even that thought was tinged with sadness as I wondered will I ever hear those sounds from you? Will there be a day I can secretly smile to myself because you chat so fast out loud or laugh so unrestrainedly. I hope so my darling.

Breathing While Drowning

> You were in the beanbag tonight with your Sesame Street frame in front of you. You were actually watching them and occasionally hitting them with your hands. You seemed to think you were pretty clever. Life is more interesting to you of late, a definite improvement. We have to see the neurologist tomorrow, maybe a few decisions to be made. Bye my lovely girl. Hope you have a great day tomorrow.

Every joyous moment underwritten with regret, disappointment, and fear.

We had the beautiful balance of Cassi being so joyous and free. So clever, so alive, and so determined to do things her way. Actually, both of my girls were stubborn now that I think about it. They must take after their dad.

Near enough is not good enough when you're dealing with life, but maybe it's okay for other stuff. Maybe I didn't have to be so driven. Where would I be, who would I be if I'd stayed still, accepted matters, and remained obedient?

Wednesday 20th May 1992

> Epilim doesn't seem to be helping much. You are still having as many seizures as before. I don't think you are achieving any great strokes of advancement either as yet. Basically no change of note.
>
> The physio group session talked about you. Results,

> well they've decided you're "athetoid" type. Your muscles at the end of the line like hands and feet work well but the interim ones like arms, legs and neck don't have enough tone.
>
> According to the physio "statistically" prognosis for physical development is poor. You will probably never walk unaided. Mentally you may be very alert and bright. I could've told them that already.

Labels and judgements and perceptions—all battles to be fought every day to be the person you want to be; to do the things you want to do. Social norms of conformity and boxes is the alternative, always boxes. It pisses me off reading this again. So busy putting people in boxes instead of working with individuals. Looking back, I realise that the physio was probably a first-year practitioner and doing her best with a busy workload. Unfortunately, the experience coloured my views on physiotherapy and physiotherapists for a long time.

I wonder now whether Jacqui could sense all the angels around Dad, all the special people in our lives: Mum, Nanas, and Granddads? Did she know they were all there to love her and us?

I've had some experiences in the last few years that lead me to believe the world of now and the world of later are closer than we think. If we're open to it, we can feel these things occasionally. Especially after meditation or when I am really home in the here and now, I can feel them around me. The messages can be pretty strong. There are lots of ways of being: clairvoyant (clear seeing), clairaudient (clear hearing), and clairsentient (clear knowing) are just a few. I'm clairsentient. I just know things, and sometimes there is no real reason why. Most of this is recognition of patterns and the subconscious pops up with the answer once the conscious mind is relaxed. I've slowly learned to trust this gift.

The lessons I learned about myself and the world that I realised then—and that I realise now—mean a lot of different things.

People seek power over others for a lot of reasons, but others can control your fate and your future only if you let them.

Lesson: lots of people are scared of those who outshine them, those who show up their own failings or lack of motivation. So I say bugger that, keep shining, get out there, and live the life you want. Don't wait. Don't be a victim or a martyr. It's not nearly as much fun as living the life you want; I know: I've been both and, even now, I can slip into martyrdom from time to time. The thing that pulls me back? My life belongs to me. Everything I think, feel, do, and believe matters—and that's what counts.

Your dreams are your own and no one else will own and love them for you.

Lesson: dream big and then be it and do it, whatever that dream is. Even those you love and who love you and want you to have your dreams can't make it happen if you don't believe in yourself and do it. Don't be contained by other people's small thinking, don't let them put you into a box.

It can feel so much easier to live a small life, a life without purpose or direction—to leave the choice of the life you lead to someone else. To live in someone else's future rather than your here and now. Or to think you'll follow your dream in a couple of years, when the kids are grown or when you've paid off your house, or when something else monumental happens. Just freaking get on with it. You will never know if you don't start. It's always worth the struggle to follow your dream. Always. Anything worth having and being is worth working for. It teaches you so much about yourself.

Someone asked me the other day what my one word was. Great question! I'd been speaking about what I do and why I do it. She asked whether it was *resilience*. When I thought about it, I said that it had been *resilience,* but now it was *gratitude*. I am so incredibly grateful for all that has happened in my life, for all the people in my life. And that gratitude brings me so much joy.

What's your one word? What's the cornerstone word of your life?

Chapter 3

The Programme Years

The road of trials continues, and we battle more ogres and dragons, some from unexpected quarters. "The one thing worse than being told that your child has a disability is being told that nothing can be done".

I read this a while back on the website of the Grow Foundation for kids[1], and it landed in my heart with a boom. This is exactly how Strack and I felt with the bucketloads of pessimistic answers we got about Jacqui's life from conventional medicine. When we questioned their opinions, most people became uncomfortable.

Patience was never really a problem for me when I was a child. Even as a young adult, I was fine waiting. Drifting was okay, doing things as they came along, going spontaneously from one thing to another. Once Jacqui's disabilities began to manifest, I found that my sense of urgency, my patience for inaction ran out.

This is why I get impatient with people who are marking time and not reaching for the possible, let alone the impossible. Apathy fills me with frustration. Near enough is not good enough. Mediocre is the death of life for me. It doesn't have to be perfect, but it can't be nothing.

After two years of heart-wrenching searching, we found a programme that gave us hope. We dived into it 24 hours a day, 365 days of the year. This was the Institutes for the Achievement of Human Potential (IAHP) founded by Glen Doman and Carl Delacarto in 1955. The Institutes is a group of non-profit institutes whose work in child brain development has created programmes to help brain-injured children achieve wellness and well children achieve excellence through individual sensory, motor, and nutritional programmes.

We were lucky enough to have an office of the programme in Victoria only about two hours away from home. The Grow Foundation for kids is working to get the programme back to Australia so it can be available for more hurt kids.

The Institutes for the Achievement of Human Potential (IAHP)

In 2015, the IAHP celebrated six decades of work in the field of child brain development. "Sixty years ago there were no child brain developmentalists. It was thought that once the brain was injured there was no remedy. Brain-injured people were often medicated, warehoused and sometimes – forgotten. For sixty years The Institutes for the Achievement of Human Potential have been teaching that brain growth and development are a dynamic ever-changing process that can been speeded and enhanced by stimulation and opportunity. Thousands of parents the world over have learned, when they come to The Institutes, that "The brain grows by use. The hottest word in neurophysiology today is 'neuroplasticity.' It's a wonderful new word. It means 'The brain grows by use'".[2]

How does cutting-edge work get to be mainstream? When does the body of evidence convince us to adopt new approaches?

Think about Schemmelweiss and his handwashing. It took eighty years and then some before this simple behavioural change was taken seriously and began to save lives. So maybe sixty years to recognise work is about par for the course.

Why do some of us resist change so strongly? Birthing Jacqui gave me a reason to change, an imperative, a life–and-death scenario. No contest. Yet even though I love change and love helping others through change, there are parts of me that don't want to change. These are the parts that tend to hide deep inside, the parts that say *you're not enough*. Get over it, get on with it. Think about it: it's not true. Feel it: it's not true. You're living proof that you are enough—just ask anyone other than yourself.

One of my favourite ways to think about change is from brothers Chip and Dan Heath. Their ideas were introduced to me by one of my dearest mentors and friends, Dr Cathy Balding. The Heaths wrote, *Switch – How to change things when change is hard*.[3] They talk about the rider, elephant, and path. *Rider* is the logical, *elephant* is the emotional, and *path* is the process. If you can direct the rider, engage the elephant, and clear the path, change is not only achieved, but also more likely to be sustainable.

The only part of that model that is missing for me is the body, the energy, the mindfulness. You need to connect that. If you help people be present and feel what change and success is like (and practice this), the change can be sustained even longer.

Thursday 3rd September 1992

Jacqui, your Dad will be really agro. He's gone to take you to swimming at the hospital and he's left your togs at home and his! He hasn't rung about them yet. I hope they work out some way to have a swim. It's such a long way.

We made a major decision concerning you yesterday. We visited the Australian College for the Development of Human Potential. We are going to try a new type of programme to see if we can get you walking and talking.

> You have shown so much interest and enthusiasm for the world latterly that we are filled with this sense of urgency. Every day that we don't help you means you have wasted a day, and it's another day to catch up.
>
> This programme sounds really promising 'cos its emphasis and approach seem to be positive. They will try to get you "well", make you catch up to other kids and get into "normal" mode. Your Dad and I are excited and hopeful. I'm sending the form in today. Fingers crossed that it won't take too long to get an appointment.
>
> Father's Day on Sunday so I'd better head down the street to get something for dear old Dad and Grandad too.

The whole philosophy of the IAHP was that these kids were hurt and we could make them well. They put the kids front and centre, and they poured everything into them that they could. Filling them with conscious stimulation that they missed out on because their physical and neural pathways didn't stream properly.

Thursday 17th September 1992

> Jacqui Bree, in 2 months we'll be at the Institute learning how to get you well. We've only spoken to a few people so far but they all seem keen to help. It's almost as if everybody was waiting for us to discover this course of action.

Breathing While Drowning

We needed volunteers, allies to help us with the programme. We had a twenty-four hour, seven days per week roster to fill, and it was a lesson for us. So many people—including family and friends we thought we could count on—stepped away from us, and so many strangers appeared in our lives and became lifelong friends.

> We had a sad day yesterday. S aged 4, died at 0400 on Monday 14th September. S was a little boy very much like you. He had been born prematurely and had a few setbacks early on leaving him with cerebral palsy. On the night he died he apparently choked on some mucus and his airway obstructed. They said he wouldn't have woken up, just kept sleeping.

I think this is wishful thinking and kindness on the part of the medicos. It is also a warning and a practice for us.

> It is all very close to home. Because your behaviour was so like his it frightened me a lot. I wanted to rush out and buy you a bedroom monitor or an apnoea mattress, anything to stop it happening. I couldn't imagine life without you. Then in the next breath I think of despite the tragedy of losing him how lucky they are that he is safe and they no longer have to worry about him or plan what has to happen when they die.

How easily I conceptualised losing a child at that point. My child was still with me, and I couldn't imagine a life without her. It is so much easier in theory.

> I suppose that is the 2nd biggest worry about you. No 1 is will you be happy, as happy as you could possibly be? Will life give you joys more than sorrows? And no 2 what will happen to you when your Dad and I are dead and gone? The best answer would be that you don't need us. That you are totally independent, married with kids of your own. At worst I hope we have you financially set so that you can have a house or lifestyle which suits you. Maybe Cassie will be involved. I can't say. She loves you dearly and gives you cuddles and kisses even if no one is watching. She still asks me questions why you are different from other children but she seems to be getting it straight in her mind now.
>
> I must take a leaf from her book and talk about when you walk and when you start talking and when you go to kinder etc. Instead of my trying to play it down and say maybe.
>
> I've had lots of cuddles with you these past few days as I've been on holidays from Sunbury but not from Kyneton. I'm trying to take some of the work from your Dad to give him a rest but also I'm trying to get to know you better. You reserve your best smiles and faces for your Dad. Every time he speaks you crane your neck to see where he is. I love to watch

the two of you together. That relationship is so precious. He can be so gentle with you, or teasing, or rough and you respond so well to each mood. To be honest I feel a little jealous sometimes. You do respond to me but not as well. I don't do the rough and tumble as well as your Dad.

Poor old Dad. I give him hell yet he is so good to me. I know I've been rotten and bitchy at the moment, PMT, but I can't help myself. I know he wants to make love but I can't bring myself to be enthusiastic. A large part is a fear of an unplanned pregnancy, another part is exhaustion, another dissatisfaction with my body, its fitness and condition, no privacy, a few snatched minutes is all we get together. I often think of him when I'm away from him and I love his cuddles and love him to touch me. I guess I would still like it more if he told me he loved me occasionally. I have no doubt that he does for me and you girls, but you know me, words have that magic and there's nothing like hearing your praises sung over and over.

Today I will be better. We have a lot to do before we get you started on this new programme. Your Dad and I both feel really positive about it. We just know you are going to do so well that you'll show everybody!

As long as I stay employed we'll be laughing.

> You have been off the Ceclor for about a week now. I nearly started you on another lot on Monday but decided against it. We gave you another 12 hours and you did well. You're off the Ventolin as well. To try and help get your ears cleared up we've got you on Bactrim 2ml at night and Demazin. Your ears have a fair bit of fluid in them apparently. I must do some reading up on ENT. I'd better write some pearls of wisdom for Cassie now or I'll be in trouble. Hope you are sound asleep my darling.

We get sucker-punched with the whole sex thing. It's only recently that I've spent some time thinking and being different with this part of my life: conscious loving as a part of a conscious life. Wow, what we've been missing! There's another book to write just there. The work of Janet McGeever and Gene Thomson is brilliant and has renewed our joy for lovemaking no end.[4]

Suffice to say that, at this point, lack of emotional awareness, physical difficulties, and cultural expectations all keep knocking off the self-esteem and adding to the I'm-not-enough pile.

<u>Tuesday 27th October 1992</u>

> I start this entry with more sad news. Grandma died on 19th October 1992 at her home. According to the doctor she suffered a heart attack and died very quickly. She was still on the couch in her dressing gown.

Breathing While Drowning

Your Dad is still really sad. He expected her to go on for another 20 years. She was 72, but it always surprised people to know her age because she acted 10 years younger. She was very independent and maintained an active interest in many things. I think it will be hard on your Aunty Barbara. She spent a good deal of time helping her, babysitting etc. Your Dad and I feel a bit jinxed, as though each time we think we've made a forward step something comes along to knock us down again.

It still feels unreal at the moment. Sunday 18th Grandma was partying on with all the other rels at home for your birthday and your Dad's. She left bright and chatty with Mel and Grandad.

Your Dad feels a bit cheated too I guess. He never had a chance to prepare or say Goodbye as we did with Nana. I think Cassie is starting to think that a "Death" happens every week.

I hear her playing games with her dollies saying this one hasn't got a mum or dad because they're dead! Death is a part of life but at the moment we seem to have more than our fair share.

In one way I s'pose you can say Grandma is going to help even more than she could have coming up for your programme. Hopefully your Dad will be able to put some money aside for you girls for the future.

I think, in fact I know, we would rather have Grandma with us. But, she was lucky. She died quickly, living life to the full right up to the end.

> I can't help but compare Nana's long, slow, painful battle over 12 agonising months that left her a shell, a mere whisper of her former self. It brought back a lot of memories, hurtful ones mostly.
>
> Enough on the past. The present is you are sick again! Another virus — non-specific. We were just getting used to you being laughing and well. Only a few weeks till we start your programme. We already have about 45 volunteers to help. We are both anxious that it gets off to a good positive start so we'd like you to be well thanks!

Is it any wonder we closed ranks? People kept dying all around us, people we loved and people we had counted on. And what a childhood for Cassi and Jacqui; they saw the cycle of life and death so frequently.

Friday 6th November 1992

> Jacqui, yesterday you did a piddle in the potty! It was more luck than management. You had a bladder up to your eyeballs so we dashed and grabbed the potty and plonked you on. Well the looks you gave us said "Hey you guys what am I supposed to do now?" You looked amazed and bemused. We had to pad the seat a bit for your skinny bottom. However, you managed a big piddle and we cheered and hooted. That gave you a big smile.

Breathing While Drowning

What is it about parents that we get so excited about the bodily functions of our children? It's a kind of rite of passage. Our kids must think we are crazy sometimes.

Sunday 15th November 1992

Well Jacqui, here we are! At the Australian College for the Achievement of Human Potential, Healesville. You, of course, are sound asleep. Naturally some of the tests couldn't be done.

Already there have been a few eye openers. There is more concern about your eyesight than we had anticipated. We haven't had to wait all that long so far. However, I'll bring a book tomorrow and some munchies. Only 2 more rounds to go. Your Dad is writing a letter to his Uncle Willy in Scotland about Grandma dying.

We, or at least I have pinned a lot of hope on this programme. I want nothing less for you than to be normal. I want to see you run, laughing and talking into school. I want to see you grow up happy, experiencing everything in life. Getting married and having children of your own.

I don't think I'm asking too much. I ask the same for Cassie. I hope she isn't running Grandad ragged. He looked pretty tired when we got to the caravan this afternoon. Of course he had already put the annexe up by himself. Or rather, with Cassie's help.

Name a mother would not want exactly the same thing for her child—to be normal. Looking back, "normal" was a more innocent wish. Underneath that wish was a wish for the freedom to choose, the physical, mental, emotional, financial, and social freedom to choose.

That's what drives me now to get the message of conscious confidence out. To give people the chance to realise they are enough. They do have the confidence to choose the life that expresses the very best of who they can be. And kids, let them choose what they want to do with their lives. I see so many people channelling kids into boxes for their future. Support their natural inclinations to learn, but leave their dreams to them. You have your own life to dream; don't force them to live yours.

Thursday 19th November 1992

Well Jacq. Finally, we know what you have, and coincidently what you have not.

You have a PROFOUND, DIFFUSE, BILATERAL, BRAIN INJURY TO THE CORTEX, THE MIDBRAIN AND THE PONS! It's a mouthful, but at least we know it.

In the same breath, we know how to fix it. The Institutes for the Achievement of Human Potential, Healesville, VIC, AUST have the programme to do it and we are the family who can do it. What's left of us anyway! It is going to be hard, difficult, tiring, agonising, time-consuming but it will work.

I want nothing less than to see you run laughing and yelling into school after Cassie with nobody noticing you ever had a brain injury. I know you have it in you. And I'm sure we'll find it in ourselves somewhere to help you as much as you will need.

Breathing While Drowning

> Cassie was really excited when we told her we could make your head better. She shouted "Yes", "Yes" and "Yes". She wants to help and learn to read alongside you.
>
> I can see your Grandad is still a little apprehensive but he's getting caught up in the emotional possibility that you might be made well. I discovered tonight that in his own way he describes you as epileptic and retarded.
>
> Words which horrified me and I had to be careful not to be angry. But the anger quickly passed because now I could say to him quite calmly but forcefully. "Now, you can tell them she's brain injured."
>
> We are armed to the back teeth and now we have to go out and fight for you in the big bad world.
>
> All it takes is love and we all have that for you. Sleep peacefully my love for tomorrow you begin the long, hard road to wellness. We can't and won't rest until you are better.
>
> Talk to you soon. Mum

We learned to fight, sometimes out in the open and sometimes in the dark. Once we found our cause, we armed ourselves to the teeth and chased the dream—the dream of a life fulfilled at its highest potential. I turned anger into passion and resilience, and we devoted ourselves to not only keeping Jacqui alive, but also to helping her learn and grow like her sister.

We were fighting time. Every moment was precious, but we were gathering a small army of allies, people who were prepared to help us fight the ogres and dragons ... even if they didn't really know what they were.

Tuesday 1st December 1992

Jacq, Cassie opened the first box on the advent calendar today. Hopefully, next year you will be able to help her open it. In fact, you might even want one yourself. I'll buy you 10 if you ask for them.

If they are able, what parent would not give their child anything they wanted? In fact, even if they are not able, a parent will find a way.

Yesterday we started on the Programme from the Institutes for the Achievement of Human Potential. You did reasonably well. Even stayed awake most of the time you were supposed to. Today, however, you were unwell. Temperature 38.6, snuffly and grouchy and sleepy. We didn't get as much of the programme done as we ought but it was only your second day.

The programme is pretty full. We have to start you at 7 and you aren't done till 8.30-9. At least that's the plan. I don't think you've read the rules yet as you didn't play fair last night. You had niggly teeth and stayed up till midnight.

I really feel positive about this programme. I can sense it is going to do you a lot of good. It has kept us really busy already.

Breathing While Drowning

So much optimism, so much hope. Trusting it because it feels right; the logic fits, and it gives us something to do. Just do something, anything!

Saturday 5th December 1992

Jacqui, tonight you are exhausted. Today you were all go-go-go! I left you sound asleep on your mattress on Cassie's floor. She isn't in her room she's at Grandad's. She'll be going to a work Christmas do with Mel.

You did really well on your Programme today. Day 6 and already making progress.

It was a good day all around as you stayed awake the whole time.

You finally crashed about 2015 hrs and couldn't even manage your last bottle.

It's hard trying to juggle your meals and drinks. You have to be constantly aware of protein and fluids as well as nutrients and fat content, etc, etc, etc.

We have just a little bit more to do and we'll be fully set up for you. Today you did a big pooh with minimal assistance and no enema! Amazing or a fluke? Time will tell. Your diet is better already.

Some people are turning out to be really good friends. They are managing to come back twice in the one week. Hopefully by the end of next week we will have given the spiel of the programme to everybody and we'll be able to get down to serious business.

This is how I honed my project and change management skills and learned how to organise, teach, and negotiate. Learning to form teams, juggle the programme elements, tell the story, and keep it all together. And once you find out there's a way to do it, you build your capability, own it, and get creative. These actions make the process yours.

In recent times, I recognised what Brendon Burchard teaches: that there is a process for doing things, a methodology that makes it easier, less overwhelming. And you can concentrate on the journey when the path and the signposts are there for you to follow.

> *Your Dad has high goals for you too. Tonight when I said I can't wait to see you learn to read his reply was "soccer!" Huh! I said and then he explained he wanted both his girls in the backyard playing soccer with him. That means you Jacqui would be able to run, yell, coordinate and everything.*
>
> *Your Dad's goals are the same as mine. At least in the main.*
>
> *Sleep well my darling for tomorrow is Day 7.*

Having goals is so important—writing them down and sharing them makes them real, gives us hope and direction. If we don't dream, we die. Sometimes it takes us a lifetime, but we still die without realising our dreams.

According to Leonie Dawson, 80 per cent of people don't set goals.

I know, I know. All the coaches reading this are throwing up their hands in horror. But wait, there's more: of those who do set goals 16 per cent think of their goals but don't write them down; 4 per cent write them down but don't regularly review them; and only

Breathing While Drowning

1 per cent actually write them down and review them regularly. The 1 per cent of people who do so are the top achievers in the world.[5]

Without getting into the whole "what does success mean to you?" and "top achievers of what?", write your goals down or draw them or cut out pictures or make a clay model of them—whatever works for you.

I've seen this work over and over, not just for myself, but also for lots of others. Dream big.

It's like the magic of journaling: once you put it on the page, it's a different story. Journaling helps you clarify your thoughts, feelings, and beliefs. It brings your stories to life. It gives your dreams a chance to happen.

Sunday 13th December 1992

Day 14 coming up. Day 13 was fairly flat, a bit of a disaster. It was 31°C and you looked hot. We barely saw your eyes today, I mean yesterday. You managed to sleep through most of the sessions.

I'll have to make you some knee pads I think, 'cos your little bony knees are getting a bit red and worn out with patterning.

I'm sure once people relax they will be more gentle with you. Your Dad and I are getting quite comfortable with it. The days are busy but mostly rewarding.

I love to see the way you react to the different people who come in. You've had some good days in the last fortnight, plenty of smiles and giggles. Also some not so good ones, sleepy, grouchy and yucky.

> It is still going to take time to get the Programme to be a total way of life.
>
> We have to spend more time touching, massaging and tickling. We need to brush your hair more often I think as well.
>
> The Incline Plane is a bit of a dud at present. We have to refine the programme. For a start we have to have only 1 person encouraging you. Next, the really bright light. Maybe? Not sure if you are having a tired day do we just leave you or do we tickle and cajole and hope you'll feel like it another day.
>
> I had to defend your right to be on the programme the other day. One of the surgeons, the Paediatric one was rubbishing the Doman-Delacarto. He soon changed his tune when I started to answer back with some knowledge. As it turns out he didn't even know who ran the place or what sort of people/staff there were there.
>
> But he was instantly prepared to rubbish them.

This is many people's reaction to things outside the norm. Rubbish them (judgement) and you won't show your ignorance. People won't take your power or realise that you don't have the answer for everything.

> Naturally he asked if I had seen his cronies at the hospital. I was able to say "Yes", all of them and not one of them any help at all. After going there weekly since she was 5 months old, she has made no progress what so ever.
>
> Being back in theatre is not too bad. I'm a bit fumbling and slow, but it's coming back.
>
> We'll have to ring the Institute and see what we can do about you sliding down that Incline. I think it's getting a bit out of gear. Only one person should be encouraging and going by what was said and what is written it is a bit confusing. Basically we want you to start crawling.
>
> I heard a rumour today that your Dad was a wonderful person. A patient, kind and loving soul. Mind you we had already known that for some time. He is managing really well at the moment except for being tired, tired and tired.
>
> The auction of Grandma's house was a fizzer yesterday so that is still on his mind too.
>
> And Christmas, what can I say! The Festive Season is upon us in all its manic intensity. I figure once it's over, life might go a bit easier.

How many times did I wish for a normal life, a quiet life, an easy life? None of that fits the definition of remarkable. Jacqui's paediatrician used to say after every exciting or dramatic event in Jacqui's life that she wished for us to have a really boring time for a while. And I would say *yes please* to that! And then we would look at Jacqui and wonder what the next thing she had up her sleeve was.

Now I say, "Ditch boring and bring on excitement, change, life, love, and joy. And lots of laughter, lots and lots." And this can be a quiet life. I'm not convinced on the normal and easy bit though. Life is too freaking short to waste doing things over and over, unless that's what floats your boat.

Tuesday 12th January 1993

Jacq, you started Week 7 of your programme yesterday. Out of 15 inclines you went 1.0 metre on 14 of them. About 2/3 in less than 1½ minutes. Mind you, you were so grouchy. It's a wonder you did anything at all.

You've had a bad ear infection and been on the antibiotics for a few days. I think I'd like to check you out. This is the first infection you've had since the Programme started.

You are making progress, not only with your inclines which are amazing but also in other areas. Your bowels are better, you haven't had an enema since Boxing Day. Pretty amazing!

Apart from the last couple of days you've been managing your food really well. Last few days it's been back to the old chuck, spew method. We couldn't do masking Fri, Sat or Sun as you still had a temp. You are so much more alert and aware of the things around you. You are listening carefully to all the new noises.

Breathing While Drowning

You have done more crying and grouching in the last few weeks than you've done in your entire life. At least something is getting through. The VSD is a bit of a worry at the moment. The light is helping a lot, your pupils are improving. The noise is a bit of a fizzer. We deadened the sound for a couple of days. It didn't really help. We turned it up today. You cried a lot but most times it was before you even got to the room. Who knows, we've rung the Institutes so hopefully we'll have a message today. We should also ask them if we can change the white wall more than once a day. I had another question but I can't remember it at the moment.

Your face is a bit of a mess at present. One cheek, the left is all splotchy 'cos that's the side you lie on the most. Also that left ear has a pressure area on it. Difficult to get rid of as you tend to go for that side being underneath. Under your chin you have a large sore, the result of a little pustule which I burst, then it got moist so I put some betadine on. In the morning you had blisters around it, so we washed the betadine off and covered it with Tegaderm. The latest thing to do is enclose these sorts of things and leave them alone for 48 hours to heal of their own accord.

Anyway I put it on at 9am and by 3 o'clock your small lesion was 10 X the size and all raw. It was clean however and it has stayed that way.

The scab is lifting at present and the skin underneath looks pink and healthy. You also have bruises on your shins and sometimes your arms.

Some days I worry that we overwork you and some days I worry that we don't work you enough. I keep thinking "Every day you aren't well is one more day the other kids are getting ahead of you." But I can see the improvement and I know you are going to get well. I still dream of you running, laughing into school with Cassie.

Cass is having a bit of trouble coping with all the attention you're getting. Most days she's pretty good but every now and then she has a "wobbly" day. It's understandable she is only 4 after all. Kinder will be good for her this year.

I'm going to teach her to read so that she can have her own Programme and I can spend some constructive time with her.

We are going to nominate a day or afternoon which is hers to spend it the way she wants to or do something that she'd enjoy. At the moment she's down at Balnarring with Mary and Co.

She rang last night and we had a good little chat. She told me her news and then wanted to know all about ours. Sounded like she was having a great time, not missing me at all. The house is so quiet without her.

Your Dad is really tired too. The majority of the Programme falls on him. He manages superbly most days. I am a bit jealous of 2 things. 1 that he

> spends so much time with you and 2 that so many other women spend so much time with him. They all recognise him as a "great Dad and husband".
>
> I have a wonderful family all round and getting better all the time.

I don't begrudge Ian any of the praise he got; he is a wonderful father and kept the programme and house together. But for myself, how hard was it not to be recognised, not to be able to share the difficulties of a working mother, not to be able to talk to someone about my trials and tribulations. Even at the Institutes, we were the only family with a working mother. It was the best way for us.

Friday 15th January 1993

> I made the mistake of calling the Institute the day before yesterday. Now you have to do 30 white walls instead of 10! We also discovered you were 4 VSDs short of quota. Then we thought we might as well add the 3 extra masks up to 30.
>
> Now you have a really busy day. As if you didn't before.
>
> You are going well on the Programme. I can see lots of improvement. Only 11 weeks till re-visit. But boy are you grouchy.

The grouchy was aliveness, poking Jacqui out of her comfort zone, her cocoon of ambiguity and nothingness. Bombarding all her senses with stimulation from all kinds of sources: physical, mental, and emotional. Things a well baby would get naturally through seeing, hearing, touching, smelling, and tasting.

Sunday 24th January 1993

The grouchiness has passed. You finally decided that you didn't like the VSD with its loud noise, so now it's a quiet buzzer. Much more civilised. You are doing really well in lots of ways. Little things are improving all over the place.

Less, can't remember what I was going to say. You sit up straighter in the highchair, less vomiting, you eat more. You can point your toes now. You are also looking around more with eyes wide open. We go ...

Sometimes the entries dribbled to a stop as I nodded off in the wee hours.

Tuesday 2nd March 1993

Boy was I tired when I wrote that last note. All those little scribbles mean I closed my eyes and was dropping off to sleep.

Well it's week 14 and you are firing on all cylinders.

Today you did 40 inclines! It was your first day at it but you were great.

Breathing While Drowning

You have so much more style and determination now.

Your arms and legs are really trying hard to coordinate and work.

Often you can bring your left arm forward by itself and your legs can bend on occasion too. You've been hard to pattern of late, stiffening yourself and refusing to cooperate. We are waiting to hear from the Institute to see if there is anything we can do.

Tonight I put you to bed at 8 o'clock. When I went to check you before I went to bed at 10:30 you have given me the biggest grin and cheeky look. I think you're asleep now though.

Jacqui you have made so much progress in a lot of ways. You are much more alert, bright, more interested in the world. Your vision is steadier. I'm sure you see a lot more and a lot more clearly too. You are aware of sounds all about you. You have had only 1 ear infection since going on the Programme. And you haven't had any temperatures for weeks.

Now the bowels, something I should have mentioned at the beginning. Jacqui can open her bowels by herself. Lots of it too. Afterwards you feel pounds lighter. Jacq you love to see who's coming next to help you

We were absolutely blessed with the family, friends, and strangers who rocked up to our door in pairs three times a day, seven days a week. Though all the days were governed by the same schedule, we learned to tell them apart by when the regulars arrived—Nora is here, so it must be Tuesday.

Many of the patterners came for us but stayed for Jacqui. They saw her come alive. The sceptics became our greatest champions. Nora had an adult son with Down's Syndrome, and she confided to me after seeing Jacqui's progress that she wished the programme had been around when he was young. My heart bled for her. She was our oldest patterner, somewhere in her seventies, I think, but regular as clockwork.

Sunday 7th March 1993

> Jacqui, you are a monkey. Ian said you were laughing fit to burst tonight. Of course I was sleeping before coming to work so I missed it. I miss quite a lot of things working. You just love your Dad so much though. He gets all the best smiles and laughs. If you hear his voice you crane your neck trying to find him. I guess it's a penalty I pay. I get a bit jealous at times but I know it's for the best.

But what about me? Getting used to being at the bottom of the pile. Just because I chose (did I?) working, I didn't feel I could express how I felt to anyone. Poor me. There's that victim and martyr mentality again. I write so often about missing out and I found it had a name: fear of missing out (FoMo). I can see it may have started in my childhood and then been pumped up with Jacqui's birth.

Breathing While Drowning

As humans, we are born with a bias to fear and negativity—this is our natural inclination. I notice that I don't write anywhere near as much about the wonderful feelings of helping so many families birth new babies, about helping ease the suffering of people dying, about helping people recover from illness.

Get over it and get on or choose differently. Your life belongs to you. Sound familiar? Everything you think, feel, do, and believe is important and that's what matters.

Just as other people tried to put me in a box, I got really good at putting myself in one. Nowadays, I'm more inclined to let that stuff go, to be conscious of my choice. I can choose to be a victim, or I can choose to be joyful.

> *He is coping much better at home than I would. I'm a better mother when I work. Sounds strange but true.*

This is something I often said and came to believe. It helped other women who were working mothers or struggling with new motherhood when I told them this.

I still believe these words today, but I approach them from a different perspective. Rather than being seduced by the masculine, the boon of societal success, I can have it all because now is all. I am who I am, the sum total of all of me.

> Work is looking up at the moment. I've been asked to start some antenatal classes for the hospital. Very exciting.
>
> Not as exciting as when you go back to the Institute in 14 weeks' time. I want you to have done so well they are amazed.
>
> We'll have to help you work hard over the next month. I'm surprised you weren't sick today (Sat) Friday you were terrible, a runny nose and sneezes all day, a temperature by the evening. But Saturday you were great, barely a sniffle. We dosed you up on Vitamin C, it may have helped. More pooh today by yourself! I hope you are asleep. Bye my darling baby.

I even felt guilty about being excited for myself. And rather than say, "You go, girl!", I reiterated other people's needs before my own.

Christie Marie Sheldon had the perfect way of expressing the importance of looking after yourself. She likened it to when the oxygen masks are used in an airplane emergency. You need to put your own mask on first before you can help other people. Fill your own battery in order to help others.[6]

It fits so well with Marianne Williamson's words: "As we let our own light shine, we unconsciously give other people permission to do the same".[7]

Breathing While Drowning

Monday 15th March 1993

Jacqui, you have achieved major improvements over the last few days. Thursday 1.3 metres Friday 1.4 metres Sat 1.5 Sun 1.6 and today you start 1.7 metres. It's hard to image how you began with 0.2 0.1 or zero. You are now getting a lot more style to your crawling. First it was legs, then arms, bend elbows, pushing hands and now its legs again. Both legs bend up and you push off a bit sometimes from the wall sometimes the floor of the incline.

You smile as you go too. You seem so pleased with yourself when you do a fast crawl. You are trying it a lot more on flat surfaces too. I don't think it will be long before you are off and racing. You still have a persistent rash on your lower left cheek. It almost disappears then a day on the incline and it's back.

You were having a few more seizures just before this really dynamic spell. I wonder if it was the brain moving to a new district.

Three weeks today and we'll be at the Institute. Both your Dad and I (and most of the volunteers) are hanging out to see what they say and what your programme will be like after this assessment. I'm sure you are a bit bored with it at the moment.

Despite you having such a good day I'm a bit sad. I know I have to keep on top of it, sometimes it's more difficult than others. Sue and Victor and

Co came for the 4pm session and tea yesterday. Jenny and Co came after tea. All of which was fine, but a few comments left me feeling a bit down.

The kids were all down the back and there was a head count. "Yes all 5 are there." Jacqui Bree should have been No 6.

All the comments on the others. Nobody seemed to think how Ian and I might feel or bother to say about Jacqui in the same breath. I'm probably just a little sensitive at present.

I guess I'm feeling a little frustrated too. I want so much to be home with you and your Dad and sister helping with the programme. And yet I've been offered antenatal classes at the hospital. Something I've always wanted to do. It will need a bit of time, quite a bit. But these next few years are so important for you.

Another thing that's been worrying me is X. It is now ½ way through March and we have not seen them since December. Pretty slack on their part. Anyway, its X's birthday and we're invited, to come for afternoon tea.

Problem is, I hear via the grapevine that you and your programme are "not really their thing". So I'm not sure whether I'll go or even send Cassie. You, certainly are not going. It makes me a bit sad to think of it at all. Obviously, they have a problem with the whole concept of you, I'm not going to expose

> you to the negative vibes and discrimination. You have plenty of volunteers and strangers who can help and are positive.

It's so easy to judge others. Running up the ladder of inference, assuming you know what people are thinking, singling out the bad and focusing on that to the exclusion of the positive.

The hurts so close to home from family and friends found me unprepared. It's hard when it comes from people you love who don't know how they are hurting you. And if you don't say anything, how can they know how to stop or how to help? How can they tell you how they're feeling?

Expressing my vulnerability and asking for help weren't really lessons I learned in my family or in my experience. We tended to embrace the keep-it-all-inside-and-look-like-you're-coping-even-if-you're-not mentality. Plus, as a nurse, I was expected to be the epitome of equanimity, sailing calmly and confidently through the chaos and pain.

Now I work hard to avoid assuming things about other people—either their generosity or lack thereof. I have no idea of their stories or their thoughts or feelings. I've only lived my life. I can count on myself. So I try to live the unexpected joys, and bring the joy to every moment.

> On a brighter note, Dad went crazy with the bankcard and bought a wok and an overlocker for me. The overlocker is great. I whizzed up 2 pair of pants for you this morning. And a dress and headband for Cassie yesterday. Of course Cassie now thinks I should be making stacks of things for her.

There is joy in creating, in being able to make something from something else.

> Soon, after programme, soon. She was a little sad last night too, watching the other young ones playing. She wants you to be well.

The learning, joy, and pain that Cassi experienced with her sister's life and death were deep and life-changing emotions. Her story is for her to tell another day.

Saturday 4th April 1993

> A new day and a new book. Its 0446 Jacqui and I hope you are asleep. I've got a spare 5 minutes and my thoughts are with you, Cassie and Ian. Monday we head off to Healesville, to the Institutes for the Achievement of Human Potential.
>
> A few babies and a few contractions later here I am again.
>
> It's an anxious time at the moment. We are keen to show you off at the Institutes, but worried they won't think you've done enough.
>
> I was worried they wouldn't think I'd done enough.
>
> We'll motel it this time, a luxury. Cass will have a couple of day's holiday with a friend before Grandad brings her over. She is excited too.

Breathing While Drowning

> *I've been to a funeral today, I mean yesterday. D died on Wednesday. She was 4 years old. Another friend of yours from playgroup. That's 2 in 6 months. I'd better write some reports before I fall asleep.*

How hard is it to watch children die, to see their life unrealised, their potential not reached? But is this the wrong way to look at it? What if their soul is here to learn a short lesson and to teach *us* a lesson? If I follow my increasing belief that our highest and best gift is our freedom of choice, these young souls made that choice to learn and teach in their very short time with us. And despite it being a heart-breaking experience, I feel like my obligation is to freaking learn that lesson and get on with my life, make the best choices I can for freedom, love, learn, and live.

Sunday 2nd May 1993

> *Another letter to my baby. Jacqui you don't look much like a baby any more. Over the last 4 months you grew 100% in height, chest, head and weight for child of your age. Truly amazing! Now you have to grow about 500% to catch up.*
>
> *You started back so joyfully onto the programme when we first returned but now you've slowed down. It seems as soon as we turn our back on you you're asleep. I'm a bit worried about that. We are persisting with you, trying to enthuse you with life and vigour. Some days it's not easy, believe me.*

> We still have heaps of people coming in at the moment. Some days I think I could scream so that we could just be a family again.
>
> Peace and quiet, on our own. But then I look at how much you've improved and it all doesn't matter anymore.
>
> You are starting to hold you head up much better now. You occasionally turn it from side to side.
>
> Constipation is gone forever, I hope. I tried you last night with chopped up pasta and spinach. You gagged a few times but managed to keep it all down. We have to challenge you a bit now. You must sit in the highchair for all meals and drinks. Your Dad is the worst culprit for picking you up when you're supposed to be on the floor working. We have to keep you prone as much as possible so you get the idea of crawling.
>
> The best you can do at the moment is 180 degrees with your head as the pivot. We've got you on extra vitamins, but you've been on them for a week now with not much improvement. We'll ring the Institute Monday if you're no better. Your Dad was wondering if it could be the masking making you tired.
>
> We'll see later today.

How hard is it for an introvert to never have a quiet space, to always feel surrounded, assaulted by other people's energy, noise, needs and demands? These days, I'm better at recognising what I need and giving myself and my family space. We are still really close and are happiest when it's just us. We can be a party on our own. We bring the joy.

I believe my positive energy and efforts to live mindfully are a big part of this. Following my own dreams helped. With meditation and eating better (removing meat and gluten from my diet), I calmed down immensely. The occasional lapses and overloads with gluten and sugar see me turn into a scary woman.

Sunday 16th May 1993

A lot has changed in the last fortnight. Several calls to the Institutes has made some adjustments in your programme and you seem to have caught up.

You were really tired for the first 4 weeks. However, the last 3 days you've been brilliant. Awake, alert, looking, doing, feeling. Yesterday for the first time anyone would have been convinced of your intention to play with a rattle which you had in your hand, left and returned your hand to it several times. All the while looking at what you were doing. Coming down the incline you've developed a much better style. Arms and legs are all trying now. The light in your eyes is bright and consistent.

Friday night you were so beautiful. I was bursting with pride. You had been put to bed a little earlier and I went to check if you were okay. I turned on your light to find you bright-eyed and bushy tailed. A big smile was in evidence too.

I checked your nappy, dry, so I turned you back on your tummy and you looked really worried. An idea occurred to you. You made your drinking motion with your tongue. I asked if you were thirsty and wanted a drink. The biggest smile hit your face instantly. You were delighted I had fallen for it. I couldn't help it. I had to get you up and give you a drink. Well, your Dad did really.

There is so much life in your eyes now. You can hold a glance for longer too. You laugh more and talk more. The time is coming, your time.

Your Dad and I are pretty tired, exhausted would be the word. Somehow we manage to get through each day and night and start off the next one. Grandad has been a good help. I know we wear him out but he goes home happy. Ian got the family photo framed and gave it to him tonight. He was a bit teary but really pleased. Other people who I thought would be more help aren't.

Mind you I can't talk. Your big sister has taken to shouting at us when we discipline her. But she is gorgeous too.

Hope you are sound asleep my beautiful girl. A big day of programme ahead.

How easy is it to ask for help? Not at all. Even now, I'm not the best at asking for help. I spent so many years being self-sufficient and resilient that it often takes someone else to point out that I don't have to do it all on my own.

Sunday 11th July 1993

Jacq, so long since I've written to you. But you are never long out of my thoughts. Your programme keeps us busy. You seem to be really up and down at present. Yesterday you were unwell. You have a head cold, new teeth coming and are tired from being up all night.

We all seem to hit a bit of a lull just before we go back to the Institutes. Everyone gets a bit down, including you. I think you get a bit bored too. I'll ring the Institutes on Monday and ask what to do.

Trying to motivate you down the incline is difficult at present. Maybe if we could put things along the sides it would help. Until you get a bit faster its taking you a lot of your day to do just the distance. This means we don't have all that much time to let you play after an incline.

You seem to be really tired this semester. Not much stamina.

Despite your head cold you have been really well up to now. No unexplained fevers etc. You have done a new one on me though. Crystals in the urine! Like fairy dust. We'll send a specimen off tomorrow or Monday. The paed seems to think it will be okay. Just Calcium oxalate crystals.

The philosophy of our house is very much tuned to you. If you have a good day, we all have a good day. It you have a lousy day, we all have a lousy day.

There is some good evidence on matching vibrations here. Emotions have energy. The energetic vibrations of each person affect those around her or him. The most powerful vibration tends to win out over the others and change the others to be close to the same frequency. A grouch makes everyone else grouchy. When someone walks into a room full of joy, it's hard not to smile and be uplifted. Because our home, our lives revolved around programme, Jacqui's energy took the lead.

> Your Dad is struggling a bit at present. He's got the pre-revisit blues. The bulk of the programme and your care fall to him and its difficult most days to make it all come together. So when you don't make any progress he feels it, almost personally. Winter is hard too, difficult to go outside with all the rain.
>
> I surprised him Friday night with a dinner for 2 at the pub. It was good for him to go out of the house. We met friends there which was good and bad. They had their 3 months old, alert, cute and cuddly.
>
> Your Dad talked a bit yesterday about how he felt. You missed all of those milestones. We have to hark back 5 years to when Cass was young.
>
> Your Dad said, and I agreed, "I want her walking now!" Then he decided crawling would be okay. We both think that if you can get motion then all the rest will fall into place a little easier. It's going to take some time is all.
>
> We also talked about more editions to the family. We had seen the newborn baby of one of our patterners when we came over to see the paed.

Breathing While Drowning

Your Dad wanted Jacqui to walk and a new baby boy in a cot. Not much to ask. We discussed it but we'll leave it till you are much further into your programme. I feel I've got room for at least 1, if not 2 more babies, but at the moment what we've got comes first.

I know your Dad feels very keenly that he is the last Strachan in Aus and it's up to him to renew the line and keep it flourishing.

I have to be strong for all of you and keep the family in sync and in order. Your Dad is feeling the strain a bit at present. Hang in there Jacq. Hurry up and get well then we can do normal family things together. Like go for drives or picnics etc.

I have so much to say to you but so little gift for saying it.

You are growing more beautiful each day. The light in your eyes is almost always on. I hope the programme can help. I just want you totally well. Too much to ask? I don't think so. We took you to the chiropractors the last two Tuesdays. Interesting, I don't know if it helped or not. Your Dad is still a bit sceptical. Time will tell.

I'd better go and do some more work. I have my second class on Tuesday. I hope it's a bit better than the first. I was a bit scratchy & disjointed. I'm sure I'll get better with practice.

This is a really important entry because it depicts me being strong for everyone, holding everyone together. No time for vulnerability, only shame and guilt sprinkled with hope and joy and love. I put it out to the universe that I had space for two more babies. And we made space for our two beautiful sons.

I had so much to say but so little talent for saying it. I spent too long writing to myself, sharing my deepest thoughts with the written page. How uncomfortable do we feel as Australians, as women, as adults sharing our vulnerability? Really bloody uncomfortable. "No worries, she'll be right, mate." Sometimes I just wanted to scream, "Ask me how I am and don't take fine for an answer!" I'm not fine—nowhere near it.

And sometimes I wanted something that we were not going to get … maybe ever. How important are intentions, and how do we manage when sometimes it's just not going to happen? How do we manage the other?

Do we feel guilty for wanting a normal life? Is this why Jacqui died? Alive, we would probably never have had a normal life. Actually, come to think of it; yes, we would. It would be normal for us because it was ours.

And what is normal? Why do we yearn for it anyway? Why do we want something so intangible? We're always looking for the future state, for the ideal, for something we don't have. We don't take enough time to be here in the moment, really living and loving every second, experiencing every sense reeling with feeling. Who said we all need to be the same? How boring would that be?

Breathing While Drowning

Monday 2nd August 1993

Jacqui, a mixed day. We're at the motel in Healesville. We've had the first day of the Re-visit assessment.

You've lost 1kg in weight! I'm shocked. Both your Dad & I were sure you would have put on stacks. You've grown 3cm in length and 1cm in chest (120%).

Max was really impressed with your action down the incline. He was also impressed with your vision and behaviour when he spoke to you. It bore out what we already know — that you are one clever cookie. And bold! We tried patterning and showed him how you misbehave. It's given him food for thought. He was very interested today. I could almost see his mind working. We will have some interesting things on Saturday, I feel

Your Dad and I are both disappointed with your weight. I am also disappointed with your head circumference. But on the plus side, Max is extremely pleased with your intellectual and visual progress.

Your Dad and I a bit numb I s'pose. We still have to wait for the conclusions.

Cassie arrives tomorrow with Grandad. So we have one peaceful day left. It's been raining. I hope it's better tomorrow. We don't have much indoor entertainment.

> *Jacqui, don't get me wrong we're still thrilled with what you are doing but we want you to be walking today not tomorrow or next year. We haven't got time for you to make slow steady progress, we need you to be better, well now.*
>
> *I know we sound impatient but you have lost so much time already. There is so much you have missed we don't want you to miss anymore.*

This is how I live life. This sense of urgency, as if I might miss something if I don't go fast; FoMO. Balance this with mindfulness and every moment is a gem, each has its colour and movement, taste and smell, texture and temperature. The sense of urgency translates into a sense of progress, of learning, of reaching for the next evolution. If we stay the same, we stay the same. The words just reek of stagnation. If we move and learn, we grow. There is so much out in the world to explore, and so much of the inner world we can explore. Our brain is capable of taking in so much more than we give it. Our emotions and energy are unlimited.

We are unlimited beings spending time in a limited human body. And even so, we use such a small amount of our potential. Never stop learning.

There's a concept called *cognitive surplus*: the shared, online work we do with our spare brain cycles. The ability of the world to volunteer and collaborate on shared projects represents ancient human motivation to create shared design for generosity. There are a trillion hours of need up for participatory grabs[8]. It's a fascinating idea and leans towards a whole human consciousness: we are all connected. How good would it be to contribute your cognitive down time to the greater good of humanity?

Tuesday 24th August 1993

Jacq, so much to say and such a little time to do it. Your head grew 200%, chest 125%. Overall a growth rate of 2 ½ times faster than before programme. You had quite a good week. Then when you got back you got a throat infection, bronchitis then mumps! At least we think its mumps. We'll get the blood test results tomorrow.

Your face is almost back to normal.

Today you have been whizzing down the incline. Face blew up Thursday 19th August.

Friday 27th August 1993

Jacq, I think I'll write a book. Title "Jacqui Bree, what will you be?" I've just finished reading about Doran (Scotson 1785). I'm inspired, if I wasn't already. Your life is too important. We have to motivate you and ourselves more. I'm going to get Cassie more involved too. Big paintings might be a good start. Your Dad is really tired at the moment.

Saturday 28th August 1993

Of course there has been no time to do much yet, not even thinking. I am determined. Your Dad, as I've tried to say before is really tired. He's starting to get more frustrated and angry that he has no time to do what he needs to. We started to have a serious talk tonight but, of course, we were interrupted. We just have to become more obsessive with the programme. We don't have any more spare time.

I think I'll try and get some big paints and pictures of bright toys/animals etc and I'll get Cassie to paint some bright pictures around the rooms. We have to give you more incentive/motivation to see and crawl. We've changed the living area around a bit. It should work out better.

Jacqui, I want you walking and talking. I'm sure you'll be able to crawl on the flat soon. You are really enjoying your intelligence programme. You are learning to read words now. We need to show you more big, bright stuff.

My heart aches for your big sister. Like you she is bright and clever. And like your Dad she is frustrated. If you were crawling I'm sure it would be easier. She could then get more involved with games to entice you along. Her imagination is remarkable. It is something I've tried to foster. In some ways it makes a safe place to retire into when the world gets a bit dicey.

Breathing While Drowning

And isn't that a prophetic line for both Cassi and me. We both use our imagination to disappear from the real world for blocks of time. We are both great readers and love fantasy. And we are both really good at hiding.

> I see so much in your eyes and in your face. You are trying so hard to communicate at present. Often it's just your mouth working hard but no sound. We'll increase your masks and try to help you get a bit more breath.
>
> I know one day you'll be able to say "I love you" and give me a hug.

This makes me want to scream, "Share your freaking vulnerability before it's too late and the moment, the person, and the life is gone!" Tell someone you love them right now; say you think that person is fabulous for whatever reason; share the freaking feeling. Stop reading this and go do it now—even if you have to call them, text them, Skype them, or write them a letter.

You may be amazed at what you get back if you open that door just a crack.

> I've worked 82.5 hours this fortnight – too much. I think we'll have to cut back on work/money and budget for less at home.

Now here is an old story I've been telling myself for years. You have to work hard to earn money—too hard. It's all just your own stories about money and work and worth. The choice is yours, and I deserve to have it all.

> I saw the obstetrician on Monday. He said my prolapse was "impressive". I've got to see a physio who specialises in that area on Wednesday. He said the only real cure is surgery in a major way. But I explained I still wanted another child or two so surgery is out of the question. It just makes everything that much more difficult. Some days I feel like everything is falling out.

And here is another priceless gem—talk about being disconnected to the feminine! How about your uterus falling out of your body!

And I feel like everything is falling out. No wonder I tried to shut it down, to keep it closed, to hold on for dear life. Holding tighter and keeping it all inside just meant the feminine disappearing more and more from my life. So my body tries to tell me in a really obvious way that I need to do something about it or I'll lose it forever.

> Also, my right leg tends to give way at the moment, usually when I twist or turn. It improved slightly when I saw the chiro but not totally. Sounds like I'm falling apart doesn't it? Your Dad wants to trade me in on a new model. Sometimes I think it would be a good idea.

Breathing While Drowning

Falling apart—lots of falling, lots of drowning in overwhelm, in the real world, in by being a working woman and mother, by being the mother of a hurt child, and by being a wife.

"Not good enough!" is what this screams; you're not good enough! Let's trade you in for a better model, one that is good enough, one that can do it all.

> You did reasonably well with programme today. Not brilliant but you enjoyed it I think.
>
> I have a mission, a mission impossible "Make Jacq fat!" Maybe or maybe not. I also have a secret wish. "Crawling by Christmas". Can you do it? I hope so. I'm going to try and get you there by hook or by crook. I think we can do it.

A few things here: again, the encouragement, optimism, determination, and stubborn resilience to keep going, to push people beyond their limits. And then there is the visionary leadership, the engagement in the excitement of possibility and potential.

I can see the subtleties and read the body language, see the life and potential. If I could see the potential in Jacqui, then how much easier is it to spot in people who can speak and move?

On the other hand, I realise that what I wish for is not everyone else's wish. Sometimes people don't see it; sometimes they don't want it; and sometimes they don't believe they deserve it or can have it. Sometimes they don't see that the dream picture I can help them paint as a coach, by putting brushes into their hands, by opening the doors to imagination through confidence or whichever switch is needed, could become their real world. If you can imagine it, it can be yours.

As I learned to coach, I realised that telling someone is easy, showing them is just as easy, and letting them do it for themselves is the most powerful thing in the world. They then remember, are proud and confident, and can do it over and over again.

Sometimes it's hard while coaching to see someone reaching for an answer or understanding. It's almost as if I can see their neural synapses trying to fire in different directions. Often, I witness them sparking into a big nothing, but then comes the part I love: I see it in their eyes when the spark ignites and the brand new way opens up like a kaleidoscope of technicoloured wonder. I witness their hearts beating faster—*maybe it could, maybe I could.* This is the point of courage. This is the moment when leaders are born, when people change their lives.

As Benjamin Franklin said, "Teach me and I forget. Show me and I remember. Involve me and I understand."

Saturday 18th September 1993

Jacq, up until yesterday I would have said no way were you going to crawl for Christmas. Then last night you made my day, week, month at least.

You had had a better afternoon, then after tea you were lying on your floor. You started to laugh maybe at us having tea or maybe at how clever you were about to be. You lifted your head by yourself and turned it purposefully to the left (your non-favourite side). A few minutes later you turned back. You didn't just flick your head like when you get a fright. This was a planned action to look in the other direction. You thought you were so clever. The next time you even paused and looked forward. You repeated this process several times

> and Dad even caught it on video! Naturally we cheered and told you how great you were. You laughed more and kept throwing up your head. Your legs were trying to crawl too. I'm sure it will help when its summer and you can have bare toes.
>
> We've been doing extra patterns 'cos you've been too tired to come down the incline. We've also been continuing to mask after tea which have probably helped.

This was a brilliant day; I saw hope in motion.

But I can't help thinking the following as I write: yes, but in fewer than two years, she will be gone.

Sunday 19th September 1993

> Jacq, I'm a bit more awake tonight. I've just cut out 60 Australian paintings for BITs. We're trying to get ahead for next revisit as we've been told we'll have to do them next time. Ian said you had a good day yesterday and worked quite hard. You did more inclines than you've done for a while.

Learning to anticipate, planning, and being proactive, are all great lessons for project and change managers ... and also parents.

Tuesday 28th September 1993

Believe it or not, your Dad and I are in bed before midnight. Your Dad is reading Doran. He's up to Chapter 13. Mary told him to get a wriggle on today as she wants to read it too.

After I got up I helped you with the last session of programme. It seems that your head control is getting much better. You no longer allow your nose to get crunched when you roll over and you are balancing on your belly more often. These episodes used to be months apart, then weeks. Now, sometimes they are only days. We are doing masking as often as possible. I'm sure it is helping. The last 2 nights you have gone to bed awake and chirpy but then gone to sleep fairly quickly. Laughter is now an everyday event. Still joyous and special but more familiar. Your big sister was tired tonight and grouchy. Half her problem was that she was too hot. In a spencer and a winter dress and it was in the early 20's.

I'm sure you can be crawling before Christmas. We just have to get those flashes of brilliance more consistent. Yesterday morning was a prime example. I had you in front of the lounge room window in the sun. You were looking out the window. You actually saw and tried to follow firstly Polly (the cat) who was outside and came and sat on the window sill. More amazingly you saw a few minutes

> Later some sparrows fly onto the bird feeder and then away! Fantastic!
>
> I think you've put on about ½ a kilo at the moment. So the "make Jacq fat" campaign is going reasonably well.

What a joy to remember these moments, to feel the smile crack my face and see you there in front of the window; ponytail and bright green eyes.

Thursday 3th September 1993

> Jacq you keep having these glimpses of brilliance. It's fantastic but frustrating. We know you can do fantastic things but you just run out of puff at present. You did remarkably well over the last 2 days and now you're tired out. You tend to hit the proverbial "wall" in the blink of an eye. Talked to Max today. All going well. Continue to do more inclines but help you with patterning a bit more often. Continue more masking, as much as possible. Introduce words as often as required. When we think you've got it, next one. He even asked how we were going. So I told him frustrated at times but basically okay. Only 3 weeks and 2 days till revisit.

Stick to the plan.

Sunday 3rd October 1993

The fish and chips we had for tea keeps coming back to haunt me. I missed most of your day as I was asleep. Ian said you were very bold. Awake, smiling, and looking but not working down the incline. We are going to friends for tea today. Nice to have a rest from the cooking. Actually I think I'll have to cook anyway to give you something. It's hard to get up at 4 and get your mind into gear for a meal and all its preparation.

F phoned tonight with all her cares and woes. She actually sounded quite cheerful. I'm sure she doesn't understand the extent of your problems or how it affects the family dynamics.

Oh my, oh my. I can't help but read what I wrote and cringe. Talk about the pot calling the kettle black. I was so quick to judge, so wrapped up in my own pain and woes. How self-righteous was I? And did I tell anybody how I felt? Did I share? Nope, still hadn't gotten that lesson sorted out.

At the time, I was like a kettle boiling. If the lid had come off, I would have erupted and burnt everyone and everything in my path. As it was, if you got too close and jiggled the lid, chances are you'd get hissed at. Back off!

Breathing While Drowning

Mel and Dad stayed for tea tonight. Dad seems pretty good at the moment. He is helping us a lot at the moment. I hope we aren't wearing him out.

Jacq, will you be crawling for Christmas? It might make things a lot easier. We could be a bit more mobile then. We could pattern you on the kitchen tables and you could learn to crawl on different surfaces at various people's homes.

Sunday 10th October 1993

On Wednesday 6th October 1993 Jacqui B-ee said "koala". I heard it as plain as day. I also had a witness, Sue Fox, who agreed totally with me. We had shown you the word and a picture then in a quiet voice you said after me "koala".

Now that I know you can do it I'm going to nag you I'm sure. Your crawling is getting better. I'm sure once we start respiratory patterning you'll get even better. Your voice has been helped a lot by the extra masking. Your head is so much stronger after all the rolling too.

Sunday in 2 weeks we will be at the Institutes. Hopefully they'll tell us you are excellent and growing in all directions. Your face and body are certainly altering. I hope the campaign to "Make Jacq fat" works. I'll have to really concentrate in the next 2 weeks. I s'pose you must get sick of mushy food. Maybe not 'cos you've never had anything else.

If you could just get the sleeping at night right you'd be much better off. Then all your energy could be spent during the day on your programme.

We've had quite a few successes with potty training. You are doing extremely well. Yesterday we switched to a cheaper brand of nappies in an effort to save some money. So far, so good.

I wish Mum was here to see you. She would have been a great help, not only in the physical sense but on the emotional side too. I miss her dreadfully, just as much today as I did the day she died. She would have been so proud of you. You try so hard sometimes and get nowhere it breaks my heart.

How hard it is to read these words, now years later. Trying hard and getting nowhere. All about change and learning and that there has to be a combination of factors for it all to come together, not just the physical, the process, the careful planning, the *SMART* goals. It's all a matter of fine tuning, having everything humming, interacting and working.

In fact, more and more, I realise that what's needed are the emotional and energetic goals; the *DUMB* goals, as Brendon Burchard says[9]. People need meaning in their lives; they have to know their work is for a purpose, that their life means something to someone, and that they're leaving their mark and making a difference.

Over and over, science and everyone else says we need meaning in our lives; if we're not moving, we're dying, rotting on the vine, wasting our chance.

Breathing While Drowning

> You are going to get better I know. I'd just like it to be sooner rather than later.
>
> Your Dad has had some time off programme to do "other things". This meant building the cupboard in the hall (linen press). It looks fantastic after 8 years of a big hole. It still needs painting and handles but is otherwise done. I think I'll be able to fill it 3 times over by the time I'm finished.
>
> I hope this gives your Dad a bit of reserve strength. We all need it at the moment. There always seems to be this pre-visit depression we have to get over.
>
> With only 2 weeks to go we are starting to get excited again and want to show you off. I would put you down as excellent this time. I'm just crossing my fingers to keep you well till we get there.
>
> I wonder how all the other kids are getting on.
>
> Judy is going to come on the last day for the new programme. Dad (G'Dad) will be there of course. I might see if Cassie can have a day at Barbara's. Maybe even spend Thursday night after the party at Grandad's. That would work out the best then I think. Details for later. Hope you are restfully and blissfully asleep.

I found journaling the best way for me to reflect, to unload, to debrief, to rejoice, and to plan. It allowed for "building a bridge between our present and our future selves".[10] There is something about seeing the words appear on the page that allows the emotions to flow and fixes them in my eyes and mind.

Sunday 17th October 1993

Jacq, I left you in your Dad's arms at 2215hrs last night. When I went down to get changed for work you were yelling in your bed. Of course when I took you down to the lounge room you were all smiles. I'm sure it was 'cos you wanted to see how all the kids were going. 3 of Mary's kids were there for tea. At least you are well, touch wood. Yesterday I was nearly demented. I was sure you had a UTI. As it turns out you may just have been tired. Anyway we sent off the sample. Cassie slept at the Z's last night after spending all day at the Geelong Show. I'm sure she had a great day and didn't miss us at all.

Your Dad and I are thinking about having another baby. We've talked about the pros and cons and think that maybe if we start in Jan/Feb then by the time its born you'll have been on programme 2 years and you'll be 4 and Cass will be 6. That's a big enough gap. I hope you're walking by then.

It will be difficult but we think this is going to work out the best for everyone. It is important for both you and Cass as well as us to finish our family. There is enough love for one or two more yet.

The baby will be good for you to watch and chase. Good for Cass to see how it's supposed to go. That's if the baby doesn't have a significant brain injury. How am I ever going to get through another pregnancy? It's going to be interesting!

Breathing While Drowning

On the IAHP Program, our Jacqui Bree woke up and began to live and grow. Life revolved around both our children as equally as we could and things eventually got back onto an even keel.

We gained some stability, some routine and could see Jacqui improving. We even got to the point where felt we had enough room in our life for another child. There was much soul searching on our part as well as genetic testing. Jacqui was unique, her disability had no obvious cause, no reason why.

Friday 5th November 1993

Well Jacq, you made it to another birthday. Now you are 3! You had a great day 'cos you were on a revisit and we had a party at Grandad's place with all your cousins.

Each day was a milestone, and each year was a miracle. Birthdays were so important.

Saturday 12th November 1993

Jacqui Bree has chicken pox. Cassie asked me why it was called that. I'll have to find out for her. You had a great day yesterday though, despite the spots.

This is week 2 after revisit. Revisit was fantastic! You got a seeing victory. You read and comprehended your words and BITS amazingly. I was left in no doubt that you knew exactly what you were seeing.

> You were also given an object in your hand, not seen, then 2 similar objects were shown to you and you had to pick which one you'd been touching. Correct picking 4 out of 4 times.
>
> We were all amazed. You were delighted to be showing off and also seemed to gain maturity and confidence right then. As if you now knew you could get your message across. You've joined the world in a big way.

This is the joy of being capable: suddenly or gradually understanding that you can do things, that you can learn and achieve and interact and grow.

> This programme is really exciting. Very physical though. 20 inclines by yourself. 10 inclines patterned. 4 patterns. Min 20 masks. 5 words 3 X day. 5 categories of 2 bits 3 X day. 100 rolls, 50 somersaults, brushing and 1 hour respiratory patterning. And 3 X 10 minutes on the Gravitron, at least that's what we're calling it. It's to help you crawl better and hopefully bring some of the cross pattern movements out more often.
>
> Up until you got sick with the chicken pox you were doing really well. Here's hoping it continues when you get better.

Breathing While Drowning

> We went to the cemetery to see my Mum's grave today. I took down some roses and some for Dad. It was the first time I'd been there since she died over 2 years ago. It was very sad. I told her I was doing my best and I missed her a lot. Not even physically but emotionally I needed her to talk to. She could always balance things out and would have helped me with you a lot. Maybe it's better this way. I have to cope with life without her and I've changed my thinking a lot.

The separation from the feminine, from the nurturing facet of life, from the wisdom, from the balance is sorely missed. *Better that I cope alone, tuck myself inside, and be strong*, I thought. *Don't let anyone in; don't let them see; be the good girl you've always been taught to be. Be happy with this gift of a hurt child.*

The fact is that a woman's relationship with her mother is central to the woman she becomes. Losing her mother early has a profound effect on her life, and her mourning never really stops. As Edelman notes, *"Instead it evolves over time, often leading a woman to a place where, instead of actively grieving, she can describe the feeling as a sense of 'missing' her mother, and where she can even begin to see some long-term positive outcomes of early mother loss"*.[11]

This idea describes my grief surrounding Jacqui Bree. Add to that the fact that I had already been grieving while she was alive—grieving for her normal life, for the things she could never be or do. Now I'm at a place where I can see the positive outcomes of losing her before she was five. Her life continues to be such a gift.

Grief is not linear. I'd been taught the Kübler-Ross model[12] in nursing school. Kübler-Ross taught that grief had five emotional stages: denial, anger, bargaining, depression, and acceptance. Most people know about these stages. I'm sure the nursing teachers gave me more than this, but what I recall is that it's a progression with an end. Kübler-Ross's model has more detractors these days.

For me, the circular, complex, twisting nature of life and growth and grieving seems like an apt description. Even laying this book out in chapters and following The Heroine's Journey stages one after the other doesn't do justice to the journey. You can be in more than one stage at a time, and you can go back to some stages until you find your way through.

My friend Ronnie told me a story of a woman who walked down a road and fell into a hole that she hadn't seen. The next time she walked down the road, she saw the hole but still fell in. The next time she walked down the road, she saw the hole and walked around it. Finally, she came to a crossroads before she walked down the road and chose another route.

I love that story because, sometimes, I forget that the road has a big, deep hole in it. I fall into the old way of living and being. Before I know it, I'm back in the big, deep hole … drowning in grief, in busyness, in denial, in anger, in depression.

Saturday 27th November 1993

Jacqui Bree, you've been busy. Chicken Pox is over and gone with, minimal scarring. You are getting back your vim and vigour slowly. We finally made it to the naturopath. He was really interested and enthusiastic about you. So far you seem okay on what he prescribed. He said you were allergic to cheese which is a bit of a pill as it is so high in protein. Never mind we'll just have to be more inventive. I've been keeping pretty much on par these last few weeks for meals. No fish and chips yet. Maybe that's what Cassie craves. I've cut down the nuts and dairy products in an effort to give the male sperm a fair chance. We're going to try and conceive another baby next month. It all sounds a bit cold and clinical but I'm sure it won't be at the time.

We've talked it over a lot for the last few months and it's now or never. Both of us feel the need for at least one more child. It will be difficult but still beneficial for all the family. With the state of my uterus it has to be fairly soon.

I wish I could talk it over with you. You are getting closer and closer to crawling. We mustn't get impatient though. We have to allow you to build up strength slowly.

Its tiring being back on programme but we know you are getting so much better. Leaving no stone unturned it will mean a lot of hard work still to come. I love you Jacq. Every time I hold you I feel a great sense of joy. I wouldn't trade you or your sister for anything.

To be honest I occasionally feel sad at what you have missed but you are catching up at a great rate.

During respiratory patterning you are breathing through your nose, steadily and unlaboured. Your eyes are brighter too. More often wide awake and looking.

On the incline there seems to be a lot more movement in your legs and arms. You are a bit concerned about going off the end though. Maybe we need to make it a bit softer, certainly a bit longer as you are coming off to your knees now. I can't wait for the day you take off on your own.

You had me tricked yesterday. About half way through a mask you started making pig noises so I took it off. Then you laughed and laughed, you were being cheeky, not puffed at all. Ha! Behaviour I would expect from any 3-year-old.

You've got an appointment at the hospital to ultrasound your hip next week. The paed thinks it might be a bit loose/shallow. I think it's okay. I certainly won't let them put it in plaster or anything. I s'pose it's wise to check it out.

Otherwise she was quite pleased with you. 7cm growth in 12 months, heaps of head and chest growth and lots of smarts.

Wednesday 1st December 1993

24 days till Christmas! Hard to believe! Yesterday was the 12-month anniversary of commencing your Programme. What a long way you've come in that time. I'm sure the next 12 months will be just as amazing.

Jacq if you could just crawl. I can't wait for the day when you lift your head off the floor and crawl over to me.

Today you were trying so hard. You're starting to get the hang of the Gravitron I think. We've begun to let you try to get to the next rung yourself. Sometimes there is a definite movement in the right direction. I think you still enjoy the somersaults the best. I hope you went back to bed okay. When I left for work you had just got up again. Amazingly the crying stopped when you go to the lounge room. Ha!

It was really novel to have you behaving like a normal kid, to come to life and have some behaviour!

Thursday 16th December 1993

Still a few up and down days. You are getting over a virus that I generously gave to you last week.

Glimpses of brilliance is what you are giving us. You have these little bursts of showing how well you can do things by yourself. Then you'll have a day like today when you spend most of it asleep. Frustrating to say the least.

Little bubbles of brilliance too far apart burst like soap bubbles, but if you strengthen them, they become a string of beautiful jewels to wrap around your life.

Don't forget to give introverts time to recover, to regenerate their energy and ideas.

> The other day you were being shown a picture of a lion. Both your Dad and I performed a growl for you. It must have tickled your fancy 'cos you laughed and laughed at us. It shows you have a real sense of fun and humour. Your laughter is becoming more the norm than the exception, which helps a lot. But you have to crawl. I know you'll go in leaps and bounds then.
>
> Your Dad said you lifted your head up a few times on the incline the other day. A hope for things to come.
>
> I realised that L wanted to talk to me yesterday. She seems incapable of getting involved. Maybe because she can't maintain her status quo. I would really love to have someone to talk to about deep and meaningful things but there isn't anyone prepared to take me on.

Again, I was so judgemental. She had been a good friend, but we had been drifting apart for a while, taking different paths in life. What are the beliefs anchoring me here? No one could be feeling exactly as I felt. No one could have any idea about how I felt (including myself!). No one else's problems could be anywhere near as bad as mine. That's a pretty arrogant thought.

Breathing While Drowning

Having no emotional connection to your own stuff cuts you off from others. Be tolerant of differences and be a bridge. Extend your hand, but not for so long that your arm aches. It's like a carousel; there is a window of opportunity to get on; otherwise, the hand extends to someone else who wants it. Yet it can come around again. The messages get louder and louder for a while, but then they'll drop off completely.

> Your Dad and I had a big talk the other night on the way home from the pictures. We decided there was no aspect of our lives that you and your brain injury hadn't altered in some way. It colours the way we view everything. We also decided that most of the things were positive. We had become more caring, tolerant, open-minded and understanding of a lot of other people's problems. It changed our priorities and made us look at our lives really closely. We now know what means the most to us and what isn't that important.
>
> We love you dearly and would never give you back. We also won't give up on you because we know you have the potential to be really well. I hope you are having a fantastic, restful sleep and so a good day.

More tolerant … that's on a sliding scale, of course. We were getting better and better all the time. Better insight into yourself helps you realise that we're all human, all imperfect beings.

Veronica Strachan

Sunday 26th December 1993

A few words before I fall asleep. Christmas Day was a bit of a fizzer. You barely opened your eyes. I'm sure you must be getting the sore throat your Dad has had.

We just can't seem to get on top of them at the moment. I know we're all a bit run down and very tired. We went to Dad's for lunch and Barbara's for tea. Too much food and all in one day. I would've had a better day if you had been having a good one. Like the one you had the day of Nana Brethie's party. That was an excellent day. You programmed in the morning and had the afternoon off. The kids were many and noisy, which you enjoyed.

Aunty Margaret bought you a drum and cymbal set. When you got into the present you were excited and started to laugh. She said it was the best thank you she could've had.

F ignored you again on Thursday. Couldn't even be bothered even saying hello or goodbye. Never mind, they're not worth talking to these days.

I hope you slept better than last time and have a great day.

Sometimes you have to let go of people who bring the negative and who don't get your message or share your beliefs. It's said that you share the energy and vibrational level with (and become the average of) the five people you spend the most time with.

Breathing While Drowning

I can see how, once I started to pick myself up in later years, I changed everyone around me. I often look at who I spend the most time with and notice that I'm happy. Energy affects everyone around you, and you can change the energy in a room by dialling it up and consciously being the positive source. Bring the joy.

Wednesday 29th December 1993

Jacqui, when will you crawl? We've waited long enough now. You are 3 and more so why isn't there more for you.

Thursday 30th December 1993

Jacq, you had a better day yesterday. It's so lovely to hear you sing out to your "Dad". That word is getting very clear. You won't say Mum though. Maybe I just don't hear it enough.

You are trying really hard to crawl but still seem too weak or your head is too heavy to get it all together. I just want you to crawl yesterday.

Maybe we'll talk to the Institutes tomorrow and see what they say.

Your bowels have been playing up too. But I think we've finally got them on the right track. Exciting stuff eh! I think I'm too tired to write.

Being too tired was a state of being, as it was for most parents. For us, every moment was stuffed with things to do: programme, food, rosters, work, shopping, housework, and on and on.

Sunday 23rd January 1994

Your Dad and I spoke yesterday. He said from his head he feels it will be the end of the year before you crawl. In his heart he wishes it sooner. I didn't get my wish to crawl for Christmas, maybe next year. Easter is still a fair distance. I'm sure that the respiratory patterning is helping you. That in combination with the naturopath things, maybe. The Programme is slowly grinding up to full pace. Most days you achieve all bar a few inclines. We're discussing ways to make your day work better for you. We might try and let you have a big sleep in the morning, miss the 11:30 session and work after tea.

It will be okay in summer but unknown in winter. Judy has expressed interest which will help.

We have to let you work at your full potential when you have the urge. You still seem to crash the next day though. I left you tonight laughing to yourself in bed. Your smile and laugh is still so infectious.

> The message will get through, I know it. I want you crawling before a new sibling arrives. I think a large piece of linoleum is the go. To put on whatever floor you are on to make it slippery and easy to crawl. I'll get a piece next time we go to town. You must get every opportunity to crawl.
>
> When you are feeling good, everyone feels good. When you are feeling tired, worn out — everyone is down. You rule the house with your 11.5 kilos. Not bad! We will win in the end. I hope we don't lose Cassie along the way. You are both so precious to me. If I could take it all on myself, I'd shoulder all the pain. But it isn't possible so I have to teach you both how to cope with the world and life in the best way. We shall see.

There's an important point to note here: be careful not to leave anyone behind who you love and who needs to come along. Don't take anyone for granted.

No one person can take it all on—that's not the point. Each person has his or her journey to take; we walk alongside for a while, even help each other, carry each other, but at some point, we have to step out on the path towards our own destiny.

Sunday 30th January 1994

Jacq, we look to this year with a lot more hope than the last. I'm sure this year you will crawl. I want you to be able to crawl to get your Christmas presents. You are starting to get really restless in bed at night. Turning 90 degrees both ways and ending up out of bed one morning last week, very exciting!

We took you to the zoo again on Thursday though this was a twilight session with a jazz band backing. You enjoyed the zebra, giraffe and some of the big cats. A great moment was when the lion roared for you. Eyes wide and listening carefully. You saw a lot more than you usually do. The music and people were good also.

It's not that we didn't take Jacqui to see things when she was young; it's that this time she really was watching and listening to the world.

Breathing While Drowning

Thursday 3rd March 1994

Well Jacq, you have pulled one out of the bag. Last Saturday 26th Feb, my first weekend off in over 18 months. You were in the highchair having lunch and I thought that you had dislocated your left elbow. Naturally it wasn't that simple. An X-Ray showed a cauliflower sort of opacity next to the elbow joint? A bursa filled with calcium, or who knows what. Anyway it's time for another visit to the hospital to see an orthopaedic specialist. Next Tuesday 8th March I just want him to say "Nah, don't worry, it's nothing!"

You had the most brilliant day today. Awake all day and still going when I left for work lifting up your head and crawling around in a circle. It won't be long before you're going forward. You have been doing really well with the bowels at the moment, and of course all the piddles in the potty too. We'll have to try you with a toilet seat and see how you go. That will be more portable than the potty.

Your words are becoming clear and overall you are doing brilliantly. I think you are missing Cassie though. She is at school full time now. You have learnt a new word though. You demand "school" when you want to take Cassie to school. You love to get into the classroom and see all the kids.

> *You are impressing all the volunteers as well at the moment. They all think you are doing brilliantly. Revisit is only 4 ½ weeks away.*
>
> *Because you were getting bored with the programme we changed it around a bit. 2 days of 8 or more patterns and ask no output from you, then 1 day of regular programme asking you for some work. It helped a bit. Now we're doing a day on and a day off. That seems to be working much better. I'm sure you'll be stonkered tomorrow after all your hard work today. I hope you went to sleep. I've been really tired the last few days as has your Dad, maybe we'll catch up next year.*
>
> *We made the mistake of telling you we were all going to Queensland after next revisit. I'm sure that's why you've presented the elbow.*

It often felt as though we couldn't put a trick right. For each step forward, we took one or two steps back. And they were rarely small—they usually involved hospitals and doctors and complications.

This played into strengthening my pattern: nothing comes easily. If you want something, you have to work for it. No free rides. I don't deserve it; I'm not enough.

Ugh! I'm so over that conversation in my head. I deserve everything I want, and the choice is mine.

Tuesday 22nd March 1994

Well he did more or less say Nah. He said he viewed with some trepidation your anaesthetic history and decided to leave it alone.

Good plan.

Wednesday 6th April 1994

As you can see I was pretty tired last entry. Today we've been at Healesville, lectures on nutrition, oncogeny, philogeny and active respiratory patterning. Judy sat in on lectures with us today. I didn't have a chance to ask her how she went but I'll catch up with her on Friday. She's coming to hear about the new program.

This visit you grew 4cm and your head was the same as it should be 100% growth. We are now going to plan more mobility programme.

The period straight after revisiting was always extra busy. Sometimes there was new equipment to build or word cards and information bits to prepare. There were always rosters and scheduling and new nutritional challenges.

But this time there was another reason for lack of writing ….

Tuesday 7th June 1994

Jacqui, it's been a long time. So much has happened to me and to you. We had a holiday in Queensland which you thoroughly enjoyed. We tried to do a bit of programme when we could. The best thing of course was the stimulation of different surroundings and views.

You enjoyed Underwater World the best I think. There was a touching tank and the assistant spent a great deal of time holding things for you to touch and carefully explaining them to you. We spent one night with F & G on the Gold Coast. It was good to talk to another couple who know so well what our lives are like on program.

You have been doing really well on this programme so far. Unfortunately, you got really unwell with gastroenteritis after we took you swimming. It took a couple of weeks to get over that as it was closely followed by a cold.

I think I'm getting too tired to think. I'll write again in a little while.

Jacq, I'm back. I haven't written the big surprise yet. Around Dec 11 you will have a younger brother or sister. I'm about 14 weeks now and slowly improving. That's the major reason I haven't written for so long. I've been too sick. I thought I was getting better but I lost dinner last night. It must finish soon. The baby is growing. I'm going to see the doctor next week. We did talk to everyone we could think of before we decided to have this child. We even got your chromosomes checked. All perfect! So we figured it was now or never. There were lots of reasons we elected this course.

Most important we felt we had enough room in our hearts/lives for another child. We had always planned on 3 or 4, you just put it back a bit.

The baby will be great for you, someone to compete with, or someone who is smaller than you anyway. A little sibling for Cassie, she's really excited. It will be good for her to see a well kid develop too. Good for Mum & Dad.

The way my body is deteriorating it was a choice between a baby or a hysterectomy.

Interesting choice to have to make. Talk about the feminine separation!

I know I'm talking as if this baby will be 100% okay. We have however, examined closely the possibility of the child being brain-injured like you. I guess that would be the worst case scenario. We talked about it a lot, over a long period of time and decided we could do it. It would simply mean 2 kids on the programme instead of 1 (Hardly simple – but possible)

> *You give us so much happiness and joy (along with the heartache) that we could not possibly imagine life without you just the way you are.*
>
> *And yet that is changing so much. You are developing at a phenomenal rate and still have a long way to go.*
>
> *We just need to get you crawling. If you were mobile life would be so much better and easier for you. The world would be at our fingertips. So much to see and explore. I can't wait Jacq. My internal deadline is another 13 months till the other baby crawls. If you don't start soon you are going to get left behind. We are still getting glimpses of potential from you. You just need to put it all together consistently.*
>
> *I know you can do it, cos you're such a smart cookie. Just do it soon Jacq. okay?*

There are a lot of *justs* and *if onlys* here. I can make all the deadlines that I want, but if it involves someone else, it really doesn't matter because the choice is up to them every time. I can feel the push reinforced over and over. I remember thinking, *If I just work harder, if Jacqui just works harder, we will get the outcome we want.*

But was that the outcome she wanted?

I find the word *just* all over the place in conversations between women, but it doesn't appear much in conversations between men. It comes across as an apology, kind of like saying: "If you don't mind, I'll just do this or ask you to do that." I've made it a habit to reduce my use of the word *just*. I have no need to apologise for being me or speaking as an equal.

Breathing While Drowning

If only—two words that convey so much envy, regret, optimism, scepticism, guilt, and shame. For me, the biggest lesson here is as follows: don't live with regret. Life is too short; freaking get on with it.

Tuesday 14th June 1994

Jacqui, today you moved 4 inches forward across the floor! What a red-letter day. I feel like shouting outside in the street but I can't yet 'cos no-one else saw you. You had completed the 1:30 session and were on the floor waiting while I got your custard ready. I had just your head on a piece of sating and the clock just past your head. When I came back you had your shoulders well in the satin and the block level with your head.

I had to believe it, there it was proof and you were still trying to go, pushing with hands and feet.

If you can do it once, you can do it again. The last few days have been superb for you. It was Cassie's birthday party yesterday. The night before we had wrapped up her pressie of a dress and stockings from you and Ian helped you write your name on the card.

When I got you up on the Monday you were so excited and smiling hugely whenever I spoke about Cassie and birthday and party and kids. You were delighted when Cassie opened your present and later when she tried it on you knew exactly what was happening, giving big smiles of approval.

You worked hard first session but didn't want to sleep straight away. Eventually you did, but you woke early, in time to have lunch and be dressed waiting for the party to arrive. Your eyes followed every move the kids made and when you were in the circle for pass-the-parcel you were wrapped. You watched the kids play the other party games and sat at the table enjoying the noise and clatter.

Cassie had a fantastic day too. I'm glad you didn't miss it. I hope it bodes well for your birthday.

Jacq, now that I know you can crawl, given the best opportunity, my heart is lighter. Maybe we will have to send you to kinder next year. Maybe that's what your internal timetable is doing. The next few days will tell. I hope. I hope. I hope.

I almost forgot to write about what else you are up to in the mornings. School mornings only. We get the message very clearly. "Go school, go school." You want to take Cassie to school so you can go in the car and see all the other kids. Ian says you smile broadly at everyone.

This morning you yelled "go school" at me after I told Cass to get ready so I told her to go and tell Ian that you wanted to go. Cass came back with the message that it might be bit late. Not to be deterred, you called out to him "Dad, go school". How could he refuse? So with the biggest grin on your face, off you went. Amazing.

Breathing While Drowning

Monday 27th June 1994

Jacq, you are doing really well with your programme at the moment. On the Gravitron you are making remarkable progress. All by yourself you are getting significant forward motion – often getting half way down the ladder. You get so excited about it too. You know you are really clever. You seem to be having a few good days together then a sleepy, grouchy day.

Today, your Dad let you have an afternoon sleep, you worked well in the last session but then wanted to play all night, so were still awake when I left for work.

Crystals in the urine are still a concern, so we're cutting down the magnesium slowly. It's a catch 22. Constipation or crystals!

I'm feeling much better although still very tired. Your Dad has been his usual strong, hard-working self.

You seem interested in when we talk about the baby. We are still undecided whether to have you come to the birth or not. We'll decide when the time comes I think. Cass is keen to be there.

We only have about 6 weeks before next revisit. If you can continue as you did in the last fortnight, then I'm sure you'll be crawling by revisit. I hope so.

Hope you are asleep you cheeky little girl. You and your Dad both need the rest.

Letting Cassi see the cycle of life was an important choice, but you will need to ask her whether it was a good decision.

Wednesday 28th September 1994

Jacqui, it's been so long since I wrote to you. Revisit was good and bad. You didn't put on any weight and your head didn't grow. Your chest and length did. You were good with your reading and speech. Some progress but not enough. You need to crawl. Then everything else will flow on from there.

We had a weekend at Janet's in Wodonga which you enjoyed.

We went to a wedding last Saturday which you slept through completely. Your Dad took you to the zoo the next day which you really enjoyed. He said the carousel was a big hit.

The programme you have at the moment is very active. We are doing lots of things for your vestibular function. Somersaults, rolls, spinning both head up and head down, rocking and pitching as well as the usual masks, patterns, inclines and Gravitron. This leaves not much time for intelligence including maths!

You are making good progress too. Your head is much stronger. Your words are clearer too. You are becoming more and more chatty. Your Dad is worried he'll be overrun by talkative females.

> He is working so hard at the moment. Not only is the programme very active, but I'm very inactive and unable to help him much with lifting you around. We really need you to crawl so you can help yourself.
>
> Ian is also building a new chook pen. It's very palatial and like the Taj Mahal. It will be a shame to let the chooks dirty it up. Your Dad has been having a lovely time building it. It's the kind of thing he loves doing.
>
> You also have your first pair of real shoes — boots actually. You need them to practice standing and to spin head down. I hope this programme helps you crawl. It is coming up to 2 years on the Institute's programme.
>
> Another potential customer came by to look yesterday. I hope they start, it would be so good for their little girl. But it's a decision they have to make. You can only hope.

What would I tell someone who was thinking about whether to start or not? Start. What advice would I give to her or him? Ask for help and look after yourself as well. It's absolutely worth it, no matter the outcome.

Monday 3rd October 1994

You were having a tired day but we patterned all day, so hopefully tomorrow will be better.

Your Dad and I seem to be running on empty at the moment. We are both really tired and because I'm not sleeping well, neither is he. I think I'll have to try sleeping in the spare bed in your room. Your Dad hasn't been well. He's had a bad sore throat and it has knocked off most of his reserves. Add to that he built me a beautiful chook house and on top of it all he'd doing programme mostly by himself. It is a really physical programme too so he is getting really tired.

I know he is worried about you wondering when you are going to crawl. Me too. You are getting stronger every day but it needs to go faster. If you could just lift your head consciously like you do unconsciously (or asleep anyway) then I'm sure it will come soon. I keep trying to tempt you with things like "when you can walk you can go out and feed the chooks etc etc. Please Jacq keep trying. I'll try and do more. When I get up. Only 4 more weeks of work then I'll be home and surely it will be a bit easier.

You must be putting on weight 'cos you feel much heavier. You haven't been vomiting as much either. Just crawl Jacq and we'll be happy. Not really. I want you to run into school laughing, with nobody knowing that you had a brain injury.

Breathing While Drowning

We all so need that sense of belonging, fitting in, and being accepted. It is part of our DNA. I didn't belong; she didn't belong. We just wanted to be normal—there's that *just* again. We wanted to be normal. No apologies.

Tuesday 18th October 1994

Reluctance to relive the events of Sunday 9th October have kept me from writing sooner. How to begin?

As I'm driving into our street after night duty, feeling tired and a little sorry for myself as usual, I saw an ambulance turn into a driveway near ours. I thought someone must have had a heart attack. When I get closer and realised they were in our drive my first thought was "they've got the wrong house" then my heart started to beat faster and I drove quickly into the drive.

As I got out the ambulance man was heading towards the door. I asked him "Did you get a call to come here?" He said "yes". With my heart in my mouth I thought of you. As I reached the door Cassie opened it and I called for your Dad. No immediate answer so I kept going down the hall into your room. The sight twisted a knife in my heart. You were unconscious and sort of grey, there was vomit all over the bed and your Dad was doing CPR on you. With his eye red and his voice hoarse he said "She stopped breathing." My first response was to shake you and try and wake you up. When this elicited no response I started mouth to mouth on you. After a few breaths I tried to listen to your heart. I couldn't hear it, but my heart was beating so hard I don't think I would have heard it anyway.

The ambo then called his base and told them what was going on. I yelled to Ian to call The paed and tell her to meet us at Sunbury. He dashed off to do that.

The ambo picked you up and I kept doing mouth to mouth till we got in the ambulance. The thought came into my mind when I first saw you. "How long had you been unconscious or without oxygen?" Was it going to be worth you surviving? The thoughts came and went quickly because overwhelming all those doubts were the thoughts "I love you, you are my baby, I couldn't bear to lose you," and I just kept going.

I found out the beginning of the story from your Dad a few minutes later when we were all at the hospital.

He had heard you coughing before 7 but hadn't thought anything unusual as you often cough. He heard you again just after 7 and went in. That's when he found you had vomited. Some larger solid bits then lots of semi-fluid. He saw immediately that you weren't breathing. He had put you on your side when he went to bed as you usually breathe better and you had been breathing nosily. When he went in you had got yourself more on your back with your head back too.

Breathing While Drowning

It must have been terrifying for your Dad. But to put it in plain words. "He saved your life!" Without his quick actions you would be dead and I would be writing my last entry. He cleared your mouth and started CPR, he was unsure whether you had a heartbeat or not so he just kept doing the lot. Between breaths he called to Cassie. It took a few times because she was watching telly.

When he got her to come she rang the ambulance for him and he asked for help immediately. Cass unlocked the front door. Your Dad kept you alive for 20 minutes or more till I came home. I can never repay that debt.

At the hospital I kept giving you mouth to mouth and I said to the nurse to call The paed and tell her to come to here instead.

Your Dad arrived and helped me cut your clothes off so I could see your chest. We tried to bag and mask you but couldn't get the inflation at all. We got ECG dots on and joy of joys your heart was beating at 135 beats per minute. That moment was my first ray of hope.

The GP arrived a few minutes later and so did the helicopter. He wasn't able to intubate you so I kept breathing for you and amazingly you tried to take some breaths on your own. Not enough but it was a start. The GP put an IV in and The paed arrived. She also tried to put an ET tube down but was unable to, because of this we couldn't use the helicopter.

So your Dad, Anne and I piled into the ambulance and drove a hairy 40 mins to the city. I kept breathing for you every 30 secs or so as you were only breathing about 5 breaths a minute. It was the worst ride of my life.

We arrived at CAS and after a couple of mins they called the ICU Registrar to see you. She was able to get you breathing with a bag and mask.

Then came a bombshell. "Because you had a brain injury" "Did we want to continue full resuscitation and put you on a ventilator as this would probably happen again, getting worse till you were finally gone."

I was speechless and looked at the doctor as if she had 2 heads. She obviously took that as "yes continue". She gave you some Valium and then Pancuronium to allow you to relax and the ET tube slipped down quite easily. A nasogastric also, lots of tape and then up to ICU. I remember, strangely, the porter yawned while he was waiting. A world of meaning.

ICU staff moved quickly to connect everything to machines. Within a couple of minutes you were looking pinker.

We then explained to the registrar what happened.

What followed was an anxious few hours while you were unconscious. Your Dad made me go home for a couple of hours. I went with Grandad to his place. I lay in bed and the tears came.

Breathing While Drowning

"Why didn't they just assume we would want every effort made?" "Take all my strength" "This was not meant to be an exchange pregnancy." "I couldn't bear it if you died" "be strong" "don't die".

I got a couple of hours dozing then got up and came back to the hospital.

I had spoken to Cassie and told her how sick you were but how proud I was that she had helped your Dad to save your life. She was at the Brethie's so it kept her busy.

When I got back to ICU you had woken up. For the next 12 to 14 hours you stayed awake. You were very frightened and wanted to hold my hand all the time. Every time the staff came towards you, you cringed and watched them anxiously. It must have been very scary to be awake and have an ET tube and nasogastric in and have the oxygen forced into your lungs when you were trying to breathe yourself.

You also had an IV, they couldn't get an 'A going. ECG and oximeter on.

Eventually you conked out after a big piddle and having your nasogastric replaced. Then you slept for a day and a half.

They were able to take you off the ventilator after about 30 hours and then just had to wean you from the oxygen. Once you woke up on Wednesday morning things were looking up. Nasogastric tube out. Mary and Sue helped me give you a bath.

> Your face creased from ear to ear. Hair washed and looking good. Then O2 tube and IV out. When your Dad came we were all packed and out of there in about 5 minutes flat.
>
> It wasn't until that Wednesday that I felt you were going to be okay.
>
> When you looked at me you knew and when you laughed I knew that you were okay.
>
> It is totally amazing and wonderful. Apart from a sore throat, hand and croaky voice you escaped without even pneumonia, no antibiotics either. One very lucky little girl.
>
> At the moment you are in good spirits but very tired and weak. You also have developed an interesting cough, sounds like an old lady clearing her throat. Your voice has faded to a whisper too, very sexy. But this morning you tried hard and got a couple of squeaky words out.

One step forward and one step back. Scariest time of my life up until then.

This is the first time I had the thought that her hold on life was fragile, that there was a possibility that she may not survive. There was a possibility that it may not be my choice. Despite all that your Dad and I and everyone else did, she might leave us.

It was reality slapping me in the face, reminding me that, dispassionately viewed, she may not survive. But I could not be dispassionate about her.

Breathing While Drowning

How dare they! What right had they to make that judgement? To dismiss your existence based on statistics—What did they know of you and your purpose in the world?

I was so angry and wanted to scream at them and at the world: "Don't you know she's loved? Don't you know she's my child, my little girl? Don't you know she is a real, whole person? She laughs, she cries, she feels, she needs, she believes? Don't you know? Don't you care? She loves having her hair brushed. She's ticklish. She cheeky, she loves her dad and her big sister and her mum."

As her mother, I couldn't do anything less than everything to save her life. I couldn't let her go. She was a part of our lives and had her own life to live.

This was my love/hate affair with Western medicine. They offered no help in the day-to-day challenges or in seeking new health options and well-being tips, but they were great in an emergency, at picking up the pieces of a catastrophe.

As I kept breathing for Jacqui Bree in the hospital and during the long drive to the city, I repeated the following over and over: "This was never meant to be an exchange. Please live. This was never meant to be an exchange. Please live. Breathe, Jacqui. Live. Breathe, Jacqui. Live."

The journal doesn't hold any record of the talks Strack and I had, of holding each other tightly, grappling with the possibility that Jacqui may die.

Monday 6th February 1995

Jacq, so long since I've written and so much to tell. It took me a long time to relax after your brush with death. You slept in our room for quite a few weeks before I could bear to let you go back to your own room. Your Dad and I hardly slept a wink listening for every breath. You had a lot of trouble and we used the vaporiser and little drinks often. Eventually you got yourself reorganised and were back on your tummy, breathing easily and in your own room.

It took ages to build you back up to where you were before the aspiration episode. But eventually your hand healed and your voice came back. In a way I think the whole saga made you more alert or maybe emotionally stronger. Intellectually you didn't miss a trick.

You had another revisit to Healesville. Despite being so weak and having spent all that time recovering you did amazingly well. The only down side was a 1kg weight loss, otherwise everything else was >100%.

The emphasis is on more patterning, more masking, more success in movement. Almost every night before we fall into an exhausted sleep we discuss how we can get you moving "if only" litters our discussions constantly. We just haven't found the right switch yet. You are getting stronger and there is more quality of movement but you haven't quite got it yet.

Breathing While Drowning

> *The intelligence programme is full on this time too. No rest for the wicked.*

It was as though Jacqui got as much of a fright as we did. It must have been so scary for her, especially because she could not express herself through language or move away from pain. After this episode, Jacqui seemed to throw herself into programme and life with gusto.

> *Angus Peter Strachan was born on 6th December 1994. We had done 1 day of programme in the 38° heat and he decided that was enough. At least he waited till we were back in Gisborne. You are enjoying Angus. He has changed the routine a bit but mostly he fits in with what goes on around your program.*
>
> *You tend to laugh at him when he cries. I think you picked that up from me because we don't take him too seriously. The first few nights he was home you didn't sleep well. You yelled every time he did, most concerned. I had to take some time explaining that it was the way babies communicated and he was okay and just getting his nappy changed. You were much happier after that.*
>
> *You love giving him hugs and cuddles though he can be a bit rough at times.*

We felt we had enough room in our lives for another child, and baby number three, Angus Peter, arrived when Jacqui was four. He added a lot of joy to our small clan, and his big sisters loved him dearly. He brought smiles to everyone. He was such a happy baby. His dad was really pleased to have a son to carry on the family name and to even up the gender balance in the house.

It felt right. It was us getting on with life and dreams, moving forward.

Thursday 9th February 1995

Jacqui, you are working so hard at the moment, really putting in some good efforts both on the incline and the skateboard. I have a sense of anticipation I feel you're going to make a breakthrough in the next few months. I know I've said it before, but this time other people are noticing. They are beginning to hear the words in your speech and treat you more as an intellectually alert child.

We've been talking a lot about going to kinder next year and lots of your friends have gone this year. I wonder whether that gives you extra incentive? Angus has been a good help too, I think.

Jacqui our dreams for you are endless. We want you to have every opportunity Cassie and Angus have. I want mostly for you all to be happy. Cass worries me a bit at present with the way she talks to me and Dad, she's becoming a bit of a smartie pants, nah, nah, nah, nah, nah, nah sort of thing. I hope you don't pick that up.

Breathing While Drowning

How hard it must have been for Cassi to find a way to be in our family. At times, it's hard enough to grow up in a home full of love. Add a child with a disability, hospitals, brushes with illness, young friends dying, and grandparents dying. Focus on programme twenty-four hours a day. Not easy, and it's no wonder she wanted to rebel. How else could she get our attention?

> We are going swimming again every 2nd Thursday to give you a break, hope you stay well.
>
> Your Dad needs a bit of a break from programme but it's difficult with my old broken down body at present.
>
> I'm restricted with lifting and certainly no bouncing on the rebounder!
>
> I'm working hard on the pelvic floor at present though because I want to get back to helping you more. I miss having you to hug and hold.
>
> I'm sure you've put on a stack of weight since last revisit. I reckon you're up to about 13 kg. You can see there is more muscle and more flesh about you.
>
> Christmas was good. You enjoyed the lead up parties and the actual day performed pretty well in the a.m. Your sister was up at 0545 so of course you had to get up too. You were really good through your Santa sack but then faded badly so you went back to bed for a couple of hours.
>
> I've made you a new bed, bigger, thicker mattress and covered with a single piece of vinyl. You quite enjoyed the hoo-haa of making it and the first sleep. Mind you of late there hasn't been all that

much sleeping going on. You have done a couple of all night awake shifts. Just to keep us on our toes.

We are just keeping our head above water with the intelligence programme. Barb is colouring words in for us but otherwise we are doing it all ourselves. Books seem to be the hardest things. Inspiration is sometimes difficult. Your Dad continues to amaze me with his strength and perseverance. I've convinced him to start Badminton for a season. He really needs some time to himself, totally away from family. It will be good socially and physically. So far I have to swap only 1 shift this month. We'll see how it goes. I worry about him a lot. I wouldn't be much good without him. He is my other half.

Sometimes it's a bit scary loving someone so much. It still amazes me that he loves me and will do anything I ask that he possibly can. He is such a good man. The more important fact is that he is my best friend. I tell him all my secrets, my dreams and my day to day happenings. He always listens and is interested. Sometimes it's hard to share him with all the people come in for programme. I can't help but wish you were well and we could have more time as a family. But that's only on the really bad days. You are doing really well at the moment and that makes it all worthwhile. That's what makes the difference.

Sleep well my darling, dream of crawling, walking and talking. I love you very much.

Breathing While Drowning

Strack and I recently celebrated thirty years of marriage, which is no mean feat in this day and age. Love has never gone; we're still best friends and holders of all things precious for each other. We're still the main witness in each other's life, the go-to people for help and laughter and love. We work hard at keeping our love strong and present.

Sunday 12th February 1995

Jacq, last night I dreamt you were walking. You walked over to me and I reached down and hugged you. Wishful thinking? Maybe, but it's coming. The last 6 days you have worked really hard. You were on the floor with Angus on Friday night and you were trying so hard to crawl. Your legs were pumping and you were pushing hard with you elbows and hands. Best of all you even lifted your head up a couple of times.

We put you near the couch and you pushed yourself forward by straightening your legs. You only went a few but it was fantastic. Your whole body was trying and your eyes were so alive. Of course you had a huge smile on your face.

Saturday of course you crashed and had a totally tired day. That's okay as long as you come up again today or tomorrow.

Dare I hold out hope Jacq. Are you going to crawl soon? I know you can do it. I want it to be now, yesterday even If we can keep you well, I think it will be soon. Sleep well.

Always optimistic, seeing success in every moment and milestone.

Monday 6th March 1995

Jacq, no breakthrough yet. It's just turned midnight and my thoughts are with you. Asleep? I hope so. More or less a day off today (Sunday I mean) All the family patterners were absent or partying so we had a day off programme much to your delight.

We called up to Petra's place in New Gisborne to see her Scottish Highland calf, born 2 weeks ago. Pretty cute. Then off to Barb's for lunch, Jessica's birthday then Mary's for arvo tea, Ben and Carly's birthday. You stayed awake most of the day which was good as it was quite hot. Usually you go on strike on hot days, especially if we have a session off.

You were happy to take it all in today. I wish you were putting out more. Your Dad and I are in a bit of a lull at the moment. Our reserves of enthusiasm and resolve are low. We know that programme is the best thing for you. It's your best chance at independence and "wellness" but at the moment we feel the weight of the years pressing on us and mostly your lack of mobility. I know you are going to do it. I'd just like to know when.

I see you in my mind running and talking. I don't care if you tell me off, I'd like to hear you try.

We'll start afresh in the morning, another day, a new beginning. Crawling, crawling, crawling.

Breathing While Drowning

> *I couldn't sleep before work 'cos I kept thinking about you. We heard from G & F that one of the kids on your group was misdiagnosed and in fact has a degenerative muscle disorder and has only about 2 months to live. Scary and tragic. He was about 2 months older than you, with a similar injury.*
>
> *Stay well my darling. I'll go and do a book for you. Love you.*

See-saw, emotional roller coaster, life and death—all days, all day. Work was about life and death, too: the intersection of people connected by life and death. It was draining, but I loved it. I still love the health and well-being sector.

Tuesday 7th March 1995

> *When I left tonight you were wide awake. Grandad was minding you. You had an excellent day. Some really good efforts on the incline and on the skateboard. We took some video, hoping to get the interim report sent off by the end of the week. You've watched a few kids pass you now with crawling etc, maybe it has helped. We talk a lot about kinder and school and Angus is watching very carefully.*
>
> *You are becoming a bit naughty at times though. Cassie had a school excursion to Queenscliff. You woke up really grouchy, all through breaky and*

showering. Then when we spoke about Cassie going on the excursion and the bus etc you decided loudly that "Dad, go to school!" You were happy to see her go to school then came home and grouched some more. When volunteers came still grouchy. Your Dad was talking to you and said he knew what was wrong! "You just wanted to go on the excursion with Cassie." Well you instantly changed and laughed out loud, big smiles etc. Very naughty.

Then back to grouching for the rest of the day.

Ronnie Zeinstra said tonight she could see you beginning to crawl. 3 weeks she suggested. It's nice to hear it said by someone else. I hope it's true.

Go to sleep Jacqueline Bree.

Wednesday 15th March 1995

A quiet night so far. You were asleep when I left, hope it's a good relaxing sleep. You've had a bit of "gastro" for the last few days and have been putting up with not much work. A bit of patterning and intelligence only. I don't remember what I was going to say. It's 0330 and the body is at its lowest ebb. I want you to walk Jacq. We need you to do something spectacular 'cos we're dragging our flag at the moment. I know and feel deep in my heart that you will walk but just at the moment I'd like to know when. More patterning I guess. We'll have to give you more choices to help with your problem solving, maybe that might tip the scales. We've posted off the video and report for ½ way this session to see what Max says about you. We might have to go to Healesville for a day next week or the week after. We also have to go to the Independent Living Centre to see if we can come up with some way to support you in the bath or shower and a better arrangement for your highchair.

It's frustrating 'cos it means time off from programme as well as travelling time there and back. I must ring tomorrow and make an appointment.

Sunday 19th March 1995

You are probably still awake even though it's 0525. Cassie had her Suzuki Book party yesterday. You were wide awake and trying to crawl and be part of the action. You love parties like any kid and of course you knew all the people there. Grandad got a special smile, he's a bit of a favourite. And I must admit you had a taste of the chocolate cake. Cassie promised you and you remembered so we had to oblige.

Stay well and I hope you are asleep.

Monday 3rd April 1995

We've had Interim Report and a long phone conversation with Max while he watched the video. Plan of attack remains the same. Keep you well and keep you working. You seem to be doing this with some consistency of late which is fantastic.

You are putting on weight. I'm sure and actually getting some muscles to be proud of.

It seems like you want to work at the moment. The things we talk about make you keen to try. We are chatting about kinder and Angus catching you etc. You are enjoying swimming once a fortnight also. Ian says he's building up your repertoire.

We've lowered the incline a fraction to make you put in a bit more effort. You are doing this most of the time too.

I wish I could be home with you more. Some days I hardly see you at all. It's hard on your Dad, especially with little Angus Peter needing attention also.

I've done a heap of night duty of late and it makes it difficult. Never mind I have a few days off coming up. I need to put in a big effort. You need food and we all need some new items on the menu?

Your voice is getting louder and more interesting. Other people are sometimes picking up things that you say.

Breathing While Drowning

> I surprised your Dad and took him out for tea and the movies the other week. Tea was good, movie was lousy, Pulp Fiction. It took some organising. P minded you, of course you were awake when we got home. Ian went and picked you up, as you came to the lounge room you cracked up laughing. Very bold.
>
> I hope you are asleep now. Another week about to begin. Will it be this week? I wish I could see it.
>
> This weekend we're off to Ocean Grove for a holiday. Only 3 days but it should be a nice break. It's the beginning of school hols. Easter coming again. It flies so quickly as you get older. How old will you be? How are you going to manage at kinder and school? Will they let you attend? I don't want you to go to a "special school". I want you to see yourself as normal and well as possible.

So often, it was about trust. It was hard to trust someone else enough to leave Jacqui's life in their hands. We had very few people in that inner circle.

Trying to sneak some time off was always riddled with guilt: *We should be programming.* I've learned to mistrust the word *should*. It usually means something I have to do rather than something I want to do. Something someone else wants me to do; something that I feel obliged to do. *Should* is another word I'm trying to remove from my vocabulary. It's a flag to re-think the matter.

Friday 14th April 1995

A sleepy day Jacq. Hope you're not coming down with something. When you have a great day we see it all coming together. On a day like today it feels like it will be forever. It must be frustrating for you too.

Almost every night your Dad and I talk about the day before we go to sleep. Invariably the subject of you, your crawling and walking and your future come up. We search for answers, are we doing enough? Could we possibly do any more in the day without compromising our sanity and your health? Should we be doing something else? When will you crawl, walk, talk, sing, play the piano and run over and give me a hug and tell me you love me? How will you manage at kinder, school, life, loves, marriage, sport, living, past your next birthday? Who knows?

Most days we fall into bed exhausted and the answers don't come. Repetition doesn't help.

There are times when repetition doesn't help. Sometimes, you have to learn to let go to change something. Einstein's definition of stupidity was doing the same thing over and over and expecting a different result. Yet "practice makes perfect" is a mantra from my childhood, one I still repeat to my own children. So, in some cases, it does. If you learn something, it's good each time you do it and strengthens your ability to do it again. We were working on the principle of neuroplasticity—retraining the brain, creating new neural pathways.

> I looked at your beautiful face the other night. You were lying on your side at rest, skin clear, breathing quietly. Beautiful angles and shades, pointed nose like mine, dark lashes long and curved on your cheeks. It made my eyes misty looking at the wonder of you. You looked so well.
>
> I love it when your eyes are opened wide, so big and round and green, and <u>knowing</u>. Programme has helped you be a part of life. Will you still be my friend when you're older? Who knows? Someone has to play the dragon and someone has to work. Your Dad is a much better mother than me. I'm too impatient and selfish. I don't finish things off properly. Good in the planning stages, not good at completing. Fairly d & m for Good Friday
>
> Be well.

All of this before any Myers–Briggs, any assessment. I knew I was a starter who came up with the ideas, the spark. I was much less strong when it came to completing. Impatience still dogs me most days; I have a chasm to fill with ideas and tasks every day, and sometimes I feel like a ravenous wolf, gobbling everything in my path.

And there's the martyr. Who said someone has to be the dragon? Who says children need that? All these notions are self-imposed based on the stories I told myself, the stories Strack and I heard as children. There's no need for it. All you need is love in all its shapes and forms: respect, loyalty, compassion, kindness, and courage.

The wonder of Jacqui, of any child—the amazing human being—a miracle. She was so beautiful.

I remember saying to a friend who was trying to interest me in getting my master's degree that each of my children was a master's course: watching them grow, interacting with them on so many levels in so many different ways. And I was hoping to graduate soon.

Friday 26th May 1995

Coming home from work tonight I began to cry. Reasons, I'm not exactly sure. Floodgates opened, luckily not much traffic. I read back a little through your book. I thought you'd be crawling before this. I set myself goals and we never get there. I love my family but maybe I'm not good enough for them. I'm not strong enough, too lazy and selfish. Otherwise you'd be okay. I miss my Mum, I need someone to unburden to but your dad works so hard with you I can't express all my fears, it might all be too much.

Please learn to crawl J.B. give us some hope. Maybe tomorrow. I'd better go back to bed before your dad misses me. I feel better after a few tears, maybe.

Sleep Princess.

Like a boiling kettle, every now and again the steam would blow the top off and escape with the build-up of pressure. How hard would it have been to ask for help? For me, it was really hard.

Breathing While Drowning

There were people I let in a little, once in a while, and those friends who stayed, but I didn't have anyone I could talk with about defeat, about the fact that I might not be able to fix this.

This is such a difficult mix: separation from the feminine, the road of trials, facing all the ogres and dragons, going to work. But you are not enough; you are yearning to reconnect. I had so little control over what was going on, so little insight. I was pushing through, forcing. What would have happened if I had surrendered at this point? I'm not sure that would have been the best option for anyone.

The downers were so often on my own, whenever the spirit refused to be held back by the mind any longer. Driving home tired me out, the quiet of early morning did too. The real me emerged to take the public me down a notch, deeper, past the surface.

Sunday 28th May 1995

> Don't know why I hit such a downer the other day. I know both you and your Dad and I have hit the pre-revisit blues. We are both stretched really thin physically and emotionally. We haven't found the right switch for you yet. We will, fear not. Maybe more of the same, maybe this time we'll find the right combination. You look at Angus and I can see you watching and weighing up what he's doing and what you're capable of doing. You really love it when he comes and grabs you or your toys.
>
> You had a lovely lunch out with me and Angus the other day. We planned to go to Sue Howard's. I didn't tell you till the morning we were going 'cos I didn't want you to get so excited that you stayed awake all night then crashed the next day.

Anyway we went after first session and I thought you'd snooze on the way over. No way! The entire hour you spent awake, watching and listening. When we finally got to Sue's I said we'd arrived and Jacqui and Sue were waiting for us. Well you just burst into fits of laughter. So excited. Jacqui Mary was good with you, you played Barbies together and she read you a couple of stories.

You've got a couple of newborn. I can't remember, oh yeah. A couple of new tracksuits so you don't look like orphan Annie now.

You loved to be doing different things and meeting kids. And when you laughed, the whole world laughed with you. It cracks my face even now thinking about you. It's such a great reminder to live in the moment, to be there, and to feel the joy.

Sunday 25th June 1995

Jacq, I was hoping I'd have some exciting news this week but I guess it will be next week now. At last revisit they asked if we'd brought a different girl along. You put on 3kg in weight in 6 months, the previous 2 years you had only put on 1kg! 300% growth of head and chest, fantastic! 3.5 cm in length, also superb and almost 100%.

Breathing While Drowning

The day we went over you had a great time. You were talking and laughing, holding things and did really well with your skateboard. Max was quite impressed.

We are waiting now for them to get back to us. We have a bottle of gas O2 80% and CC2 20%. With this we hope to drastically improve your muscle tone. They have only been doing this particular programme for about 10 years so are not as knowledgeable as with the other programmes. We thought it might be this weekend but it looks like it will be Monday or Tuesday.

You got fired up after revisit and seemed to be doing okay. Unfortunately, you got the flu from Cass which has knocked you for six. It's perhaps just as well we didn't go this weekend; it gives you a chance to recover.

Two steps forward and one step back. Still full of hope and dreams.

Tuesday 4th July 1995

We finally started the Gas programme on Thursday last week. We had to go over to Healesville and let Max see how you managed it. Nothing brilliant as yet but we have great hopes. I'm happy for you to surprise me anytime J.B. you want so much to be a part of whatever the family are doing. You try and chat away to us. Sometimes we pick up most of what you are saying, but most of your words are still unclear. There is still more variety of tone and volume coming in, which is good.

Since you got over the flu you seem to be quite bright and are working reasonably well.

We don't have your new floor programme yet. Hopefully it's going to give you the right combination and you will crawl. That will be a start.

We have to go in to the hospital to see about some equipment for you. A highchair, a bath chair and a toilet support. More forms coming up.

Stay well Jacq.

You enjoyed your visit to the Zoo. It was the culmination of a month talking about butterflies and moths. We did pasting and made caterpillars and sticky taping and made butterflies. Each time you seemed to quite enjoy it.

This month's theme is going to be cities. Probably not as exciting as butterflies but we'll see what we can do.

I've had no more tears Jacq, but I still have a pain in my heart for your lost childhood. It colours how I view everything in life. But we wouldn't give you back ever.

Breathing While Drowning

The pain in my heart got worse and worse. For so many years, it was like a stone in my chest, dragging my shoulders down, keeping my life dark. It was the physical sensation of strain in my chest, and until I let it go twenty years later, I didn't realise how constraining it had been.

Friday 18th August 1995

Jacqui Bree, what will you be? Better, I hope. You succumbed to a second dose of the flu and are ever so slowly getting back on track. The gas hasn't done the stupendous job we anticipated although there is some improvement. I think Angus is going to crawl ahead of you. He is up on all fours rocking, ready to take off.

Cities as a theme was a bit of a fizzer but we did finish on a high. Yesterday we had a trip to Melbourne. The weather was superb 23°C, not bad for a winter's day. You were awake with a giggle and a big smile first thing this morning and that seemed to set the mood for the day. We drove in to Melbourne Central and Daimaru. Arrived in perfect time to see the giant fob watch open and the music and birds working. We looked around Melbourne Central then got on a train to Spencer Street Station via the underground Museum Station. You loved every minute of it.

We talked to you about all that was happening and you carefully looked around and watched and reacted to everything you saw. We collected Mel

> from her building (MLC next to Rialto) then went up to the Observation Deck. 'Cos you were in your pusher, Ian got in for free and we had a ride up in a special elevator. Walked to Southbank for lunch. Hopped on a tram and back to Melbourne Central. Everyone we met seemed particularly nice and helpful. I was amazed at stuffy old Melbourne. We had a much better day with courteous cheerful service, carpark attendants, ticket seller for the train, Rialto staff, tram conductors and shop assistants.
>
> We headed straight up to Lancefield then to music for Cassie. Apart from 10 mins on the way to the car you were awake the whole time. Looking absorbing watching.

Stuffy, old Melbourne indeed. My favourite city in the world was magic that day. I remember being awake and alert for Jacqui's visit. People so often surprise the hell out of me, and I still think Melbourne is the best city in the world.

Monday 28th August 1995

> Well, you've done it again. Fantastic day on Thursday so much so that we talked expectantly about how well you'd done and were going to do. Friday after being grouchy Thursday night, you vomited when Ian picked you up. That continued with food and bile then nothing. We let you rest

but you started vomiting blood in the afternoon. I let first one pass thinking many things mild and severe but after the second one I let panic rear its ugly head. A phone call to the Paed and we were on our way to the hospital. They expedited your arrival and after a brief visit to CAS and IV inserted then up to the ward.

Tuesday 29th August 1995

Your Dad stayed with you overnight and by the time Cass, Angus and I got in at 0930 you were smiling again. I was really pleased to see that smile. You started on fluids again and we have you discharged by 3:30pm Sat.

Since then you've been tired but cheerful. We've filled out the interim report and will send that off today. When we were talking last night about going to Brisbane we realised that there would be 3 birthdays while we were in QLD. We mentioned this to you, i.e. your birthday in Brisbane and you started to laugh joyously, real body rocking stuff. It obviously sounded good to you.

We booked the tickets tonight, last night actually. Can't wait. It would be better if you were crawling Jacq.

This was my last entry before Jacqui died. A record of joyous laughter, holiday anticipation, a birthday milestone, and, of course, a wish for crawling.

And perhaps the vomiting of blood was an intimation of things to come.

The lessons I learned about myself and the world that I realised then—and that I realise now—mean a lot of different things.

On the Programme, our Jacqui Bree woke up and began to live and grow. She was dismissed by so many as not having anything to give or be. She changed the lives of everyone who met her.

Never underestimate the power of the spark of magnificence that's in all of us.

Lesson – Among so many things this taught me to not judge a book by its cover. And never to judge the limit of any person's potential. Sure, I loved Jacqui to distraction, and it's different if that person is your own child, but the things I learned from her I experienced many times over the years. A good lesson. Stay the judgement, be present, be innocent, and keep a beginner's mind. Don't have preconceived ideas of who people are and what they'll do.

Of course, this is contrary to everything I do as a project and change management consultant, leader, and manager. This is all about risk—identifying what could happen, judging situations and people, and guessing what they will be and do. Yet, even though this is what I do, I can still be open to the moment, still be surprised by people's responses. After all, they're human, just like me.

But is it exactly what I need as a coach. To be open and unbiased about the potential of every person to imagine and achieve their dreams.

Breathing While Drowning

The Programme changed the way I thought about life and friendship and community. People I never expected to, came over week after week to help us. People I counted on were not there because it wasn't their thing—all of them changed because of Jacqueline Bree. I remember Nora particularly well. Our oldest volunteer, well into her sixties, had a son with Down's Syndrome. For her, helping and watching Jacqui grow and come alive was particularly poignant. She told us that she had been sceptical initially and had only come for us as parents. But as she watched Jacqui grow, she became one of our biggest believers, and she even expressed that she wondered what her son's life would have been like if the Programme had been around when he was growing up.

Compassion makes the world a better place. We need more.

Lesson: in later years, I realised this was one of Jacqui's greatest lessons for me: learning compassion. My community gave so much to us, to me. It was incredibly humbling to be the recipients of compassion. It's a core component of being human.

Keltner stated, "Humans are tribal beings, we're motivated by a desire to help, in fact there's good evidence that it's part of our deep evolutionary purpose and vital to the survival of our species.

"Compassion is not the same as empathy or altruism, though the concepts are related. While empathy refers more generally to our ability to take the perspective of and feel the emotions of another person, compassion is when those feelings and thoughts include the desire to help. Altruism, in turn, is the kind, selfless behaviour often prompted by feelings of compassion, though one can feel compassion without acting on it, and altruism isn't always motivated by compassion.

"Charles Darwin was the beloved and engaged dad of a really rambunctious group of children. When one of his daughters died at age 10, Darwin started to have these deep insights about the place of suffering and compassion in human experience".[13]

It was an incredible moment when I read this. Charles Darwin had also loved and lost a child. And the life and death of that child had given him lessons he thought about deeply and shared. It took me a while longer to get to the lesson, but I made it almost twenty years later. And I'm sharing it with you as I try to share it with everyone I meet. *Compassionate* is one of my words.

In *The Descent of Man,* Darwin argues that sympathy is our strongest instinct, sometimes stronger than self-interest, and he argues that it will spread through natural selection because "the most sympathetic members, would flourish best, and rear the greatest number of offspring."

"Our babies are the most vulnerable offspring on the face of the Earth. And that simple fact changed everything. It rearranged our social structures, building cooperative networks of caretaking, and it rearranged our nervous systems. We became the super caregiving species, to the point where acts of care improve our physical health and lengthen our lives. We are born to be good to each other".[14]

Initially, people came through generosity and curiosity, but they always stayed because they came to know Jacqui. She was surrounded by love, positive vibrations, and good energy. Generosity is its own reward—to give with no thought of receiving, purely to see the light in someone's eyes.

People can cope with an amazing amount of work, worry, and wonder. Adversity defines people in many different ways, and some people find resilience.

Lesson: resilience is more than persistence, which helps us continue in the face of difficulty or opposition to our views or actions. Resilience is a capacity and flexibility to recover quickly from adversity. You get knocked down, and you get up again and again and again. How could we not become more resilient with Jacqui's life dependent on us? How could we not learn to adapt, to be flexible, to let go of tiredness and sadness and despair? To swallow all that down and keep going? Any parent has the chance to become more resilient, and any person who faces difficulty in all its shapes and forms can learn resilience—to be strong and healthy despite all the bad and sad and mad that happens. Persistence is part of it, though. Don't take the first answer you hear; don't settle for anything less than everything you could possibly do.

Often, people don't see their resilience as a gift. And for a long time, I got stuck in resilience. I got so used to managing on my own or with Strack alone that I forgot how to ask for help. But resilience opened me up to the possibility of change, to knowing that change could be good … and then better, and then exciting. It was something new, a rush of creativity. It made me a great change agent, a catalyst wherever I went. I could see the possibilities, I could see past the dross and the daily grind and the entrenched processes and ideas. I had optimism and resilience on my side. When you've battled for the life of your child, a multimillion dollar project is small potatoes. It gives you an incredibly clear perspective on what's important and what can be done. Not many people can stand in the way of resilience, and if they do, do you want to be there?

Eventually, being resilient was part of allowing me to let go of so many things that just weren't that important. Another thing resilience and Jacqui taught me was that, sometimes, you have to move on to the next thing, try something else. Life is too short to repeat mistakes and regret.

Humanity is, by nature, generous. Having always been self-contained, whole, and introverted by nature, one of the hardest things I had to do was ask for help. We could not do Jacqui's Programme alone. People came out of the woodwork to help a small child grow.

I've spent a lifetime repaying the generosity of Jacqui's community and the lessons learned throughout my own childhood. I didn't realise how powerful gratefulness could be.

Lesson: *gratitude* is the word that sits behind who I am and what I do. I'm so incredibly grateful for all that has happened in my life, for all the people in my life, for everything that I have, for all the opportunities I've had, and for those that are yet to come.

I'm not sure exactly when it changed from resilience to gratitude, but I'm so glad it did. I know that it took a consciousness and a curiosity to make the change.

A few years ago, I began searching for a way out of the ocean of grief, a way to break the chains that held me neck deep in water, forever holding myself tense and ready. With a prompt from a beautiful friend, Ronnie Z, I began listening to various experts in the transformational world and stumbled on Christie Marie Sheldon. She had the loveliest, quirky voice and an incredibly infectious giggle.

Amongst her gems was an explanation of the vibrational energy and frequency of emotions around the work of Dr David Hawkins in one of his books, *Power vs. Force: The Hidden Determinants of Human Behaviour*.[15] The frequency emitted by positive emotions is higher than that of negative emotions. You know that if you walk into a room where everyone is happy, it's pretty hard not to get a little happier yourself (and the reverse works just as well).

Christie Marie Sheldon had a great way to start you on the road to love, to raise your vibrations to a more positive frequency. She issued a thirty-day gratitude challenge that involved writing and journaling, which sounded like my cup of tea. (There's more about what I discovered with Christie Marie Sheldon in Chapter 7).

The challenge was to think of a time when I was really grateful, let my mind paint the picture clearly, and let my body feel what it was like to be grateful (and remember that feeling). It was pretty easy to remember the generosity of our army of volunteers and to be grateful for their time and love, to remember Jacqueline and the joy she brought us. It was not challenging to look at my children, my husband, my friends, my family, my home, my garden, my town, my country, my work and be grateful.

Breathing While Drowning

And then, for thirty days, I was instructed to write down five things I was grateful for just before going to sleep. They didn't have to be as momentous as the initial memory, but as I thought about the five things, small or huge, I had to remember how it felt to be grateful. And with that feeling in my body, I was told to write down the five (or more) things.

Before the challenge, I'd gone to bed thinking about all the things I didn't get done, the stuff I still needed to do the next day. This was not a good recipe for restful sleep. I was focused on scarcity; I didn't have enough and wasn't enough.

As the challenge progressed, I began to see that my day was full of small, joyful moments, and I realised I had done and achieved lots of things and had lots of conversations that were great. And then I started to recognise the small, joyful moments as they happened. I generally went to sleep feeling much calmer and woke up looking forward to the day.

For just over two and a half years, I've continued to journal reasons to be joyful and grateful almost every night. I've filled several journals with more than 7,000 grateful entries. And I realised that, far and away, the things that were most important to me, the things that brought me the most joy, the things that elicited the most gratefulness were my family; a hug here, a laugh there; a chat about small things; shared meals; a smile or a touch. Chats and interactions with friends were next. It helped me realise that, for me, relationships were the way to change myself and the world. And it made me appreciate the joy that my family and friends brought to me.

Chapter 4

The Closure and Descent

Jacqueline Bree Strachan was bright and cheeky, but being born with a midbrain injury meant she struggled to stay in the world. She had a body that didn't grow or work particularly well. Without my perfectly imperfect daughter's life and death, I would not be the woman I am: scarred, optimistic, visionary, resilient, impatient, passionate, creative, selfish, mindful, and caring.

When Jacqui came along, everything changed. We were no longer a middle-of-the-road family, although it took us a while to realise this. We became a minority: a family with a child who had a disability. Becoming Jacqui's mother made me a whole lot of things most people never get the chance to be. I became the mother of a child with disabilities, and that's tough. This opened me up to a world of caring and bigotry that I would never have been aware of otherwise. All was going along with our plans for a normal life, and then our beautiful Jacqui Bree died unexpectedly. Unexpectedly for me, anyway. She had a fragile and tenuous hold on life, which I refused to acknowledge.

Jacqui Bree died early in the morning on Saturday 9th September 1995. She was four years, ten months, and eleven days old—not quite five. The prediction of Western medicine that she would not survive past five came true.

Breathing While Drowning

Life had to rearrange itself all over again. I became a mother whose child had died, and that is the toughest road I've ever walked. Some of the signposts along my road of trials: in a decade, I lost four grandparents, my mother, both my parents-in-law, three of Jacqui's small friends, and Jacqui herself.

Friday 15th September 1995

My darling, precious Jacqueline Bree, my beautiful, green-eyed little girl. Never again can I hold you in my arms, hugging your skinny body close and kissing your smooth forehead. Never again can I stroke your long, silky hair, twisting your ponytail round my fingers.

The last time I saw you was a week ago. I had been on a late shift and trying to get my act together I'd made you all tea, a new recipe. I remember watching you roll down your floor and I thought how well you had done it. You were holding your head up really well. Then your Dad scooped you up and I can see your beautiful smile bobbing up and down your Dad's shoulder and your arms trying to hang on as he strode off with you to the incline.

I kissed you goodbye and did not know I would never see you smile again.

We were busy at work. A newborn baby had been born quite sick and I'd stayed till the ambulance arrived. So it was passed 12 midnight before I left. Maybe I could have left a few minutes earlier. I don't think so.

Anyway when I got home your Dad was in bed. I checked on him. I went back to the lounge and expressed some milk, first time for the night. It was just after 1 o'clock when I left the lounge room. I can't remember if I checked Cassie or not but as I passed your door I thought Angus had been waking around 1 o'clock so if I went in he'd probably wake up. I didn't go in and check you or kiss you good night. I wish, I wish, I wish, I wish, if only I had maybe I would have turned you on your side a bit more, maybe it would have made the difference. But I didn't, I'm sorry darling girl. I went to bed.

Angus woke around 6 and your Dad got up and got him and brought him in for a drink. I wish I had got him 'cos you were okay then, sleeping well.

We got up with the alarm at 0645. Angus was still asleep in our bed.

I heard you cough, I don't remember when.

Was it when I was feeding Angus or was it later? You often coughed and it didn't register as unusual. I got up and showered straight away. Then after I dressed I went to the kitchen. I didn't check on you then. I wish I had, it may have still been too late. Your Dad finished his shower and went in to get you. I was in the kitchen and I heard him call. I knew from the tone of his voice that you were in trouble.

I ran to your room and my heart cried No. You were pale and lifeless with vomit all over your bed.

Breathing While Drowning

Your Dad had pulled back the blankets. I grabbed you and shook you to stir your breathing, no response. I commenced breathing for you, trying to give you my life. Your Dad started heart massage. We called to Cass to bring the phone, your Dad rang 000 and called for an ambulance. Then we kept going all the time willing you to live. I got Cassi to get my stethoscope and I checked for your heartbeat. There was none. We kept going with CPR and raced you down to the hospital in the ambulance.

When we got there we tried to defibrillate you and start your heart again. Each time we yelled at you to live and to come on. No response. Finally, the Paed came in and listened to your chest. She said she heard the right side was full and the left mostly also. She said that maybe this time it was too far. I yelled No that I wanted her to try. So she put an endotracheal tube down and tried to ventilate you. There was still no heartbeat. I called to your Dad what should we do. There was no light in your eyes. They were cold and glazed. You had already gone. He said I think we should let her go. The Paed said something in agreement and stopped bagging you. I took out the ET tube and gathered your little body up in my arms. Your Dad and I held you and cried, stroking your beautiful face and hair. I felt as if it was a dream, a nightmare and I would wake up soon.

But it was not. My darling Sweet Pea was gone. I wanted to get you out of that place and take you home. I rang Grandad and said Our Jacqui was dead. He cried out Oh no Ron.

We took you home in the ambulance wrapped in a blanket in our arms.

I ran and got Cassie from across the road and Angus too. When we got outside their door I told Cassie that you had died, she sobbed and cried.

We took you in and I ran a bath. Your Dad put you in and gently washed you. I gathered your clothes and got the towels ready on the patterning table. I helped him to wash your lovely brown hair.

We dried you and dressed you in some of your favourite things. Mickey Mouse jumper, black polar fleece pants, Lion King knickers, dinosaur socks, white singlet and skivvy. Cassie brushed your hair and your Dad dried it with the hairdryer. I put it in a ponytail, of course, with a matching scrunchie.

Then your Dad lay you on the couch with your head on a pillow and we covered you with your favourite Indian blanket. You looked just like you were asleep, just waiting for the next session to begin. I kept expecting you to take another breath. But you didn't. You were cold and still.

In a funny way I felt as if your spirit was still around that morning, as if you were still there with me.

Breathing While Drowning

> The whole day seemed unreal.
> People began to arrive and I was semi-organised. I called the funeral directors and said they could come and get you after lunch.

As I type the last entry, the tears are pouring down my face. I sob as I remember Jacqui's soft hair and skinny arms around my neck. It's been twenty years since you died, twenty years since I held you, twenty years since I wished you would crawl and run and laugh.

My heart threatened to burst with very real pain, and I began to drown. I was on a slippery slope, and nothing I could do could stop the slide into unreality.

I'm sure your spirit was around that day, bewildered, lost, maybe looking for the light, helping me bear the pain. One small life made such a great difference in the world, such a great difference in our family.

Friday 22nd September 1995

> Too many memories for 1 day. It's 5:30 and I've just fed Angus. He's now asleep in our bed. It's hard lying there in the dark awake. I think of you over and over. When did I hear you cough? Did I imagine it? I see the events of September 9 over and over and over in my mind. If only's fill my head. Now I start to ask why? Why did it happen? Did you stop breathing first? Did you vomit first? I don't think it would help me to know but I would like to know. What I want is to have you back to cuddle and love.

When the funeral people came to take you your Dad carried you out to the van. Just before that I gave you one more cuddle. It almost felt the same. Your body was still warm and you were still floppy and jelly. Your head still tucked in close.

Even now I still can't believe that I'll never see your smiling face, your beautiful green eyes, your silky hair. I can't hold your slender, soft hands or hug your bony body. Why did it happen? We loved you so much. We were trying to help you as much as we could. I don't think we could've tried harder.

I can't see the sense in it. You were doing so well. The last few weeks you had come so far. You were whizzing down the incline and even on the floor you were pushing against the couch and getting yourself forward. You were holding your head up beautifully when you were propped up on our elbows and also when you came rolling down your inclined floor. Jacq you were so well and going places. Who knows how far you would have gone.

Your Dad and I know you would have been running soon. I can still see you in my dreams — running to hug me and tell me you love me.

We went to Kyneton on the Sunday to see that you were okay. You just looked asleep, so beautiful. We talked to you and stroked your face and hair. Your right ear was a bit reddened from lying in the vomit. I'm sorry Jacqui I didn't do enough. My guard slipped and I feel that I let you down.

Breathing While Drowning

How many times have I told myself I am not enough? All I knew then was that my daughter was dead. Her life had been my responsibility, and I had failed to care for her and keep her safe.

Twenty years later, I can say I am enough. I'm more than enough, actually. This was not my life to choose; this was Jacqui's life. I did the very best I could—we all did—but this was not my life to control. It was my joy to love her and let her go. It sounds sensible now, but in 1995, with Jacqui's death still a raw wound, this was not something I could have said or even imagined.

My emotions around this are complex; there's a huge dose of grief and guilt and despair and anger and what I later came to realise is shame. It's the guilt and shame that shut me down the most.

There's a movement in a number of circles that exhorts us to seek abundance as our right. The optimist in me says *yeah!* and blissfully writes intentions and affirmations, notes to self, and mantras of magnificence. The sceptic in me says *yeah right!* and doesn't believe I deserve it.

Brené Brown says we live in a world that runs on scarcity. We don't have enough of anything: time, money, or love, for example. But rather than have the opposite to scarcity be abundance, Brené suggests that the opposite is enough.[1]

Strack and I were walking the other day, and I was thinking about a friend who has lived alone with a chronic illness for many years. When I thought about myself, I realised that I had enough. I was healthy, my family members were healthy. And though we might have some cash flow issues from time to time, we are wealthy. Also, I am wise. I'm in a good place—a place where I feel successful, a place where life is good.

> Your Dad says he saw your life as "fragile". You were getting stronger but still had a long way to go. You weren't strong enough to cry out or roll over when you were sick. It was like your life was on a tightrope every day. I thought of you as tougher I guess, a survivor. This time you couldn't hang on. What went wrong?

She was tough and a survivor, yet she was so fragile. I saw her soul, which was very strong. And yet her body was fragile.

> It's not as if we didn't plan for you to be alive in the future. We had things in place, bank accounts, equipment ordered, Christmas presents, trip to Queensland.
>
> On the Friday I had outlined a whole stack of Queensland and airport words. Your Dad had stayed up late colouring them all in. You never saw them. We had the journey planned. Sue was ready to have your birthday party in Brisbane. We were going to take you to Movie World and Wet and Wild. No programme for a month. You were looking forward to that.

And today, Monday 30th March 2015, I'm sitting and typing on my own while Ian, Cassi, Angus, and Frazer are at Wet and Wild in Queensland. Yesterday, they were at Movie World. Strange coincidences. What a difference almost twenty years makes.

Breathing While Drowning

So little, so young, so much life to live. Was it too hard my darling? Were we asking too much from you? Was it just luck or did you stop fighting? The hardest thing for me is that I'll never know. What if I live till I'm 94? Then I'll have 60 years without you. I don't know if I can bear it. Part of me longs to die so I can be with you. Your Dad says I must hang around for Angus and Cass and him. I feel that I'm empty inside. You left too big a hole. The pain in my heart is still yours.

We went back up to see you on Monday night. You were in the coffin this time and seemed more settled. So familiar, just asleep. Your Dad and I had written you a letter, I sprayed it with my perfume so you'd know it was me. I had to write it out again 'cos the first time when I sprayed I smudged the writing. Cassie made you a beautiful drawing of the 3 kids holding hands and one of you. She wrote you a lovely letter telling you she loved you. We also bought some of the gum tree near the swing to have with you, remember the joys.

That night I was reluctant to leave you as I knew I would never look at your beautiful face again. It was very hard. I didn't want your life to end. Your Dad was my strength as always.

I think sometimes it's the early morning that I'm closest to you because I'm used to talking to you at this time of day. They keep telling me the pain will ease and the memory fade. Maybe. I know life must go on but each day is so long and each night is longer.

The anger, denial, and bargaining is all here. Predictable perhaps, but true. It's not linear, though; rather, it's a tortuous process for me as I go over things again and again and create a pattern of thinking and behaviour that resembles grinding myself from rocks into sand. It's like no part of me is whole. I'm drowning.

I feel scoured clean, scraped raw. My nerves are on edge, and I'm tingling to the point of pain. How hard it was to read these words again and feel the emotion ebb and flow: the hope, the frustration, the exhaustion, the joy, and the love. And drowning—that feeling of being at the mercy of a giant ocean of grief, shame, and guilt. Always drowning. I rarely do things half-heartedly, and grief is no exception.

But twenty years later, I'm still here and sane and not drowning. Most days, the tide stays far away in the ocean. I can see it in the distance, but I'm firmly on dry land. I'm grounded, whole, and happy.

Saturday 30th September 1995

Three weeks Jacq. It seems like a lifetime. A life sentence. I'm still struggling to move the images of Sept 9 to the back and trying to remember your beautiful smiling face and sparkling eyes. It still goes around and around in my head. If only ... if only ...

For what reason did it all happen? What are we supposed to do now? We don't know. At present we are kind of numb, empty, lost. Life has no purpose, no sense of urgency. You gave us a reason Jacq, and now you are gone.

We had such plans for you. School, holidays, sleepovers, new bedroom, equipment. Walking, running, talking and yelling. Where do we go from here?

Breathing While Drowning

I still can't believe you are gone forever. I keep expecting you to just be asleep on the couch or the floor, not so.

It is taking a long time to pack your things away. Too painful and sad.

We've brought a big wooden trunk to keep some things as it is too difficult to imagine throwing them out or even giving them away.

I'm just remembering you laughing. Your whole body shaking with joy. Everybody who saw you laugh always had to join in because it lifted the spirits to see you enjoying life so much. Mind you, you had a wicked sense of humour.

I can still hear you teasing Cassie dreadfully because you had the longest hair in the family. There was absolutely no doubt about what you were saying, accompanied by laughter, that your hair was the longest, nah, nah, nah.

You enjoyed the tooth fairy too. You were so excited when your first tooth came out. We still don't know where it went. But Cassie carefully wrote a note to the tooth fairy and you enjoyed the anticipation and build up that night.

You had lost 3 bottom teeth already but they were starting to be replaced. The others were on their way.

I had intended taking you down to the toyshop to spend your money from the tooth fairy and last year's birthday money from Nana Brethie. There were some good Bananas in Pyjamas things to choose from. No chance now.

Jacq, we're going on our holiday to QLD anyway. It won't be easy. I'm finding it so hard to get motivated. I know it will be difficult thinking of all the things we were going to do with you. You were going to have a whole month off as a honeymoon. That tickled your fancy! We could have done heaps of things.

I've got books put away for you for Christmas. I guess they'll have to wait for Angus.

I haven't gone through your room yet. Your clothes will be difficult. There isn't anyone to pass many of them on to as I made most of them to fit your skinny little body.

I feel so guilty just being alive when you're not. How can life go on? How can the sun keep coming up?

Your Dad has made a beautiful thank you card for all the patterners, but in typical Strachan fashion we've messed up the first few. Used the wrong glue and smudged some of your picture. Never mind, the poem is beautiful.

The outpouring of grief and sympathy from our friends and family was deep and heartfelt. Even many who hadn't been able to volunteer for the Programme came and expressed their sorrow. Children should not die so young. Even years later, people would send a note or call on her birthday or anniversary. The reaching out lessened over time, but people would still remember occasionally.

Breathing While Drowning

Making memories without Jacq was really hard and so important for Cassie and Angus. I heard one phrase over and over: "At least you have two other beautiful children." All this did was make me feel more guilt and shame. *At least* is not what I was looking for. I had lost my child; my daughter was not even five before she died. I wanted the world to wail and grieve with me, to rant that it wasn't fair, to bring her back, to give me another chance.

And there was one other phrase on the day she died, while her body was still lying on the couch: "It was meant to be." What the hell does that mean? In what way was that of any help whatsoever? Add to the insensitivity the fact that it came from someone who refused to help us in any way, shape, or form. We don't have a good place for death.

I couldn't believe the religious dogma that told me of heaven and hell and everything in between. The pain was all too raw, the hurt too deep.

Wednesday 1st November 1995

53 days, forever. Our lives go on but all seems without a purpose, no urgency in the days. They follow each other in a numbing march, some worse than others.

I hated the holiday for making memories without you in them. The best days were also the worst days as I'd think how much you would have enjoyed Movie World and Amazons Water Park. Even watching all the kids in the bath together made me think how you would've loved to be in the thick of it, crooked smile flashing and eyes alive with mischief.

The best of days and the worst of days are so often the same ones. I recently discovered I'm not the only one who contemplates disaster at the most joyful moments. Brené Brown wrote in *Daring Greatly: How the Courage to Be Vulnerable Transforms the Way We Live, Love, Parent and Lead*[2] about foreboding joy. At the very moment when joy fills you, your head fills with images of disaster, pain, and sorrow. Your imagination tears up the joy, stomps on it, rips it out of you, and replaces it with the total opposite—you can't have the joy; you don't deserve it; it'll never be yours, so stop dreaming. Why do we try to rip out that bubbling joy, to tear down the sunshine and rainbows?

There's a scene in the movie *City Slickers* where they talk about their best and worst day, and for one of the characters it's the same day. Why is it that we tend to learn so much more from a negative experience than a positive one? Why do we grow new awareness and skill from being deep in the manure?

> We made you a chocolate ripple birthday cake in the shape of a J. We all tried to sing Happy Birthday with little success. Grandad was the only one who made it all the way through. Your Dad wished you safety as he cut the cake with me. I had a dream of sorts, half waking. I was in a small dark place and a light came towards me, I had Angus too. I was frightened but asked were you okay? The wall/wood or something mouthed "yes" then disappeared. Wishful thinking? Who knows, I'm not certain.

I think I was very close to her spirit; that the barrier between worlds—the veil, if you like—was thin in those early days. I was holding on very tightly, keeping her close. Keeping myself breathing while drowning. I believe that dream was real.

Breathing While Drowning

These days, I'm certain it was you. I feel you close sometimes, my beautiful, feisty girl. Strong, laughing, loving. I've done a lot of searching to find a way to help me feel, to help me live and love and laugh again. I've tried lots of different ways to set it straight in my mind and my heart.

> We cleaned out the fridge on Monday, defrosted it even. Had to discard all your frozen dinners, by the time Angus would be ready they'd probably be off. It was really hard to come home on Sunday night. Just driving down the freeway brought back the whole horror of that night. Why didn't I go in and give you a kiss? To come home to the empty house was really difficult. I went to your room then to mine. I held your ashes, wrapped in your favourite soft Indian blanket and cried for you. I'm sorry Jacqui Bree. I couldn't do enough. I can't believe that you're gone forever. Will we meet again?
>
> Will I ever have a day when I don't think about you in everything I do? When the pain of losing you lessens and fades?
>
> Sue tried hard to give us all a great holiday, Tim too but it was pretty difficult. Your Dad made the best of the situation but even he had his bad times. Not bad so much as sad. He found it hard to sit and relax, he had to be busy doing something. That's the way he's keeping a handle on the whole thing I think.

> Emotionally he seems more able to cope or organise himself or something. He keeps his body busy so his mind doesn't have time to think so much.
>
> I still have an image of the house on 9th September. Your clothes were on the back of the couch ready for you that day.

We never know when the moment will come. The exhortation to live as though there were no tomorrow echoes down the years. I say to live in the moment now, to be as mindful as you can. I believe in being rather than doing.

Take back that angry shout, don't say that mean word—it might be the last thing you exchange with that person. Love as though there is no tomorrow. Do everything now; don't wait if you can help it.

Friday 3rd November 1995

> 55 days Jacq. Last night I went to bed to get a sleep before coming to work, all I did was cried. You were so close in my thoughts. I struggled to keep happy memories of you uppermost. Every day is still hard, so many things you'll never get to see or do or learn. We had such plans for you. Why did it happen? Weren't we trying hard enough? We were prepared to do anything to get you well. Looking at video of you on the skateboard, you were so close to crawling solo it wasn't funny.

Breathing While Drowning

> Now all I have of you is photos and videos and memories. I have a lifetime without you. How can I ever be happy when you aren't here? Are you safe Jacq? Are you happy? Is somebody loving you like we did? Will I ever see you again or is death the end?
>
> We try hard to fill the days up with tasks and chores but still you are there. Sometimes I want to change the house completely, start again. Other times I can't bear it to be any different in case you don't recognise it.
>
> Your garden is coming along very well. We are all trying hard to finish it. Angus is helping by getting dirty and eating sand, leaves and grass. Cass is helping with watering and laying the path of bricks the "J" path.
>
> Daylight saving has started so we can work on it after tea too. We bought new hoses and some perennials today. I'm still trying to decide what sort of chair to have at the end of the J.
>
> Now you will always be my little girl, never growing up. You had so much to give, so much life and joy. I wish I could trade places, you deserved better. I'm not a very good mother. I'm sorry my darling sweet pea.

Guilt and shame. I was hitting one of the top feminine shame triggers: motherhood. No need for other people to trigger me, though, because I was and am really good at getting that one done on my own.

Veronica Strachan

The Initiation and Descent into Darkness

Murdock tells us that the initiation and descent into darkness is the "dark night of the soul".³ When I read her words that a precipitating event could be the death of your child, someone "with whom one's life and identity has been closely intertwined," I realise I am not alone. This is the start of my longest descent, and it was okay to go down. I can't tell you the relief and release I had reading those words. I inhaled them, took them into the darkness as a small flicker of light, a life buoy in the ocean. Here, at last, was someone who was writing about me, about how I lost my way in the world. She explained that, even though I was alive, a large part of me was dying. And it was fine to be there, to be lost. It was okay to be "filled with confusion and grief, alienation and disillusion, rage and despair [...] naked and exposed, dry and brittle, and raw and turned inside out".⁴

The descent could just as easily be the death of anyone close. Or it could be "when a particular role, such as daughterhood, motherhood, lover, or spouse, comes to an end. A life threatening illness or accident, the loss of self-confidence or livelihood, a geographical move, the inability to finish a degree, a confrontation with the grasp of addiction, or a broken heart can open the space for dismemberment and descent".⁵

For me the descent into the underworld feels like all the years since Jacqui died: the depression, the aridity of emotion. I had to go to death's door to see the limits of life and death. Not my death, but the death of my beautiful daughter.

And then Murdock writes the most welcome words I have ever read: "In the underworld, there is no sense of time, time is endless and you cannot rush your stay".⁶ You "cannot rush your stay"—the words chimed into my heart. I can be there as long as I need to be, which, strangely, made me want to leave immediately.

Pig-headed, stubborn, control freak ... maybe. Actually, just lost and stuck and looking for a signpost. That was it. That was the key that was my permission to myself to get going. Time was wasting, and I had a whole lot of living to do.

The lessons I learned about myself and the world that I realised then—and that I realise now—mean a lot of different things.

Live every moment as if it were your last; don't regret a single instant. Be in every moment as if you'll never see that person or that thing again. Bring all your joy and love to being who you are right now.

Lesson: it's hard to do this all the time, but I'm practising more these days. Mindful practice and meditation are powerful tools. I'm working on living now, and I'm not stuck on a see-saw between the past and the future. When I don't get it right, when I rant or lie lazily on the couch watching TV, I forgive myself and start again. There is a thing in mindfulness practice known as the *beginner's mind*. It is best understood as curiosity for everything you see, hear, say, touch, and feel.

Zen Master Suzuki Roshi says, "In the beginner's mind there are many possibilities, but in the expert's there are few."[7] If you cultivate a beginner's mind, a world of wonder will open right in front of you and deep inside you.

Grieve in your own time. There is no formula, there is no best time, and it's always an individual journey.

Lesson: don't be bound by other people's need to heal from their own hurt, their own grief. Don't be bound by other people's rules and expectations of when you should be feeling better, when you should be over it. You know yourself best, you know what you need. Listen, but do what you want. Grieving is intense sorrow, and it's also feeling everything else intensely. I needed to find out how to move from feeling intensely sad to feeling other things intensely.

And grieving is forever. Sometimes I miss seeing the puddle and, before I know it, I'm deep under water, floundering and flapping about. Anniversaries are hard. We try to celebrate Jacqui's birthday and remember the good days. This week it was twenty years since Jacqui Bree died, and this year it was hard. In the days leading up to her anniversary, I was writing and re-living the real days. And I found myself cranky as anything. While trying to explain it to Cassi, who had been comforting me, I realised that I was putting myself back into the same place and space that I had been over and over again. Too busy with work, too little time for family and self; sucked into that illusory boon of success that has us running ourselves ragged. And then, of course, we can blame ourselves when it doesn't all get done—see: we're not enough.

So I decided, as people pushed my buttons all over the place, that I would choose differently, I would choose to be myself, to take the time and love myself, to grieve and remember, and to exist differently. I was still sad, but I was okay with that—I wanted to feel it, to be in it, to be through it. I was conscious that the runaway train that was so often my life could easily take over again, so I gently applied the brakes and took a breath, straightened my spine, and realised that my head was well above water. I thought, *Yep, I'm in control. I choose to feel differently.*

Sometimes you can grow from pain if you let it feed your soul and teach you the lesson. You can be like a phoenix rising from the ashes.

Lesson: learning to be in the pain or the fear or whatever the life lesson is can be very uncomfortable. And why is it that we seem to learn so much more from painful or frightening experiences than from joy and happiness?

In *Wired for Life*, Sheehan and Pearse suggest it's a hangover from our survival mechanism: "Your brain is more highly attuned to threat than it is to reward. While it wants to move towards reward, it gives more attention to threat".[8]

Breathing While Drowning

So taking the idea that what we focus on (what we are highly attuned to) is where our attention goes, then "it's only logical that we would have evolved to examine a threat closely and not turn away from it until we are sure it is not going to cause us danger".[9]

Joy and lasting happiness seem elusive because "we experience a short period of satisfaction from reward, then we move on".[10]

Whatever the reason—logical, emotional, energetic, nature, nurture—the chance is there for you to take it, even when you know it's going to hurt. Until you get that pattern into your brain, your body, and your soul and realise where it takes you, you'll keep getting the lesson over and over again until you don't need it any longer.

There are some great words in Dr Wayne Dyer's movie *My Greatest Teacher*. The main character talks about a snake bite. The actual bite is not deadly; what's deadly is the venom, the poison. This is what circulates around your body long after the bite and destroys you. But if we can release, assimilate, or transmute the venom in some way, we have a chance. He suggests looking at "the most damaging things in your life, the things that have caused you the most pain and the most suffering and figuring out a way to turn those into your greatest teachers, this is what we're supposed to do for the world around us and for ourselves".[11]

This is where I'm at with the pain and loss and grief of Jacqui Bree's passing. This book is my way of thinking and feeling and going through the pain and figuring out what her life and death are teaching me ... and then I can share those lessons with the world.

The veil is thinner sometimes—the veil between worlds, between realities.

Lesson: maybe this is not a lesson as such; maybe this is more a comment. Anita Moorjani had a near-death experience and wrote a beautiful, inspiring book called *Dying to be me*.[12] The short message she had is that we are all one—all of us, across time, space, dimensions, and realities. We're an infinite being having a human experience. Sometimes we get close to the other realities, the other dimensions, and sometimes we can feel how close we are to those we love. Let them in and feel them.

Use whatever it takes.

Lesson: just that—use whatever it takes. I've seen so many people try to control grief and life; it's so very human of us. Use whatever it takes to find your way to being, to living the life you want. I found books wonderful sources of wisdom and comfort. Listening to people when the time was right was inspiring. Just allow it to happen; don't push and force yourself. If colonic irrigation is the thing that gets you moving (pardon the pun) and helps you get your shit together (couldn't help myself), do that. If journaling works, do that. If going to a counsellor to talk works, do that. If bottling it up inside for about seventeen years works for you (it did for me), do that. It's your life. Everything you do, feel, think, and believe belongs to you, and that's what matters.

Create your own definition of a successful life

What's your definition of success? Is it things, position, power? I think we all like a bit of that kind of success, I know I did and still do. But if it's only that, we stay on that scarcity roundabout; we never want to get off because there is always something else we want, even if it's for someone else.

Other things are now part of my definition of success, and they're in two groups that kind of work together, but I'm working to get them more integrated.

Group one is personal: success here is happiness, health, and wisdom—all of the things that allow me to live a life that expresses the very best of who I am, to live joyfully and bring that joy to every moment for myself while learning and loving.

Breathing While Drowning

Group two is relationships: success here is bringing that joy to every interaction, being present and compassionate, really listening, being ready to love, share, and teach—all of the things that allow me to leave someone in a better place than if I hadn't been there.

So my success is being joyfully healthy, happy, loved, wise, and wealthy.

Chapter 5

The Years of Guilt, Shame, and Despair

In the years after Jacqui died, reality for me became like the lyrics from the Eagle's classic "Hotel California": "You can check out anytime you like, but you can never leave".[1]

I checked out of life and went through the motions for the first five years. I always take things to perfection, so I took my heroine's journey of closure to perfection as well. I shut it all down.

Of course, the problem with putting up barriers to keep the bad stuff out is that the good stuff can't get in either. I couldn't leave my life because, everywhere I went, the grief came with me—it followed me to new jobs, new friends, new cities, new states. I was still inside the barriers, still re-living the loss, the pain, and the heartache in an unending series of nightmare reruns. I was still imagining the worst-case scenario for every joyful moment. I was still telling myself, *If only*. I wanted so badly to change the past.

Even now, I sometimes wonder, "What if", especially if I see a brain-injured child on the telly or down the street. One of the wonderful women I've met since my return to life is the mother of a young boy with a disability. I sometimes envy her. She has her son, and he's still filling her life with moments of joy and angst.

Breathing While Drowning

Every now and again, it still catches me while explaining what I'm writing or how many children I have, I feel the tears well up and the ocean beckoning. A friend I met by chance told me, "It's a gift to be caught like that—that's how deep your love is. Notice how beautiful it is that your love hasn't changed after all these years. And years doesn't make it any easier or shift it. It's unshakeable love." It was a beautiful way to express the sentiment, and it helped a lot. Even after all this time, there's an element of apology if I cry in public or unexpectedly. It's as if I should be able to hold it together better after all this time. But she's right: it's unshakeable love, and I will always miss my darling Sweet Pea.

Thursday 21st December 1995

Jacqui Bree 103 days. Life at the moment still seems quite unreal. It's as if we are just living in a dream and we'll wake up and it will all be gone and you'll be with us. I miss you so much. The tears still flow so often, I thought I would be all cried out. My emotions are on a roller-coaster. There are very few days at the moment when I don't cry for you. Often I'm quite good till I'm arriving home from work then the thought of the house empty of you makes me cry. My birthday was hard. Your Dad tried so hard to make it happy despite my gloomy disposition. He is battling on, keeping busy, working on your gatehouse and our house too. I've planted more things in your garden and more people have given us plants over the last few days. We've had a lot of rain which will help I'm sure.

Today we moved some of your equipment from the lounge room, the incline and your floor. It was very hard. It's like you dying all over again, bringing a sense of finality. I don't want to say good-bye yet.

Your clothes are still untouched. That is going to take some time. I'm not ready yet. We have a big photo of you and Cass & Angus on the wall in the lounge now. I can see you at a glance. I've looked at some video of you, so happy and trying so hard.

We've finally rearranged your room. I folded up your mattress, after crying all over it. We've got a bed from Nana Brethie's and I've bought a new clown quilt (from Queensland) so the room is neat again.

A few people have written Christmas cards and are unaware you had died. It makes it hard. I've had to write to a few friends and explain.

It was like a conspiracy when we did Chrissy shopping. Bananas in Pyjamas everywhere. I saw so many things you would have loved. Not to be.

I've re-enrolled at Uni to finish my degree. Your Dad is thinking of going to TAFE to get an integration certificate. He wants to continue helping special needs kids and this could be a good way to start.

It's hard to gauge how your Dad is doing. I know he has his difficult moments but I think he's trying to be strong for us all. I hope he takes time out to grieve for you properly. Men are different in their thinking so I don't know how to help him always. Maybe me being a mess gives him direction. He minds Angus and Cass pretty well, looks after them with the same single-minded dedication he cared for you with.

Breathing While Drowning

Although grief was new, we were surrounded by patterns from our families, from our own relationship, from ourselves. Because we felt as if there was so much out of control, we were looking for new ways to behave, new ways to live. Maybe me being a mess gives Ian direction, so if I keep being a mess, Ian will have something to do. Crazy? Maybe.

> I'll have to try more to help him. It's just that most days I'm struggling. There is no explanation thorough enough to justify why you died. I still can't fathom that out. No-one really to talk to who might understand.
>
> I think everybody expects us to just go on. Like we should be over it all by now. I can't foresee a day ever when I will be over losing you. Some days I feel really selfish, as if I have the most pain and nobody else could hurt as much as me.

Feeling selfish for grieving for my daughter? How hard I am on myself. How hard is the rest of the world? Children are not supposed to die this young.

> I know lots of people are thinking of me but nobody else can help at night going to bed without you. Seeing an ambulance and thinking of giving you mouth to mouth. Waking in the early hours and wishing I had done that on Sep 9. Kissing Cass and Angus goodnight and not you.

> My darling, beautiful girl will I ever see you again? Ever hold your soft hands or stroke your hair, hear your infectious giggle, watch your crooked smile. Love you Jacqui Bree.

I was getting more and more closed off, listening to the *sad* and *you're not enough* shame voice over and over. It was all my fault. I couldn't control it; I wasn't enough.

Sunday 24th December 1995

> 106 days of forever. Tonight I don't believe I can live with you gone. How can I accept it, find peace? Why, why, why? If only I'd been on an early or a night duty, if only you'd vomited later or been on our side more on your stomach. Then I would be looking forward to Christmas with joy and not this overwhelming sadness. How can time heal this pain? I don't believe I can. Did you slip quietly away Jacq as your Dad thinks or did you struggle to call out to us? This I fear in my worst nightmares. Should we have kept you on the end of a monitor? Would it have made a difference?
>
> We tried hard to find that balance between wrapping you in cotton wool and treating you like a normal kid. Did we err on the wrong side?
>
> Where is the future? Our future as a family? My future as a mother? Do I have one? Haven't I failed because I've lost you? I wish I believed in heaven.

Breathing While Drowning

> Your Dad wants to do a TAFE course to help disabled kids, he sees that as the way to go for him. Sometimes I think he has the makings of a saint. It's hard to live up to at times. If only my mind wasn't so active. If only my memory wasn't so good. Over and over and over, if only, if only, if only.
>
> Jacqui Bree I miss you so much, I can't believe you will never grow up. When will I see you again? Soon?
>
> Where is the way, where is the peace? Your Dad helps me as much as he can, somewhere I have to find the resources to keep going to achieve a purpose, an aim in life. I have no direction I'm lost.
>
> Would anyone miss me I wonder, your Dad maybe? Not many others. Already they are distant. Too caught in their own troubles to help with mine.
>
> How can I go on? Does my existence make a difference? No. There are others who would do it all better.
>
> Cass is independent, resilient and resourceful. She would manage. Angus is too young to remember. He has his Dad. Life would go on.
>
> What about Ian. Can I imagine life without him? Never. Would he be better off without me? Maybe. Do I give him purpose?

I thought about death a lot. I thought about taking my own life a lot. I came close so many times in those early days; I was so desperately unhappy. Each time, however, something stopped me. Was it more courageous to stay or go? I often thought about this question. For a long time after I decided to stay, I felt as if I had drawn death into my soul, and I carried it with me day after day. It sat on my shoulder, whispering in my ear: see what you've done: not good enough; you don't deserve happiness.

This is the first mention of a life purpose. I was thirty-five years old. Humans need connection, and mine had been severed. Covey says humans need to "live, love, learn and leave a legacy".[2] We need a reason, a purpose. I didn't have one of my own and could not even begin to accept one. So, I just got busy being someone else's worker. Helping every other woman and man with their purpose.

Tuesday 26th December 1995

Just after midnight Christmas Day. Our first one without you. Sad? Yes. I wanted so much for everything to go well today, so did your Dad. Too little sleep and highly strung emotions didn't help. But we kept it in check while all the visitors were here.

I think I made your Dad very sad tonight. I told him that the love I have for him overpowers me. That I don't have any time | energy | something to put into myself so I'm not myself. It's something that's vaguely been nagging away at the back of my brain for quite a while. Yet it is really a choice I've made. I love your Dad. He is my other half, my soulmate. I don't mind doing things his way, letting him think for me at times. Maybe the bitchiness I get is in part resentment, against him and myself for not being allowed to be myself. Confused? Me too.

Would I be a better person, mother, wife if I had more time for me? Maybe not more time but better

> use of time. Start tomorrow, no actually today. Do something about it. Life is short. Make a difference. Don't leave it all up to him. He is only 1 man, his strength is not unlimited. Let him lean on me, or at least share the load.
>
> Darling girl I missed you heaps today. You will always be with me. Always in my heart. Wait for me sweetheart. Not too long Mummy loves you

Here's the first indication of discontent with who I'm being, with how I'm being. The consciousness of who am I is beginning to emerge. It's a long road of discontent that I find myself on. I had forgotten that the search began so long ago.

I loved that man to distraction, and I still do. Now I am stronger, more whole. Now I love myself a lot more, and our love is a wondrous joy, an amazing and incredible gift that I am grateful for every day. I work to treasure our connection every day.

I feel a bit like shaking that thirty-five-year-old me and telling her to get her act together. She would try the patience of a saint—honestly! It would be another fifteen years or more until I finally voiced those feelings with my best friends and realised I was not alone.

Thursday 28th December 1995

> 2:30 am, tortured again. I did not kiss my children goodnight. Too tired? Too lazy? Too optimistic? Always thinking there will be tomorrow, I'll do it then. Too selfish? Why, why, why?

I cannot live with it Jacq. I don't know how to. Is this my punishment to live every day with the guilt of not being there when you needed me? Of not kissing you goodnight? Would it have made a difference?

Your Dad is asleep, snoring. Is he at peace? Did his best. Kissed you lots of goodnights. Heart untroubled, sleeps.

I can't. Images of you in my head. Where are you? Take me instead, is this my test? To live a long life with the burden on not kissing you goodnight? To see if I have the courage to stay alive? Or does it take more courage to finish it? I think of ways to end it, over and over. Think of people's reactions. Selfish? How would your Dad manage? He would be sad but he would survive. His duty and sense of right would keep him going. He'd do the right thing. Cass? She'd survive, maybe be glad the old dragon wasn't here to tell her off anymore. That's not fair, she would be sad for a while. Angus? Too young, he wouldn't even remember me.

Which takes more courage? To go or to stay?

Christmas was a nightmare. Like walking through quicksand. Every moment likely to go under.

How can I go on? What am I supposed to do? Where do I go?

I can't make love to your Dad. He needs me and I can't. How can I have any pleasure when you're not here? I must feel guilty. I don't deserve to have any joy. I am a failure as a mother and now as a wife.

Breathing While Drowning

> I don't want to go to work and pretend to be happy and chatty. I don't care about other people's marriages and children. I feel like running and screaming from the room. Don't they know my pain?
>
> I'm sorry Jacq I can never hold you again. I can't take back that night. It's too late. I can't live with those memories. You were so innocent and happy. You didn't deserve to die. Why did you? Life is hollow. I can never be happy.
>
> I need help but I have no one to ask. No friend who could help me, my best friend has his own burden, finds his own answers. No one in the family wants to know. Too hard. Caught up in their own lives. Don't even ask me about you or talk about you anymore. Don't ask how I am or Ian. Don't want to know. Too hard.
>
> Do I go on? How? A trip to Europe? A betrayal? You can't come. A dream from my past? How can I go?
>
> So many thoughts. Jumbled. I don't know where to turn. I love you Jacqui but that wasn't enough. I love your Dad and we made you. But we couldn't keep you. I've lost you. Now I'm lost.

I felt I didn't deserve the dream. Hammered into me over and over, cemented with tears and misery. The patterns of thoughts, the desperate crying out without being able to ask for help or share my vulnerability. I was too caught up in the game of guilt and shame.

Tuesday 16th January 1996

A bad day, a bad few days. How can I go on? My heart is empty, I cry a lot, I can't explain. I'll never hold you again my darling beautiful Jacqui Bree. I can't bear it anymore. I think of more and more ways to stop the pain. My head goes between one argument and another.

Everywhere so many reminders of you. Scraps of material, things I made for your skinny little body, material I had to make you pj's, now Angus has it. My life is torn, nothing will ever be the same. Toys we bought for you, hoping you could play with them. Articles saved from magazines with hopeful answers. Initial assessment at the Institutes so long ago.

We are doing so many things that you would've loved to do. It's like walking on glass with bare feet.

Turmoil, where are you Jacq? Are you safe? Can you forgive me? Is there anything for you to go to or is it just the end? If I die now will I go or is it not my time.

I am not a good mother. Cass and I and your Dad had a dreadful fight today. Are we bad parents? Is Cass OK? Would Angus remember me?

Can I face another day? Another night? A shower, wishing I had checked on you earlier?

I love you Ian, you be strong. I love Cassie, you will be a beautiful person. I love Angus, be like your Dad little boy, he is a beautiful man.

Numb. Hollow.

Breathing While Drowning

Even reading this now, I feel like saying, "Get a grip, move on, let it go." With that kind of self-compassion, how hard must it have been for others to support me, to reach me? I was so sad, so full of the darkness, drowning, barely breathing. It seemed so much easier to let go, to stop swimming, and to sink.

Friday 26th January 1996

I'm still here I didn't have the courage to finish or maybe I found the courage to go on. It still strikes fear into my heart imaging myself living to old age 80-90 and being there without you. Is that my punishment?

I don't see how I can continue to nurse sick people. I feel like screaming at them to wake up, see my pain, understand my despair. I don't care about them anymore.

My head still whorls with images of doom and death and I feel like I move through quicksand.

Your Dad is trying so hard to hang on to me. He is strong, but also sad.

What direction lies the future? Is there any? Am I willing to face it?

We had some of the flowers from your funeral pressed and we had to go and choose some arrangements. It is hard to think that is all that's left. What I would give just to kiss you goodnight? To feel your silky hair. A hug of your skinny bones. To feel you try to hug me back or struggle to purse your lips for a kiss.

Thursday 1st February 1996

We worked on your garden last night. The rosemary hedge was looking a bit dodgy so we dug them up all, added soil and mulch then replanted them. It looks much better. Your Dad spoke to the man at the nursery and he said they don't like their feet too wet.

Life seems quite unreal at the moment. It's as if this were a separate existence like we've stepped outside the real world. One day I'll wake up and it will be back to normal. You'll be there and programme will be on.

I guess we're just drifting, aimless at present. I must try and push on. I s'pose I've decided to stay, at least for now. There are still pleasures and Ian, Cassie and Angus. I don't think the ache will ever go Jacq. I hope I see you again soon. I'd be happy for you to visit if you wanted to.

Your garden will look good for your Anniversary I promise. Your Dad has almost finished the gatehouse and all the drainage is done. It just needs more plants now. But I keep imagining you in it which doesn't work. Be happy my beautiful girl.

The need for ending, for suicide, gradually subsided. This was one of the worst times with the balance almost tipping. The optimist won out. Crawling back to a semblance of life inch by inch, seeing and feeling the small pleasures: Cassi and Angus and Ian, my landmarks on dry ground.

"When there's no way out, there's still a way through".[3]

Sometimes it feels as though the whole ocean is between me and the shore.

Wednesday 14th February 1996

More than 5 months Jacq and still it's hard. I was talking to your Dad on the way home yesterday He said it doesn't leave your mind, the thoughts of you are always there but sometimes you can be distracted for a while. I guess the busier we are the better.

We've just been to Sydney to help Mel shift into her new flat.

The power of distraction, of keeping busy, can become an addiction. And like any addiction, if you feed it, it gets worse. Like all addictions, you need more and more to get the same buzz or numbing effect. We're so lost in the chaos of work these days. I see families breaking apart because the members are too busy to live and love together. I see so many people in the business world destroying themselves by being too busy. It's become a badge of honour: "I'm so busy." "That's good." "You must be busy." If you answer no, which I have consciously begun to do, people look at you oddly. Admitting that you don't have much paid work going on at the moment or that you are deliberately keeping a slower pace in your life elicits a kind of embarrassed smile. And then the reactions are interesting. They move between "Well that's okay for you, but I have so much to do" or "Yes, that sounds like something I want to try." There's a slow awakening to the joys of living a more conscious life.

Monday 19th February 1996

The Sydney trip was busy but fruitful. Your Dad hammered and screwed and I sewed and sewed so now she's pretty much set up. We've left her with a lot to do but she has a direction now. I wrote out some old recipes for her last night which I'll send up today.

We called in at Janet's on the Monday so the drive wouldn't be so long home.

It was really hard to leave, knowing you wouldn't be home. Your Dad admitted yesterday that the events around you dying had come back to him. He had been able to block it out for some time and focus on the good memories.

I had been doing pretty good for a while too but the last few days have been hell. My mind goes over and over you. The same questions come back to haunt me. Yet I am accepting it was not my fault. I know events were beyond my control. Has it changed the way I am? The way I think? Oh yeah!

I wonder if I can ever by truly happy. We will never forget you Jacqui Bree.

We would have made you well I know. I still hate to go home from work knowing you're not there. I still cry a lot in the car when I'm by myself. No one to be brave for. I have to check Cass and Angus before I leave and as soon as I get home. If only I'd checked you I may have kissed you or put you further on your side and you might have lived.

But I didn't and it might not have made any difference. I was too tired, too late.

Some days I struggle to bring back the good memories. The feel of your skinny body, the silky feel of your hair. Your bony fingers holding mine. Why Jacq? Too young, life too short. We loved you so much. The burden was not too heavy we could carry you easily. Were we unworthy? Was it just too much of a struggle? Did we ask too much of you?

Extraordinary, irreplaceable.

My extraordinary, irreplaceable Jacqueline Bree: beloved daughter and teacher.

Sunday 31st March 1996

Coming up to 7 months my beautiful girl. Life has seemed impossible to live these past few days. I was in a quagmire of despair and depression unable to find a lifeline. Your Dad had even given up on me. He didn't know what else to do for me. He'd run out of ideas. And still all I could think of was you and "what ifs". Everywhere I turned seemed to be against me. Like the world was just waiting to knock down my flimsy defences.

I dropped out of a subject at Uni. It was called Communication Skills but involved a lot of reflective practice and introspection so it was very difficult.

I decided to be kind to myself. And to the rest of the family. It will help us get ready for a good holiday. Jacq I wish you were coming. I know you loved the flight to Brisbane last time. All the sights we'll see would have been fantastic for you.

Jacqui I miss you so much, it still makes me cry too easily. I got to the desperate stage one Sunday afternoon and rang "Compassionate Friends". They are a group of bereaved parents. All have lost kids. They've sent me out information and some of it has been quite helpful. I s'pose it's helpful to know what I'm feeling is OK and normal.

I planted a stack of bulbs in your garden today and your Dad has finished the gatehouse. The lettering is up also. The whole area is coming together well.

We still haven't decided what to do with your ashes. I'd like a wooden urn but in a natural state. We'll find what we're looking for eventually I know.

I must go on Jacqui Bree and build a life without you with us. You will always be with me in my heart and in my head, just not in body.

Your Dad said he didn't think I knew/accepted how far you had to go to get well. How far behind many of the other kids you were physically. I s'pose I never saw you as disabled, just as Jacqui, my darling girl I knew you would get walking, I just didn't know when.

> Maybe I'm glad in a way about the suddenness. It would have been more difficult if you had been unwell. Then sometimes I think you waited till AP was here with us before you let go. It would've been hard to forgive myself if I had lost you when I was 35 weeks. AP was _never_ meant to be an exchange in any way, shape or form.
>
> As it stands now I can't find forgiveness in my heart yet.
>
> I don't think I even want to nurse anymore. I don't really care about the patients anymore, less thorough, I just want to go home all the time, spend my life with my family. I need to yell at them "what about me" "feel my pain" "heal me". But they don't, everybody shies away from me. Am I so hard to be a friend to? Death is obviously a difficult topic but surely not uncommon?
>
> Keep watch Jacqui Bree, I love you.

There is so much emotion when I reread this passage. I was on such a roller coaster, so vehemently grieving, so angry, so sad. If not for Strack, Cassi, and Angus, I may not have held on. And perhaps my optimism did make me misjudge Jacqui's chance of having a normal life. But now I'm so thankful for my hopefulness and confidence that everything would be okay (or more than okay).

In Anita Moorjani's *Dying to be me*[4], she talks about there being a spark of magnificence in all of us. I love that. I can see that spark in everyone I meet, even if it's deep inside and covered in layers of dust or *busyness*. That is one of the most precious gifts that Jacqui Bree has helped me see. Whether I'm coaching just one person or facilitating a room of people, I'm seeing the spark of magnificence. My work is to fan it into flames and to get people to hold out their hands and hearts and minds and take the warmth deep into their souls, to create and to inspire and to serve.

Sunday 14th April 1996

It's been a while Jacq. It's getting harder to write to all of you. I'm becoming more numb I guess. Not less sad or less loving you, just numb.

Ian says it's the best way to be, it helps you go on. How can I without my little girl? What's the point of it all?

Mel rang tonight, at work. She sounds like she's searching, still grieving. Wanting to make a difference, leave an impression on the world.

I can't help her much at present 'cos I feel caught in a stasis. Frozen in my grief.

Your Dad is on a downer at the moment too. He doesn't go so well in the winter when he's trapped indoors. He's finished putting your card album together and now needs some other projects to keep him going. Maybe he's better when I'm down so that he has to stay up for all of us. I've been busy studying which has left a lot of the daily chores in his lap. It gets very wearing.

The holiday comes closer, almost all organised and I'm sure that worries him a lot. He wants so much to please us all. His love is strong.

> He wants to use all he learnt from caring for you Jacq to help other brain-injured kids. We don't want the skills to be lost. I don't think I could do it yet. I'd want to but I'd end up a blubbering wreck at the moment. I'm not sure what I want to do
>
> I used to think like Mel that I'd like to make a difference. Now I'm not so sure. Maybe I want to be good at other things. Who knows?
>
> All I know at the moment is that I miss you unbearably. Life just doesn't seem right.
>
> I need to work harder with Cass and Angus, I guess 'cos they don't need me like you did makes it more difficult. They'll survive.

Giving up on making a difference. Letting go of that need to leave your legacy in the world. I was frozen in my grief. My world had shrunk to mostly Jacqui's death, grief and a little left over for my immediate family. Not much else was getting in or out. Humans need each other, we're tribal. Our survival depends on us looking out for each other, protecting our young.

Strack wanting to use the good things he'd learnt was a worthy goal. I think he got a bit side tracked looking after me, Cassi and Angus but we felt the love and care. He expresses this even now in his everyday way – but that's his story to tell.

Sunday 5th May 1996

> I think what I was going to say is that they'll survive without me. Maybe I don't feel needed enough?

I didn't feel needed enough. The complexity of Jacqui's life had given me a purpose, and now I did not have one. The other children could survive without me, so I thought they didn't need me. This is such a self-centred concept, and it's all about looking in rather than looking out. What I need from people rather than what I can give, how I can be of service. Eventually, I came full circle; I have a totally different way of looking at living, a totally beautiful way to a conscious life. Dr Wayne Dyer expresses this really well: "Be of service first."

> Your Dad wants me to pick some photos for a locket he bought me for our 11th Anniversary yesterday. I'm going to have one of you and a lock of your hair.
>
> Your garden is growing. We've planted stacks of bulbs. It should look beautiful when your anniversary comes around. Still needs more though. John and Julie gave us two bushes today, they'll help. I'll talk to you later my darling.

Sunday 12th May 1996

> Mother's Day! I was committing a neatness in my wardrobe and found a mother's day card from last year, it had on it from Cassie, Jacqui and Angus. It is still so incredibly hard my darling. Whenever I think of you tears begin. I still feel so hurt, so much anger at myself and everyone else. Why aren't you here with me? Some days it's just like it was yesterday. Some days it feels like an eternity since

Breathing While Drowning

I held you, stroked your beautiful hair, felt you snuggle up and give me a squeeze. I still have memories of the smell of your clean silky hair, pointy noise, beautiful fine fingers, big green eyes, bony knees, crooked smile.

It is almost impossible to believe I will never see you again. Basically it's a shit! I can't figure out why. Was life too hard for you? If that's the case I'm sorry, I have to let you go. I wouldn't want it to be that way. But I still feel I let you down. Over and over in my head I rehearse the way it could have been. I come home and kiss you good-night. Angus doesn't disturb you. You don't vomit, even if you do you are on your side 'cos I turn you over when I kiss you goodnight. Or I hear you cough and I get up. I wish I could take it back, maybe just one step would make a difference, maybe not.

How does life go on? Many times I wonder if I will ever function properly again, I doubt it.

The few years you were with us were the most important and best years of my life. I loved you so much and you gave me a direction, a purpose, now I'm nothing, wandering aimless.

My days are full, not as busy, but complicated enough to keep me occupied for most of them. Yet the only way I get through is by being numb. It's like I have a rubber wall around me and I just let things bounce off. But still I hurt, so many things remind me of you! Stuff Cass does, stuff Angus does, stuff your Dad does. Ambulances, kids who turn 5, special needs kids, your cups, your photos, memories, hospitals, working lates, driving home, driving to work, your garden, your bedroom, your toys.

Everything reminds me of you, even now. Where we focus is where our energy and thinking and intention goes, so that's all we see, that's where we make all the associations.

But I'm no longer numb, the rubber wall has gone … mostly. I'm getting through, I'm letting myself feel everything. I'm living "a life that expresses the very best of who I can be"—thank you Stephanie Dowrick for those inspiring words.[5] I've got the functioning happening … mostly. I'm happy with exactly where I am and who I'm being: a work in progress, an imperfectly perfect woman.

The best years of my life are now; this moment and all the other moments past and present that exist in this moment. Right now.

Monday 5th August 1996

Jacq we're home. I meant to take your book but somehow in the rush I didn't. Maybe it was meant to be. We were so busy almost all the time.

I asked Mary to mind your ashes and photo album and Mary-Ellen. I wanted you to be with family, not strangers.

The last little baby wants to be born now Jacq. So much like you, a month early to conceive and making me sick all over the holiday. I hope it has your nature. I don't know if that'll make me miss you more or less. More I suspect. As usual I'm struggling physically and emotionally to welcome this new little person. I feel this is the last and your Dad also. We will be as complete as possible without you. This will give me some direction I s'pose, but I still feel like I'm drifting, aimless, struggling to choose a path to follow. My pain is still so close to the surface.

Breathing While Drowning

And so the last member of our family, Frazer Douglas burst into being and made his own and very determined way into our lives. There was another spark of magnificence to nurture and love and bring us joy.

Sunday 15th September 1996

12 months Jacq. A lifetime since you left us. As the 9th got closer I got worse and worse. Stumbling around like I was in a fog, unable to find my way. Your Dad kept trying to throw me a lifeline but I couldn't take it. In many ways I was hoping lots of people would come and talk to me about you, but no one did. A few people rang and a few dropped in but no one wanted to talk. I need to talk about you, to hear you described in detail, to keep you sharp in my mind.

I want people to hear my grief, feel my pain, share it with me. But only your Dad knows and he is different from me. He sees he must go on. Somehow he finds the strength.

I finally unloaded a bit onto Ronnie Z. She was a good listener. Interesting that after I'd told her a lot of the what if's from the morning you died she said it seemed that there was almost a barrier or force field around you to stop us going in.

Your journey was over. Was it? Was that your reward for trying so hard for us and yourself?

I don't know but I felt calmer after I'd spoke to her and she acknowledged my grief and my right to grieve in my own time frame.

> I have to forgive myself and move on but I want to take you with me, I still spend so much of my days and nights thinking of you. Mostly it's still that nightmare day but sometimes now I can think of you happy, smiling and alive. I worry a lot about your new brother or sister. I spend a lot of time feeling sad and depressed which is not ideal for growing a healthy baby. I wonder whether all the worry I had over Mum being sick when I was expecting you played a part in your brain injury.

Good friends are priceless. Friends without judgement, with compassion, with patience and love are invaluable. You need people who can just listen and hold you.

Worry became my state of being, totally swamped the naivety of youth, something could go wrong for every joy every time. After all, the worst had happened, hadn't it?

Sunday 22nd September 1996

> Your friend from Queensland died. Her Mum was nursing her in her arms when she stopped breathing. They knew she only had a short time left and so had stopped program. She made it to the magic "5" years, but only just.
>
> Her Mum said she could see you both holding hands and running off to play. I hope so. I wish I had her faith. It must be difficult for them as they

> have no other children. Cass and Angus certainly fill in your day, even if it's only with the mundane.
>
> I've been thinking more and more about what to do. Finally gathered enough courage and talked to Ronnie Z. Admitted I was a real mess. She was great and let me just talk for ages, supplying hankies as necessary. After I'd talked over and around and through the events of September 9 she said it was as though there was a field or gate around you preventing Ian and I from doing any or all of the things we usually did which may have interrupted the chain of events.

It took twelve months to unload onto someone and to have a different view of what may have been happening. It took that long for someone to show me some compassion and suggest forgiveness as a way of getting through. I was so unaware, so unconscious about life and myself.

Brendan Burchard says: "Only two things change your life: either something new comes into your life, or something new comes out of you".[6]

For me, it was impossible to break out of the drowning cycle without something new. And I also had to be ready to hear it. This is really important. Sometimes it's a message I've heard before, but it hasn't landed. Maybe it's because I have to be drowning, in so deep that it feels like a lifeline—I'm not sure.

And another small friend let go of her fragile hold on life.

Sunday 20th October 1996

Maybe it was meant to be Jacq. Your Dad says I didn't realise how fragile your life was. The thread so thin.

Single-minded, stubborn, working towards making you well despite everything and everyone. Holding on too tight? Maybe. I know you were happy though. You enjoyed life, being treated like a well kid as much as possible. Was it just your fate, destiny, time? Whatever. People / things have been trying to bash me over the head to make some sense sink in. I reached into the cupboard to get some words for show and tell at Uni. My hand settled unseen on "ceased, free and heart"!

Is the message that simple?

Have your worries ceased with the end of life as we know it? Are you free now? To do as you wish, how you wish. Do I look in my heart and know this is the time? Do I just keep your place in my heart secure? Do I take heart in your courageous life and go on?

It seems like a message of hope. First one for a long time. I'll take it as such for the time being.

Are these messages from Jacqui or wishful thinking? I like to believe a bit of both, interpreted from my higher self to help the ego get through. I have a tendency, as do most adults, to overcomplicate things that are really simple.

Breathing While Drowning

Learning to let go. This is my hardest lesson ever. I'm persistent, stubborn, right, and in control. All of that out the window. No matter what I did, grief was there to slap me in the face every time.

Monday 28th October 1996

Happy 6th Birthday my darling girl. It was a beautiful day, full of promise like you.

It was very difficult to be positive today. The dreaded pits of depression had been building for a few days. I also had a terrible gut yesterday which didn't help.

Your Dad even though he was sad too pulled me kicking and screaming out of the darkness. We went for a drive after Cass was at school. Mind you we had already argued and were barely speaking to each other. We went to Trentham Falls. Angus was amazed at the waterfall and everything he saw. We stopped at a nursery and bought some plants for your garden. It is looking beautiful Jacq. You would love all the bright colours and textures. The birds love it and the cats too. Cassie climbs the tree and Angus loves riding his little car or tractor down around the "J" loop.

When I'm in the garden I can think of you without so much anger, more constructively perhaps. Watching things get new life after the bareness of winter is a joy. Just a few sunny days have bought all the new buds and leaves into play. There are still a few bare patches though.

Judy bought some plants for your garden today. It was good that she dropped in. She played an important part in your life and you in hers. She also bought some chocolate for your Dad and I to gorge on.

Somebody else left some flowers, yellow freesias, while we were out but I don't know who as they left no card. No doubt we'll find out eventually.

Dad rang (Grandad that is) this morning, Ian said he was a bit sad. Mary rang too. Barbara also. And Sue Mihailovic, she said it was a good day to remember as it was the day you were born into the world and you gave so much to so many people. They were beautiful words to hear. Jenny Black came as it was Monday but I'm not sure if she knew it was your birthday.

Your Dad worked physically hard and of course was tired tonight. So I'm in bed writing to you. I seem to be grieving harder, longer and louder. He says to lean on him. Maybe I'm grieving _for_ him a bit. By talking and thinking and trying to express my sadness and despair it gives him a line, something to hang his emotions on. Who knows? We are different people to what we were years ago. Not all of it due to you but you've had a big influence.

Cass was sad tonight. We had a toast to you for your birthday at teatime after I kissed her goodnight she came back out in tears. She'd been thinking about you and just felt sad. We talked about you for a little while. She doesn't like to get emotional so it was probably a good release.

> Angus Peter was happy it was your birthday 'cos he loves birthdays. Unfortunately, he won't remember you 'cos he's too young. We showed him your photo album and he enjoyed that.
>
> For me it brought mixed emotions. So many happy times, so unaware how few.
>
> I know I must in time accept that you're gone and not coming back but not just yet. I'm searching for the answer, Jacq, a way to set it straight in my head and my heart. It will come. I love you always my precious sweet pea Jacqueline Bree, be happy and safe and loved.

My interpretation of acceptance always seemed to be forgetting, and that was so hard. Surrendering to the fact that I had no control over your life was a tremendous challenge. I have no control over anyone's life but my own—unless someone chooses to give it to me.

Human beings need to know where we're going; we like a clear direction and a sense of certainty that we're going to get somewhere—eventually. We're mostly content when we feel we have some control over our present and our future and are heading in the right direction, towards wherever it is we want to go or whoever it is we want to be.

When we feel out of control, life gets a little hairy and a little scary. We all react differently.

Sunday 24th November 1996

Jacq it's been hard to put pen to paper this past month. I feel distant, numb yet life goes on. I feel like I'm watching the rest of the family from behind Perspex everything is a little dulled. It's even difficult to get close to this little person inside me. It's making itself felt more and more movements are stronger. Just under 14 weeks to go. We've been trying to decide on names at the moment. Most difficult when we've used all our favourites.

I don't know whether it's harder to talk to you or I've just not found the words. I'm trying to keep in the game, not be a burden, be productive in the family and in life. I'm torn a bit between family and work. Work would threaten to take over if possible but I try and keep it down to a dull roar.

The illusory boon of success was beckoning, and like a moth flying towards the light, I kept circling. It was so easy, so seductive to stay busy. That way I wouldn't have to think about the big, dark hole inside or the fact that I'm living life behind a wall that dulls all my senses.

The horror of you dying is still present but the sharpness had faded a little. I was looking at some photos in Angus's album and remembered you being so concerned on his first night at home. Each time he cried you called out to us. I had to reassure you he was OK. And just getting his pants changed. I think it was then you realised he was here to stay and not just visiting. You loved it when you were allowed to have a cuddle -Typical Big Sister. A little jealous if your Dad had him though. You were a Dad's girl.

These are the memories I need to have and hold tight. You gave me so many joys. You were such a happy kid. We had so many dreams for you. For a while I thought you'd have them all. It's still hard to plan a future without you. I had things put away for Christmas that I'll have to give to AP over the next few years, not fair. You were part of the future Jacq. I wish you were here.

I was grieving for this unrealised future.

Sunday 29th December 1996

Jacq I'm just beginning to surface after some near drownings. I think your anniversary, birthday and the lead up to Christmas without you was just too much. Couple that with an old body ready to give out and mid-life crisis regarding work and directions of life and it all gets just too overwhelming. I was very down and depressed and couldn't seem to lift out of it. It stinks that you l approach is blocked. I still feel so inadequate and wish I wasn't. weren't here. How would you have been? Crawling? Walking? Who knows? Happy at least and growing.

It's time to sort through your room. We were going to begin yesterday but your Dad and Cass ended up going to Balnarring to help set up the annexe and gazebo. Of course they were later than expected.

I think the hardest times are when I'm on my own, and yet sometimes when I feel the strongest. I have to put a numbing padding around your memory to stop it being so sharp.

I'm not sure how I finally came out of it. Your Dad tried talking but didn't have any answers. I s'pose I finally decided no one could help except myself. I had to have the will to do it but do I have the power to change anything? I don't know. I've decided to defer the Uni course for the first semester. Time is so precious and as this will be our last baby I feel I should spend some time just living with it and being myself, finding myself. The nursing degree seems such a waste of time. It makes me angry to think I'm wasting time on something I don't really want to do. I'm sick of doing stuff to please other people.

But as yet I don't know what to do myself. I guess time will tell.

Jacq I love you, always will, hope you are safe and happy.

Breathing While Drowning

There's a Tony Gaskins quote I love to use when I'm coaching: "If you don't build your dream someone will hire you to help build theirs". [7]

This is so important. Without dreams of my own, I spent many years helping others build theirs. I started to believe I didn't deserve to have my own, and that's not true. We all deserve to dream and achieve and live and love.

Tuesday 16th June 1997

So long Jacqui Bree and so much to tell. You have a new baby brother Frazer Douglas. He was born on February 27th 1997. Weighed in at around 4kg! He is so different from you all, a new person all of his own. A few people have said he looks a bit like you. He has your dark hair and at the moment its growing straight up like yours did so I don't think he'll have curls. He's a really happy little boy, placid and cuddly. I was worried through the pregnancy that my sadness may have affected his growth but I don't think so. Angus loves him dearly and likes to cuddle him and show him toys. Cass is pretty impatient with him but loves him in her own way, in short bursts. He had the most beautiful smile which at times is a bit lopsided and reminds me of you.

I miss you so much Jacq. That doesn't seem to go away. I'm having a lot of trouble getting through the days and nights at the moment. I feel so desperate for help but I don't know where to go. Every avenue

There is so little joy and happiness in my life at present. Work is hopeless and depressing, everybody wants to tell me their problems but no one wants to listen to mine.

I hate waking up each morning, the day stretched ahead with monotonous regularity. I have no energy, no motivation.

I made the decision to try and go on. Went to see a naturopath in Sunbury. That seemed to help for a while but there is a cycle of down and despair every few days, prompted by various things.

My body is in a pretty pathetic state too. Pushing a 4kg baby through didn't help. Bleeding for 12 weeks also stresses the system.

I still have so much anger, so much hurt. Jacq I feel guilty to be taking another breath when you are not here. Your Dad and I are so far apart we are almost strangers. We have only you kids in common. Many times of late I have felt I had to leave, somehow I stayed. I cannot bear the thought of making love. Not only is it painful but I have no desire at all. There are physical and emotional reasons. I have no right to pleasure if you're not here. Your Dad has stopped touching me with any affection at all. He wasn't listening and we did no talking. I don't know if there is any relationship to save. At present the only things that keeps me here are the children. Is any mother better than none?

> *Your Dad and I are going to give it another try. I tried to tell him some of my feelings and how desperate I felt. It may have hurt him with some of the things I said but he didn't really give anything back. He wants to try again and says he still loves me.*
>
> *I feel like a shell, hollow and empty. I have no right to feel anything. I can't say I love him, I don't know if I have that inside. Who can help me? No one, just myself.*
>
> *Your garden is growing but I need to spend more time there. It needs attention at the moment. So many things to do, commitments, so little time. I stretch myself so thin that I'm becoming transparent. Will there ever be a time when I can forgive myself?*

The arrival of our beautiful and amazing Frazer Douglas was such an unforeseen joy. He brought us together in a way nothing else could. He made his own joyful place in the family and gave us all someone to love together. He could make us smile so easily, and he was such an easy baby to please. He was always busy watching his older brother and sister to see what mischief they were getting up to.

Body, mind, and soul—I was worn out. I was sleep deprived, hormonal, and probably anaemic. I was stumbling along, trying to keep it all together, trying to stay in control. After several days of paralysing grief, Ian asked my sister, Mary, to help. She found a psychologist for me.

Friday 4th July 1997

I visited a psychologist today. The session was painful but had some positive aspects too. She seems good, approachable and confident but professional. I think I can sense this will be OK. At present it's the way to go. I can't cure myself, I need help. This is a big admission for me to make outside these pages. Mary got me her name through Sue Mihailovic. I don't love you any less or miss you any less Jacq but I have to give the others better than they're getting now. I have to feel that it's no one's fault and we have a lifetime to fill.

I hope your strength will be with me. I'll need it I know. There will be more bad days ahead but I hope there may be some good ones also. It's a big toss up at work whether I'll go or stay. The next few months will be difficult. I think I'll go and see Sue and ask her to do your chart. It may help. I also want to see Frazer's.

Frazer is 4 months old and growing well. He is so clever with his hands and eyes. It seems so easy for him Jacq. We are trying to teach Angus to read at the moment with no obvious success. He doesn't seem too keen and I guess our heart is not exactly in it. We don't seem to have the commitment. Must try harder.

> As soon as we get a sunny day I must work in your garden. It needs mulching and weeding for a good show in Spring.
> I hope Jacqui Bree, I hope!

No more hiding in the journal, things unravel and the world can see what's behind. Everything is dark. And yet, in the darkest moments, I search for the light, for control, for meaning, for answers.

The sessions with the psychologist were full of tears and recriminations and compassion. She gave me permission to let go, to realise that no one could hold it all together over the death of a child, no one could be unfeeling and let life go on. It was okay to feel sad, to not be strong, to grieve.

Sunday 17th August 1997

> Managed to get a good couple of days in the garden Jacq. All the plants are trimmed and everything is weeded and mulched. Since then lots of bulbs have started to come up. So I hope there will be lots of colour for your birthday. I'm trying not to focus so much on your dying but on your living. The sessions with Suzanne are helping.
> I missed ringing Dad on the 15th August, Mum's anniversary. I thought of her a few days ago but forgot on the day.

I still miss her terribly too. She was such a good friend and mother. It seems as if I wear out the people I love the most. Maybe it's not me though. I have to accept that it's not always my fault and that people make their own decisions, I hope you decided it was time to go. Thank you for staying as long as you did, I know it was very difficult almost always. I love you fiercely, perhaps too much. I would never have let you go of my own accord. You had to make the decision for us. You had to show us you were tired, that it was too much. I'm sorry I hung on to your soul so tightly. It was a thing of perfection, strong, innocent, resourceful, beautiful. I hope a part of it will stay with me always. I want to meet it again.

Your little brothers are growing quickly and developing well. I've applied for a new job which would allow your Dad to stay home more so they could get more attention. At the moment we seem to be constantly behind the 8 ball. Every moment requires us to do 3 things in 2 different places.

Frazer is teething and struggling a bit like you did. So he's not sleeping very well which means we're not either. The effects of chronic sleep deprivation are catching up on me. I can't make decisions properly at the moment. Your Dad is just as bad.

Breathing While Drowning

You would have loved Frazer. He's a dear little boy (as Mum would've called him). Very much a watcher and do-er. He watches his older brother and sister so carefully and they often make him laugh. His eyebrows knit in concentration sometimes and he looks really quirky. The thing I love best is his smile. It lights up his whole face, a dawning.

Angus is maturing daily, he loves to be called a little "man"! He knows he has a big sister called Jacqui and he recognises you in photos.

At the moment he is mad keen on Thomas the Tank Engine and Friends and has developed quite a collection. We'll have to be careful 'cos he's getting the idea that you can just go to the shops and get whatever you like. Must get that from his mother. He's had two haircuts now and I've kept his curls. Still lots of people are surprised he's a boy — too beautiful.

Cass is maturing slowly but surely. She's into pop music now. Savage Garden. They seem reasonably harmless at present. She still gets sad about you now and then. She talks freely about you though. She hated that it was harder to remember the way you were. Her memories were blurring around the edges. What can I say, I hate it too. Be safe and happy beautiful girl, I love you very much.

I was busy with life and watching the children grow. As I was living and loving them, my days were filled with small joys.

Sunday 30th November 1997

Jacq. I missed writing to you on September 9 and on your birthday. Too full of memories, too many thoughts.

We spent 9/9 in your garden, doing some planting and cleaning up. A few people called in and gave us support.

Your garden looked great. It was even better for your birthday. Lots of tulips, all colours, plus other flowers in fine form. We burnt a candle for you on your birthday. The kids enjoyed that 'cos it was fish and chip night.

We watched you on video on your anniversary 'cos we transferred all the camera tapes onto large cassettes. That brought many, many memories.

Quite a few tears were shed but a few laughs and smiles as well.

The best thing was Angus Pete. He sat through the entire show and kept asking to see more anytime we stopped. I think it really helped him to see you in action, from baby to later — interacting with him. It cemented the image of you in his head, you were a real person.

As you can read I am better these days, mostly anyway. I had about 6 sessions with the psychologist

Breathing While Drowning

I think. I'm sure the time was just appropriate. She told me and discussed that it was OK to grieve for as long as I wanted, stuff everybody else, I shouldn't expect so much of myself. I had to stop trying to live up to everyone else's expectations. I did a fair bit of self-analysis. I don't think I miss you any less I just think the others have more immediate needs and I have to help them. Your Dad is a big help as usual. Keeps me going, on the straight and narrow. I can still twist his arm though. We had a week's holiday in Merimbula. Originally it was planned for your birthday but that got a bit tight with time. We had a lovely week, Grandad came too. Played some golf, walked, rode and swam. The weather was good to us too. The kids especially enjoyed the joeys from 4 kangaroos, lots of birds to feed and the mini golf.

I'll write more later, too tired and silly now to make sense.

Now there's a good instruction: stop trying to live up to everyone else's expectations. With no mother, I lost my role model. I didn't know anyone close who had a child with a disability, and then I lost her. I didn't know anyone close who had a child who had died. We are so constrained by other people's perceptions, by what the world expects of us. And if we so much as slip outside the lines, there are sideways glances, turned up noses, disparaging words.

So what! My life belongs to me. What I think, feel, do, and believe matters—and that's what counts. Experience and years have taught me to value that notion. These days, people have the global village watching over their shoulder, not just their family and local community. I say you should "do what you want to do and be who you want to be, yeah" (some of my favourite lyrics by the Master's Apprentices).

Saturday 28th February 1998

Well Jacqui Bree, Frazer is 1 today.

Yesterday actually, night duty again. He has been a great help to me and to the rest of the family, bringing us back to the present and reality. He is a very decisive young man, knows his own mind. Yet he is so different from the other two. I often find myself staring at his face and wondering "who are you?" I see you in him a lot, that "I'm sizing you up" look, as though we are all a bit pathetic sometimes. He does love to play with your Dad. Angus and he will wrestle him to the ground and then climb all over him.

It has been amazing to see his progress from lying to rolling to crawling to walking. I know Angus and Cass did it too but I think because we see him in isolation he looks amazing. We sometimes verbalise our feelings about your journey. How come it was so hard for you, what interrupted the cycle?

I would give anything to have you back Jacq. But now I realise it must be only on your terms. I'm sorry if I tried too hard and hung on too tight. You had to do it your way. I know I had to control. I understand you gave me a second chance when I couldn't let go the first time, I hope it didn't cause *you too much pain and heartache. Those 11 months after the first time you seemed magically progressive as if the near miss had frightened you and made you appreciate life more. I had great hopes for you then. I was so proud of how well you'd come through.*

I am still proud of the way you lived every moment. I still miss you dreadfully. Everyday there is a reminder. Have you left us for a particular reason my darling? Have we some work still to go? We're thinking of a move interstate, maybe it will help us find the way. We're not prepared to let the garden go yet, nor the house full of memories of you. We'll see. I love you my precious sweet pea.

Have we some work still to go? For sure! And changing geography is not necessary.

I have messages to give all over the place. I have a life to lead that expresses the very best of who I can be. I have people to inspire, people to instruct, people to involve. I have joyous moments to feel, I have sad moments to grieve, and I have time to love. More than anything, *I have time to love.*

Sunday 22nd March 1998

The interstate saga continues Jacq. I have 2 job offers in Sydney. I just have to decide what my priorities are. At the moment it's a combination of wanting more family time, I hardly ever get to see and interact with Cass and our time together is so limited. If I am home, I'm so tired and moody that we usually end up shouting at each other. I can't seem to stop my tongue from lashing out. I think about her heaps, I worry we won't be friends and she won't come to me with problems.

On the other hand, is the CV and mental health state of working in a job that I hate or will take too much of me. I have one more interview to go on Tuesday. This won't involve a move to Sydney but it will mean more money but still not good hours. I'm not sure what direction to go for now and for the future. Maybe I'm intellectualising too much. It's very un-Sagittarian of me not to decide straight away. Maybe a sign of maturity? Who knows? At the moment it's giving your Dad an ulcer. He's having stomach cramps just thinking of all the organising, especially his garage. Hopefully Tuesday will help and not complicate the issue further.

Is this a sign of maturity or finally bending to the will of someone else's dreams? And Strack always worried, sometimes enough for all of us. I was often too blithely unaware of his needs, so caught up in my own pain.

Sunday 3rd May 1998

Sydney is off. The new job is Nursing Coordinator at a hospital in the city. First day tomorrow. Exciting stuff Jacq. Directions still unclear but plan of attack forming. I'm doing a management unit at RMIT with the ANF. It will be a good start regardless of which direction/area I go for.

Your Dad is still a little lost for direction at the moment. I'm trying to nag him a little to step outside his usual slot and extend himself. This is a difficult thing for him to try. He tends to hide behind his "family" a bit.

Angus started at 3 year old kinder on Friday. He was a bit shy to start but by the end had warmed up and was enjoying himself. A very important day. Since Molly shifted he hasn't had quite the contact with his peers so it's a good chance.

Frazer continues to grow and amaze me. He is such an independent body, so quick to pick up on ideas and examples set by older siblings! Still breast feeding despite 7 teeth. Your Dad laughs at me. I'm not quite ready to pack it in yet.

Cass and I are slowly forming a stronger relationship. She misses you a lot, your life and death have coloured her perceptions differently from the other kids. She wrote you a song the other day and said she hated hearing bad news of people dying as it made her think of you. She has a great deal of insight for one so young.

We've had a week of breakdowns. New hot water service, new knee for the dog. Hope the luck is about to change.

Stay in my dreams always.

There's almost a different energy in the words. They're gathering a pace, beginning to race, heading up towards the light.

Tuesday 27th October 1998

Soon time to wish you Happy Birthday my darling. My throat is dry, my tears begin. You would have been 8 years old my sweet pea. A skinny, dark-haired girl with beautiful green eyes. Looking slightly like me perhaps a crooked smile, a cheeky glance. What would you have been Jacq? I'm sure you would be crawling, probably walking by now. Giving cheek and teasing your big sister and little brothers. Angus loves you dearly and loves to watch video of your when you were still at home.

I'm not sure about Frazer. Sometimes I think he has a large part of you within him. He watches and learns so quickly, yet sets himself a little apart. He loves you on his terms, when he wants to.

Jacq, I didn't write on your anniversary, indeed I haven't written for a long time. I begin to realise I love you so hard and so overwhelmingly that the thought of losing another child makes me stand

Breathing While Drowning

back from the others a little so that I won't hurt again. I don't think that's right. I must let you go a little more my sweet girl though it causes me even more pain. Pain only for me, not for you. I don't love you less, I guess I'll just try and love them closer, I must. I'm losing my chance with Cassie. I need to be closer to her, or allow her to get closer to me.

We're holidaying in Hall's Gap for your birthday. We're trying to build some good memories, some family memories to share.

On your anniversary we worked really hard in your garden, it looks fabulous at the moment. It was a good thing to do, bring new growth from winters dying. There is still more to be done but we have made a good start at least. 3 years" growth. The wounds heal slowly.

Ronnie Zeinstra drove 4 hours down the highway from Cookardinia to be there for me/us on the day. That's the sort of love you inspire Jacqui Bree.

How can I be inspirational like you? Is that my role? Where do you lead me Jacq? What direction?

Try again tomorrow. Try harder? Hope you are safe and happy little girl. Love you Jacqui Bree, my precious daughter. Help me be a good mother Jacq. Give me strength to go on.

With almost three years gone, time begins to cover the wounds and heal. I have more searching for purpose, for meaning from events—though still for someone else's purpose. It's time to look inside and find my own answers—the things I want and the things I am. I'm almost thirty-eight years old, and I don't have a dream. I can't find the conscious meaning for my life. I'm still adrift on the ocean, and the shoreline is hazy.

Like blazes of light, good friends appear in your life when you need them. When you shut out all the bad, sometimes you find you've shut out all the good as well. But good friends will step over or through your walls. They'll ignore the thorns and see the blooms. I love these people for their souls. Ronnie is one of these treasures.

Sunday 10th September 2000

Two years and a lifetime. Yesterday 5 years since you died. Longer apart than together. I know it had been difficult this past week or so. I sensed the boys restless and wondered if you were there, thinking and remembering.

I played your song and was sad but the tears were brief. So much to do and the others which thing to get to first.

We planted a rose bush in your garden. Jo Bell gave it to us for you. Grandad made a special dash up for a cuppa. Doesn't say much, just tries to be there.

Cass and I had a little chat, she is so grown up now, so mature. We have a better understanding than we used to. We talk a little more, though still a bit distant. I think I'm at the embarrassing stage, very uncool.

Breathing While Drowning

She is excited about her school for next year. I know she will do well but I have to hope it's not too traumatic. She tends to fly off the handle very quickly sometimes. She is so clever at so many things. She likes to try everything. A good organiser and ideas person. Not really any one special friend, she seems to have a few and flows between them when it suits. I don't know what she'll be, something in movies is what she wants, maybe a producer or a writer.

Angus Peter is growing too. It is still so important to him that you know him and interacted. He worries that he doesn't remember you. His heart does. But he is such a worrier, the weight of the world is on his shoulders sometimes, life is so uncertain for him, he seeks stability always. Not an adventurer yet he draws people to him. Everyone loves him and wants him near. I don't know whether he is not confident or rather prefers his comfort zone and peace of mind. Glasses have helped a great deal with school work and he is moving in leaps and bounds.

Frazer is our Wildman, this is the adventurer, no fear, mostly anyway except for monsters and scary bits on the video. Life is a laugh and constant amazement for this child. Very chatty and worldly in his conversation but loves a car or a train. He will have to be doing something with engineering at the very least.

> And your Dad, I think OK. Physically we're both tired but still going strong. We chat about you from time to time remembering this or that. We still have the "what if" game.
>
> I'm better since I let you go. I'm sorry I hung on for so long. It is so hard to lose a child. So hard to let you go. You will always be in my heart Jacqui Bree. I will never stop loving and missing you. I hope we can meet again one day when it is my time. At the moment I have a feeling like I have so much to do and my time is running out. The future seems unknown but exciting, unexpected.
>
> I hope tomorrow goes as well as I would like. I don't think your Dad will ever shift. But that's OK we'll build more time into here and things will be fine. That's who he is at the moment.
>
> Stay safe my beautiful girl.

Two years and a lifetime. So much healing has gone on in these two years. The balm of family and love has covered the wounds and buried them. I beat myself up for so long that I didn't know any other way; this was my focus, even when it wasn't. It was the story that ran in the back of my mind for so long it became who I was being. It was behind every decision, every choice.

Now there's hope and wonder. There's still apology, but guilt and shame are lessening.

Breathing While Drowning

Sunday 29th October 2000

Almost missed your birthday my sweet sea. You would have been 10 years old yesterday. You have been gone longer than you were with us. That makes me sad for what you and I could have been. We worked a little in your garden, thinking a little of you, remembering other people who were kind and thoughtful when you were alive and when you died.

I am in a transition phase again. Moving and changing evolving towards a better balance. I've nearly finished studying for a little while and I am slowly rediscovering your siblings. I find now I have something left to offer them when I come home. I am enjoying reading stories and spending time.

It is a small thing but in fact a turning point. I am ready to start over. I have found some direction, my children love me and I them. Life is good, many things tell me that.

I think I have stories inside. I'm not sure yet what kind but I know they are there, stories to share.

Emotional resilience is what I have. Strength inside is what others are drawn to, strength I get from you, loving you and knowing you. Both of us growing, you helping me see the choices clearly. I have a lot to offer but a lot to learn.

Take care my beautiful girl, be strong and be loved always.

That was my last entry in Jacqui's journal, almost fifteen years ago.

In so many ways, I can see that time was just the beginning. I was about to move from being unaware, unconscious, and unmindful to hitching myself back to the main life preserver in my life: why? My chief word has always been *why* in all shapes and forms: good, bad, and everything in between.

And then, of course, there is doubt and shame and guilt. That voice was strong in my life for so long, and even now she can grab the tiller if I'm not careful.

Each person's journey is unique. Who am I to think anything I write would be of any help to anyone else? Shut up Blackheart, go back and sit in the corner and sulk. I don't have time to listen to you right now. Anyway, I know what you're going to say: I'm not enough. I wasn't enough to keep Jacqui Bree alive, so how could I imagine anything I do would be enough.

The story of not enough starts in childhood. At first glance, I had a loving and safe childhood. But layer that with being one of eight children, living off one wage, having working-class parents, residing in the northern suburbs, being Catholic, and being female. Now you've got plenty of *not enough* to imprint on a child. They say we take in all our imprints between the ages of zero and eight. This kind of information makes you say, "Yep, it's all the parents' fault." But I'm more of the mind now (and not just since I've become a parent myself) to say that our parents do the best they can with what they have and know at the time. And this life's journey is my own.

"These words are my own" (echoes of Natasha Bedingfield's lyrics ring in my head): "It's who I am, it's what I do. And I was gonna lay it down for you".[8]

There comes a time when you have to say *yes*, but now it's time to make choices of my own, to accept responsibility for my life, for my future. And then there's the cycle of thirteen years that gets talked about. Our life goes around in these 13 year cycles, repeating the lessons we came to learn in this incarnation. They keep coming back until we learn the lesson, then we can move on to do what we came here to do.

If I accept that, I'm the sum total of my choices and experiences until this very moment, and then I haven't wasted a drop. It's all in the cup, ready to drink, ready to inhale. It's time to take the next step in *The Heroine's Journey*.

"Above all be the heroine in your life, not the victim," Nora Ephron said.

I separated from the feminine, had my road of trials, met ogres and dragons, and experienced a deep descent to the goddess. After that, I was caught identifying with the masculine and the illusory boon of success.

In the early years, I was sometimes drowning in grief, sometimes drowning in work. Sometimes I was using work to drown the grief. I was swirling in grey and beige, not even black—just bland and flat and numb. Yet even this is not truly how life was. There were so many beautiful, joyous moments too. What the hell drives me on, how did I get out of the fugue of grief and depression? How does anyone do so? When was the turning point? When did the balance tip to the brighter side? What makes me able to keep going, when others find their way back earlier or never do? At the end of the day, I think it's love. What's love got to do with it? Love has everything to do with it. The love of my children and Strack, the love of good friends and good times.

I began to ask questions, to get increasingly restless with the status quo. Why is it easier to put my stuff last? To deliberately procrastinate so that I never address what's really bothering me? What is it I really want to do?

Now, I'm not alone here; millions of women are at the bottom of the totem pole. Is this the way it works? Are we the fabric that holds this existence together? Without us doing things for everyone else, what would happen? How would the world be?

Veronica Strachan

The Illusory Boon of Success

Endless possibilities or endless trivialities?
Management creativity or delusional mumbo jumbo?
Find the fire, nurse the flame
Ignore outliers, fly again
Inspire and drive, find passion
And then
When it all goes to mush
Start over — again ...
Tired, so tired
Wrung out, grey and beige
No passion, no fire
Just get me off this stage!
Give me another script
Let me write my own
Create an alternate reality
Keep me close to home
How does fire survive without
green earth and water
Air sparks and spits
and rumbles with laughter
How do you survive, keep going
and yet, how empty, what meaning
your dreams are not met, and yet ...

So, if I keep working, I'll be too busy to feel the emptiness and too tired to feel anything or connect with anyone.

There's this thing about not wanting to change because of what the current way gives us. Even if the current way is painful and stagnant, there's still something we get from it. The kind of thing that holds people back from change. What is it about the current way I do things that works for me? Hiding keeps the pain at bay, not sharing or looking or being aware makes it easier to kid myself that I'm okay, that my life is fine. Oh! That word is so not me anymore. *Fine,* for me, is grey and beige. These were so often the colours I chose; I sought to blend in. I chose cream curtains for the house that blended into the mud-brick walls. I wore mostly black and grey.

Now, at fifty-five, I'm fabulous and creative and joyful. I'm present and empowering. I'm focused on compassion for me and everyone I meet. I wear what I like, which is most often red and orange and green. I'm stylish, creative, and powerfully feminine. In other words, I'm finding my inner fabulousness.

Brené Brown says, "Perfect and bullet proof are seductive".[9] For me, they absolutely were. Presenting work that is as close to perfect as you can get it gives you the kudos of being a doer, someone who delivers, someone who can be counted on, someone who should be watched and given more opportunities. If I spent all the time in my head, and displayed a slick exterior, I didn't have to feel and could keep my head above water. Go with the flow, the flow of instructions from the patriarchy, from someone else's dreams and ambitions. It also meant that I didn't have as much time to spend at home in the emptiness. Seeing the sadness in Ian's eyes, seeing reminders of Jacqui everywhere I looked, seeing reminders of my failure as a mother. But it's okay because I'm successful, I'm making money, moving up the ladder, getting more responsibility. It's not all bad.

We are always exactly where we need to be, learning what we need to learn. I learned many things about management and leadership and relationships and the nature of people during this time.

My career blossomed as I threw myself into distraction. I taught childbirth education classes and started up an antenatal clinic in a small private hospital. This was great. I loved the organising and autonomy, but I soon got itchy feet and began looking for the next challenge. I looked interstate, and although every job I applied for I could have had, I ended up taking one in Melbourne. My roles included education and quality. And shortly after I began work there, I became the Director of Clinical Services.

A change of fortune made my position redundant and, for the first time, I had some career counselling. Some of the assessments showed that maintenance and operational routine were not my preferences. I was creative, innovative, and loved change. They suggested project management would be the way to go. This statement gave me permission to breathe, to look for another route, to step out of the traditional path. During the career counselling course, I applied for an interim role as an evening coordinator at one of the larger private hospitals. During the interview, the Director of Nursing stopped asking me interview questions and instead asked if the job was really what I was looking for or whether it was just a stepping stone. I responded truthfully: it was a transition until I decided what to do, and I intended to go back and study, to learn something new. Whatever she saw or heard or felt about me, I will be forever grateful. She offered me a job as a project manager, and I implemented a new IT system between their two main campuses.

I loved project management. It felt like coming home. Getting organised, planning, change, innovation, solution finding—I loved it all. From then on, each role I took had an element of change and project management about it. Even when I took operational roles, they always had an element of change with large projects attached to them. I realised I was a change catalyst; I was the spark that some places needed to fire them up and thaw them out to get things moving in a different direction. I was a good people manager, and I could inspire confidence in teams, share a vision with them, and take them on the journey. Sometimes, the teams were eighty or three hundred people; other times, the teams consisted of one or two people.

Over the next decade, I led statewide and national projects in health, often with an IT bent. I managed budgets in the millions of dollars on numerous occasions. Mind you, I am still not the greatest with cash flow for my own pocket because the numbers are too small. I learned to manage and lead people, I learned about technology and its connection to strategy.

I learned where my line in integrity was and when I crossed it. And I did. I learned that it's very often everyone for themselves, and that sleeping your way to the top doesn't only happen in movies, but that was a line I would not cross. And if you don't play by those rules, you get booted off the island. You're out in the cold. I found I couldn't be one of the mean girls, even though I wanted to belong.

Even though many fabulous things happened in that period, it is so much easier to think about the bad things, the regrettable things. It takes me a while to think about the brilliant work we did as a team, the awakening to strategic thinking I had, the leaps of intuition and the natural leadership I displayed, the lives I influenced for good. I became stronger, I realised my talent for seeing where everything goes. The inspiration I have to see patterns and connections grew profoundly. I can see simplicity in complexity; I can see order in chaos. I'm a great listener and problem solver, and I have a gift for business, organising, and leading.

Dennis Saleebey says (according to Brené Brown), "Viewing performance from the strengths perspective offers us the opportunity to examine our struggles in light of our capacities, talents, competencies, possibilities, visions, values, and hopes. This perspective doesn't dismiss the serious nature of our struggles; however, it does require us to consider our positive qualities as potential resources".[10]

This fits with the way I coach—always looking for the positive in people, the potential. I believe people have what they need, and that, as coaches, we just need to help them realise this and unlock it for use.

According to Brown, Dr Saleebey argues that "it is as wrong to deny the possible as it is to deny the problem".[11]

Strengths perspective is not just a "positive spin." Brown says, "By first enabling us to inventory our strengths, it suggests ways we can use those strengths to address the related challenges".[12]

There are several strengths profiles you can do online for free or for a small fee. Some of the strengths that came up in both of these profiles in the last two years were as follows:

Creativity—thinking of new ways to do things is a crucial part of who I am. I'm never content with doing something the conventional way if a better way is possible.

Incubator—I love to think, to ponder, to reflect. The ability to think things through is a constant throughout my day, every day. I like to take moments out of my day, my week, my month to give myself dedicated thinking time. These times are precious to me, allowing me the time and space to be absorbed in my own thoughts. But not too many; otherwise, I get too introspective and drive myself nuts by overthinking things.

Curiosity—I'm curious about everything. I love to ask questions, and I love exploration and discovery. I'm very open to new ideas and constantly seek out new information. I get ridiculously excited when I discover new things to learn.

Growth and love of learning—I actively seek out activities that will help me develop; I love learning new skills, new bits of knowledge, or different ways of doing things. I love to invite feedback on my performance, taking on board both positive and negative comments that will help me improve and develop as a person.

Appreciation of beauty and excellence, esteem builder—I notice and appreciate beauty, excellence, and skilled performance in all domains of life … from nature to art to maths to science to everyday experiences. My words and actions help people build their self-confidence and self-esteem. I see the potential and possibility in people clearly, and I help them recognise it for themselves. I love to help people use this knowledge to build their own confidence and self-esteem, and in turn to work towards achieving what they are capable of.

And, of course, perseverance, change, optimism, courage, kindness, gratitude, fairness, and love—these things are indispensable in my life.

Is it any wonder that I love coaching people and teams, teasing out their strengths, helping them become aware of their potential, and fanning their spark of magnificence into a conflagration where they let their own light shine?

We so often forget our strengths and focus on our weaknesses, the things we don't do very well.

Mel Neil suggests positive psychology is the best way to work with people and performance management, and I agree.[13] Positive is good for you—no pun intended. This seems like a much better way to go than focusing on where I was weak.

Neil's main point was that people with higher levels of well-being are healthier, more resilient, more successful, more caring and altruistic. Plus, they live longer and are more socially engaged.[14] One of the best ways to improve your well-being is to spend time doing the things that light you up, things that you value, things that are your strengths.

These are the things I work with now, but at the time, I was at the mercy of my own negative thinking. The idea of myself as a victim, a martyr, and a self-righteous woman meant I was afraid. "It's a way to puff up and protect myself when I'm afraid of being wrong, making someone angry, or getting blamed"[15]

This is different from going with the flow, which is talked about in spiritual circles. This is more like being caught up in a raging torrent of testosterone, trying to stay afloat in our Western, corporate, patriarchal, masculine.

These thoughts and concepts play into the story that I'm only as good as what I accomplish. In our world, there is always something else to accomplish, especially when I'm working on someone else's dreams. There becomes this constant thread of scarcity—there's never enough time, resources, or money; I'm never enough. I give to the point of exhaustion, but I'm still never enough. I'm powerless, and I have no control over what happens to me.

Sometimes, this seems like a good thing. After a particularly unpleasant and uncomfortable episode, I take a phone call from my CEO one night while I'm at uni. Can I act as the operational director starting tomorrow because the last person left suddenly? My heart skips a beat. Even now, I can remember knowing this was a crucial choice, a moment to decide whether I wanted to lead or follow. It was also mired in the uncomfortable knowledge that an action of mine had contributed to a cascade of events culminating in the other person leaving.

I'm not entirely sure why I was elected to approach the CEO, any of the other managers could have had the conversation. I gathered my thoughts and words, endeavoured to keep it professional, and spoke in terms of leadership style and the interests of clients and the organisation.

I decided to step up because I wanted to see things get better. I wanted to be supported and to learn, to have a chance to be better, to be successful, to be respected by my colleagues, to be in control. The road to leadership is a slippery slope, though; you have to be careful not to lose your integrity.

So, back to "I'm not enough" for a bit. Brené Brown says that we live in a world driven by scarcity and that the opposite of scarcity is *enough*, not *abundance*.

Education and knowledge had given me the language to remain professional, not personal, and to say that I (and the rest of the leadership team) were struggling with the leadership style. This language enabled me to have the difficult conversation. It was the start of me being conscious that a greater awareness was needed, that emotional intelligence had to be a part of who we were. I had IQ in buckets, but my EQ bucket was pretty empty.

Breathing While Drowning

During these years, I often felt like I didn't deserve to shine. I responded by moving on before people got to really know me, before they could see through me, before they could realise I'm flaky; a fraud. My career is dotted with brilliant projects and jobs, and that's why I'm such a good change agent. That's all I do. The time for deeply understanding myself, my needs, my values, and my purpose was still in the future. The formal education of the post-graduate diploma of business management was a great start. I used some of the tools, such as MBTI, to start thinking about myself. Having great mentoring from Anne Smyth helped me unpack a whole lot of stuff and learn to think deeply. That woman was persistent; she could see through my bluff in a flash!

I needed to be seen, held, loved, and valued. I needed to be beautiful and loved for myself, by myself.

I continued to practice my skills of breathing while drowning, following someone else's agenda, slipping into mediocre. Sometimes I think it's laziness, sometimes I'm hiding—though I'm never quite sure from what. Some days there are so many things that I'd need a truck to move them all. What's always missing is self-compassion.

What's your picture of success? For most of my life, it's been more or less the standard, even though I started off going in a different direction, determined to be different. I more or less ended up on the standard route anyway. Live a good life, get educated, get a job, get married, have kids. Okay, I've done all that ... what's next? Get a really good job, be a Director of Nursing, be a CEO, change careers, start my own company. Each step, each achievement brought me experience, friends, skills, financial abundance, and more hurt. Okay, I've done all that ... what's next?

For me this is Murdock's illusory boon of success: "No matter how successful she is, she still has to deal with the fact that the outer world is hostile to her choices". [16]

For me, it's also the inner world hostilities that keep me drowning. My life played out on a hamster wheel, going round and round and getting nowhere, even though I passed all those flags that said I was.

Meditation held an impossible dream for me: that I'd find peace, a peace I desperately craved. I'd tried a few different meditation practices, but I usually gave them away after a couple of tries or weeks, whichever came first. My mind was chronically busy, crammed with thoughts and ideas and voices. I seemed to lack the intellectual discipline required to be still and empty as many meditation practices instructed. Besides, the guru-like practices suggested were quasi-religious in my eyes, and I was leery of anything that smacked of dogma or strict rules.

Eventually, I found my way into successfully meditating (i.e., doing it for more than three weeks) through philosophy. I wanted so much to be wise, and when I found out that philosophy was the study of wisdom, that was on my list of things to do.

Philosophy is a study that attempts to discover the fundamental principles of the sciences, the arts, and the world that the sciences and arts deal with; the word *philosophy* is from Greek, and it means *love of wisdom*.

As a child, we had two books that I read over and over: *The Philosopher's Scrapbook* and *Philosopher's Notebook* by Monty Blandford.[17] They were bits and pieces of prose and stories that seemed remarkable in their insight and wisdom to a young, impressionable girl. As he says, "It will lead them along the road to better understanding of their fellow men. Its sincerity of purpose, and its blending of charm and pathos will compel you to think and reflect over the meanings so admirably expressed by writers recognised as great by literary people throughout the world". [18]

Blandford goes on to suggest that, in sharing your insights and wisdom with your community of family and friends, "you will hold their enthusiasm and will find yourself becoming a philosopher-living according to the rules of practical wisdom". [19]

While I was still young, I read Kahlil Gibran's *The Prophet*[20], and it seemed full of a wisdom that I didn't quite get. *The Prophet* was so different from the sort of writing I had been exposed to through my education. Much of it rolled right over me without me understanding it or seeing the connections to my own life.

In May of 2009, I enrolled in a course that claimed it would change the way I thought. As ever, the thing that attracted me to this particular course was its practicality. The Melbourne School of Philosophy taught "practical philosophy," and they defined philosophy as "the love and application of wisdom." Their practical philosophy course explores the meaning of wisdom, truth, consciousness, and the real nature of human beings. The "principles draw from the great philosophical teachings of the East and West, past and present to help us enjoy a deeper understanding of ourselves, our world and our fellow mankind". [21]

Practical philosophy was said to offer students an effective and novel approach to the great questions of life: Who am I? How can I be truly happy? How can I be at peace? What is the purpose of my life? How may I realise my full potential? They also promised to help me increase awareness; become more grounded and confident; overcome the limiting effects of negative emotions; be more productive; and free me from stress.

These were exactly the questions I wanted answered and the way I wanted to live: aware, grounded, confident, productive, and free of stress. Who wouldn't? So off I trotted.

The course used a "process by which philosophical principles are tested in the light of experience, so that the value of these principles can be truly known and incorporated into one's experience of living".[22]

I was introduced to a slew of different concepts that challenged my working-class education, and taught me the simple (and short) meditative practice of "the exercise," which I still use. For me, this was a big step towards becoming conscious; getting better insight, challenging my long-held beliefs, and thinking differently.

Some days, I still feel like hiding. There's this uncomfortable feeling that comes with writing about yourself—it makes my skin crawl, and the drowning feeling comes over like a tidal wave. I feel like I lose my anchor and every bad thought and action comes back to haunt me. I start to look for excuses, I look for anyone else to blame. I practice my great skill of procrastination. I waste minutes, hours and days on mundane minutiae, telling myself that they're more important. Dammit, I'm last again. My dream is sloshing in the backwater with the perfect excuse: "I'm too busy." Too busy with what, for goodness sake? What's more important than my dream of being an author, my mission to write Jacqui's story, to learn, and to share? I feel the emotion bubble to the surface, and I want to shout and rant and cry. I'm all on my own, sitting in the backyard, writing. I have only the chooks for company. Even the dogs have gone back inside for the warmth.

Business women don't care, and spiritual women don't wear suits. I check my belief on that. No, it's not true. I am a business woman and I do care. Making it in a man's world? Really good at that too, totally identified with the masculine. I believe the tide is changing. So many strong women in both public and private endeavours making a difference in the world, making the world a better place by sharing their messages and skills.

So I'm straddling the chasm between cheesecloth and Chanel. Or that's how it seems to me. I want to help people, but I want someone to help me, to free me from this burden, this gift, this mission. Of course, that person is me. I'm impatient and frustrated, angry and scared. For goodness sake, I'm fifty-four, you'd think I'd have it all together by now. Nope. Not even close.

Is this the angst of the superhero? Does the heroine do it any differently, any better? God, I feel so crappy, it would be so easy to give up. Why don't I? Why don't I live my life small? The tears are threatening. Why don't I let them overflow? Why don't I just give up again? I could go back to work for someone else, get a real job. Why do I still not know what the hell I'm doing? Why am I here?

Breathing While Drowning

What am I supposed to be? Who am I supposed to be? What the hell do I do now?

Sit with the discomfort. Yep, sitting, uncomfortable. What's next? I'm looking for certainty where there is none. I want an answer when there's only the next problem. Escape. Escape from reality, escape from life, escape from the grief as it overwhelms me again. I can't even write a story for Jacqui. How the hell can I get on with my life? I need to write this for me, just for me, I don't care if no one else reads it, I need to heal, I need to heal. I need to listen to some of my own advice. Write the dream, pick a milestone, and get on it.

My dream is a book that tells the story of Jacqui's life and how her death destroyed the life I'd imagined. But I don't want it to. I want to live, I want to love, and I want to live a life that matters. It may be crazy, but when the balance is between spending all my time with people that I love dearly and people that I don't even know yet, why am I picking people that I don't even know?

I just want to be happy and loved. So what would it take? I have to give up the self-pity and get myself together. So how do I do that? Take one breath, then another, then another. Step out of the water, feel your feet on the ground. You're not drowning. You can do this. It's your light that frightens the crap out of you (thank you Marianne Williamson). Stop being so gutless; stand up and shine. Write whatever.

Why do I get like this and then get over it? Why am I full of passion and enthusiasm some days and other days I want to hide from the world?

How can I be so inspiring for others and so uninspired myself?

What is it that I want with this book? I want a voice; I want to be heard. I want you to know it hurts … it hurts like crazy to lose a child. The hurt never goes away. It's always there waiting for you. It's there in the background, waiting to rain on your sunny day. It's guilt and its shame and its despair. Guilt that I couldn't keep Jacqui alive, shame that I'm not the kind of mother, wife, daughter, sister, friend I should be. Says who? Says who?

What do I want to do? I want to write. I need to write. I want to read. I want to love. I want to be loved. I want to dance with Strack, and I want to sing loudly and out of tune. I want to travel.

I want to find my place; I want to live a life that expresses the very best I can be. Where is that life? Where am I?

I need to think and not think; I need to feel, to heal, to reconnect. Where is that? How do I do that?

What's important to me? Ian, Cassi, Angus, Frazer, Ron, Marguerite, Lesley, Sue, Janet, family.

What compels me to better myself? Why do I struggle? Why don't I just settle? It's just not in me to settle. My head is too full of ideas, my heart too full of hope. Jean Houston captures this so well when she writes about that feeling of waking up, getting ready for the day, and being "consumed by an urge to get on with it. What 'it' is you do not know, but it is barking at your heels like the Hound of Heaven. Something unknown is calling you and you know you will cross continents, oceans – realities, even – to discover it."

If I can't have a dream, let me help you get to yours. I need to feel needed, so let me show a caring and compassionate face to the world. Forget about self-compassion and my own dreams. End rant.

And then there comes a point where you begin to ask yourself *Is this as good as it gets?* Or you realise that you've ticked all the boxes on the list, and you're not happy, not content. Even that line *ticking all the boxes* is so "boxy" and constrained. Women need more than material achievement, and I believe men do as well. We've been suckered into this get, get, get mentality. We've been sold on the material wealth thing; this idea of success is an illusion.

We need to know our lives are important; we need to know we're making a difference; we need to know we matter. Live, love, leave a legacy.

Breathing While Drowning

The lessons I learned about myself and the world that I realised then—and that I realise now—mean a lot of different things.

It's so much easier to stay the same, but even then you have to be tough to take it.

Lesson: people say they don't like change, but what we don't like is being changed. It brings up a whole lot of fears, lots of them about not belonging. There's a fear of failure and, more importantly for me, if you are too successful, you might become unloved.

If staying the same is being unaware, unmindful, uninterested in life, and ignoring the human drives that make us feel alive, there's not much point. Even though I led change in my professional life in all shapes and forms, in my personal life, there was little control over grief. I had virtually no control: it led me where it wanted, dumping me into the ocean at the most inconvenient times, catching me unaware.

In *The Charge*, Brendon Burchard writes that the ten human drives that make us feel alive are: control, competence, congruence, caring, connection, change, challenge, creative expression, contribution, and consciousness.[23] When I think about what was missing for me around this time, I can easily tick off control, congruence, creative expression, contribution, and consciousness. Most of the others were externally focused.

The most important one here is consciousness. I was unaware, and I didn't know what I didn't know. I was only just beginning to realise the depth of my unconscious incompetence in life.

We all need a little more self-compassion.

Lesson: be kind to yourself. Put yourself first and show a little care for you. It's a healthy thing to do, and it's a conscious thing to do. People who are more self-compassionate are happier, healthier, and contribute to the human race deeply.

Ordering the chaos keeps it under control. If you keep a lid on it, it's going to blow up in your face one day.

Lesson: yes, we need control, but we also need to lose control from time to time; we need to be uncertain, spontaneous, and emotional. Allowing ourselves time to rest and digest. My emotions, mostly consisting of grief, shame, despair, and guilt, were like a boiling kettle with the steam bottled up inside. It looks cool from the outside, but it you touch it, you'll burn yourself. Plus, every now and again, hot steam escapes, which scalds and scars. And then, once in a while, the lid blows off, and everything blows up in your face. Ask for help. Are you okay? That would have been good to hear more often. And have the courage to say, "No, not really," rather than saying, "I'm fine," which I said so often—lying through my teeth.

"If you don't build your dream, then someone else will hire you to help them build theirs".[24]

Lesson: you can have it all—all your dreams—if you know what they are, and if you get some direction, and if you have the courage to go after them. Living every moment joyfully and knowing your purpose is a way to be. If that way is congruent with your values, if it has compassion, and creativity and curiosity (and you are conscious and mindful), you have it all. The moments you don't, and you realise you don't, are moments of consciousness, and those are valuable too.

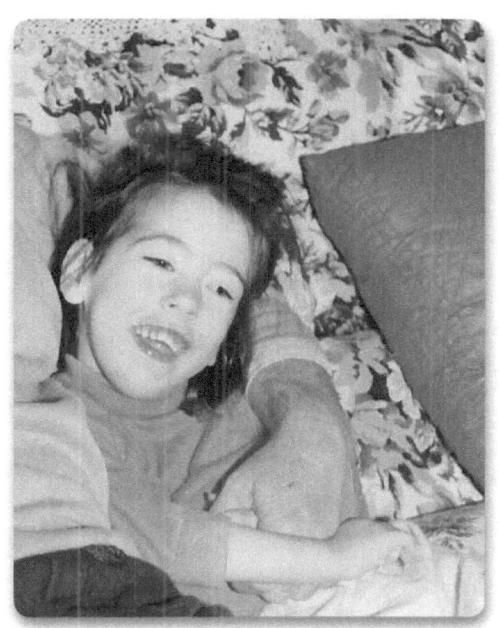
Jacqueline Bree, my little Sweet Pea

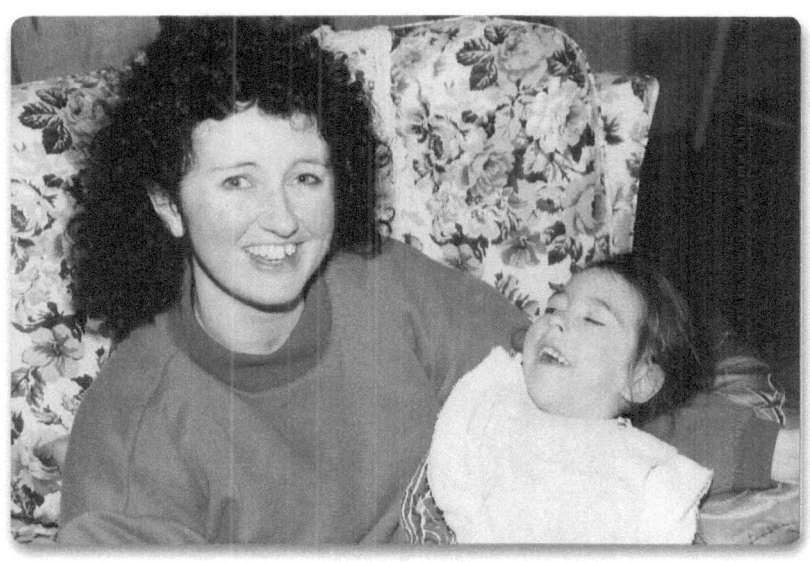
Jacqui and I getting ready for a messy drink

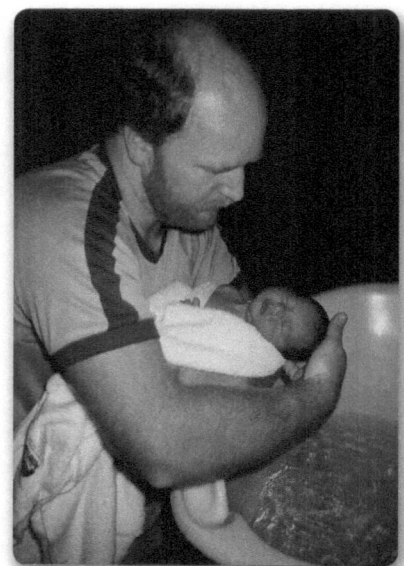
Day 1 and first bath with Dad

Day 2 with Mum & big sister Cassi

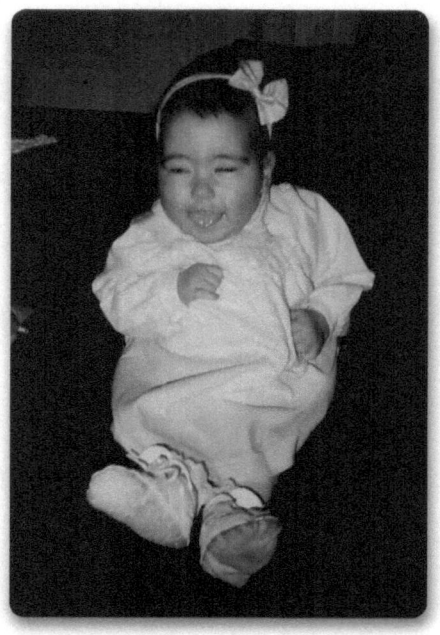
Jacqui caught in one of her rare laughs

Jacqui giving Grandad one of her precious smiles

Jacqui loving stories with Grandad

And telling Grandad a few stories of her own

Cassi & Jacqui with their brand new brother Angus Peter

The three amigos: Jacqui, Angus & Cassi

Cassi reading Jacqui a book in the park

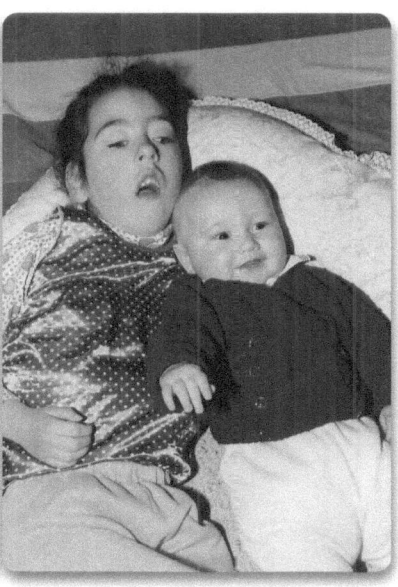
Having a hug with her little brother Angus

Jacqui on the Gravitron

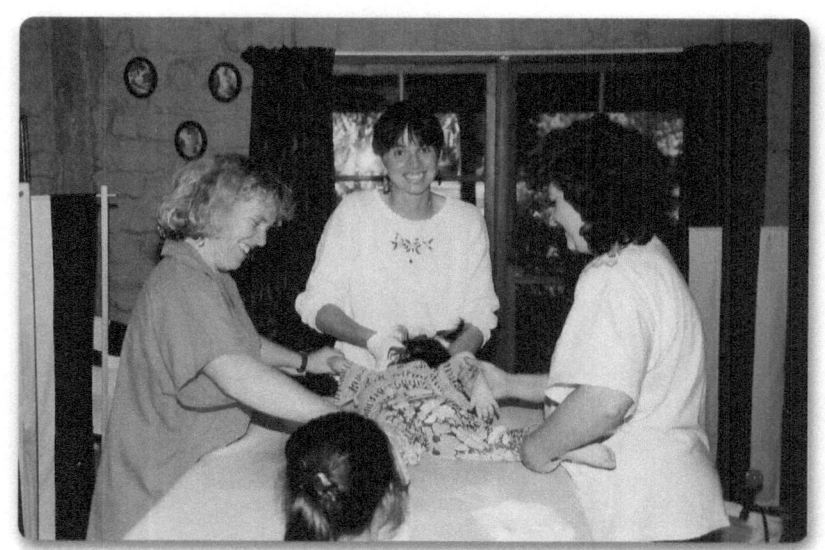

Patterning with Ronnie Z, Leanne and Jeanette

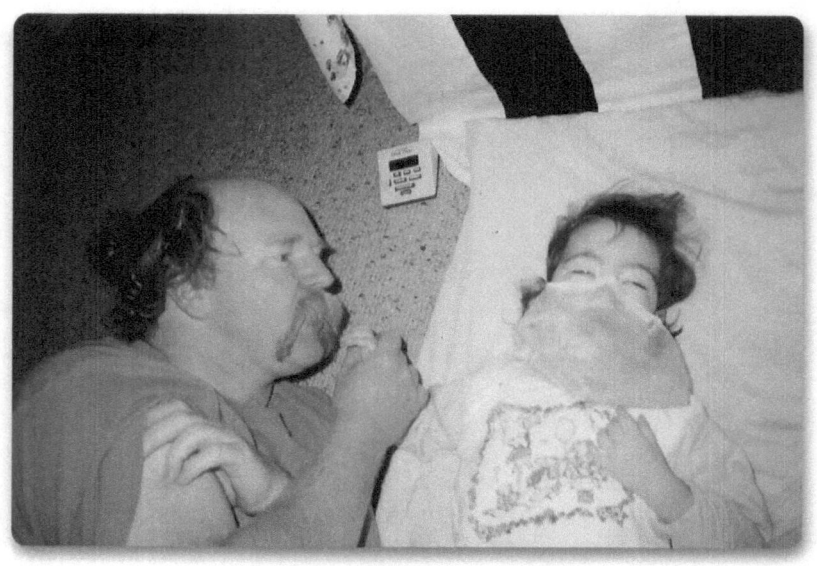

Masking with Dad watching closely

Practicing standing
with Mum & Cassi

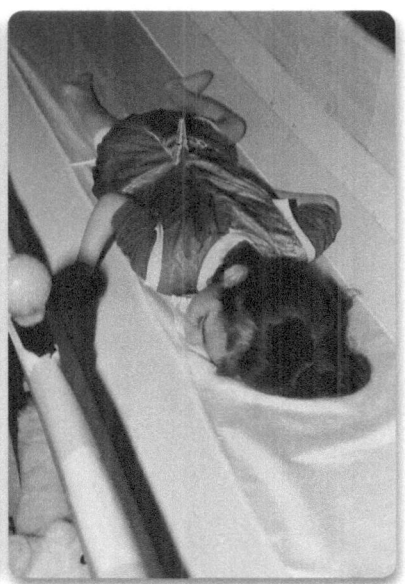

Heading down the incline
in her slippery suit

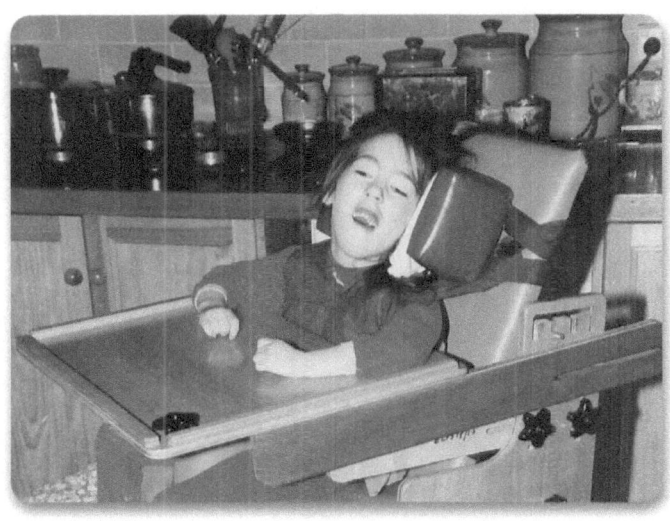

Loving her highchair
and waiting for lunch

Sue & I with the two Jacqui's

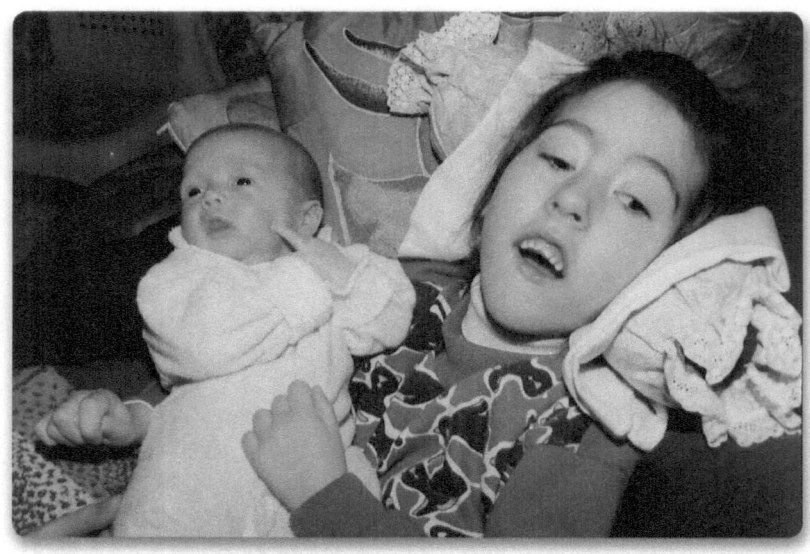
Having a hug with her brand new cousin Brittnee

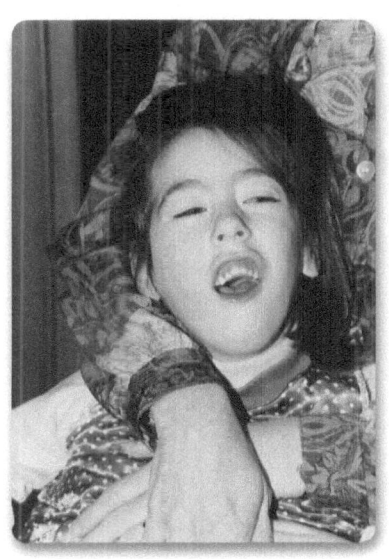

Jacqui making her feelings known

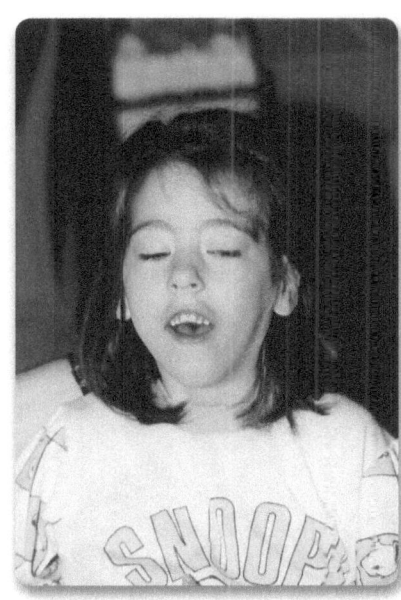

Feeling very grown up with a new haircut and her hair down

Jacqui's 3rd birthday at Grandad's house

Patting the
Clydesdales with Dad

Making
caterpillars

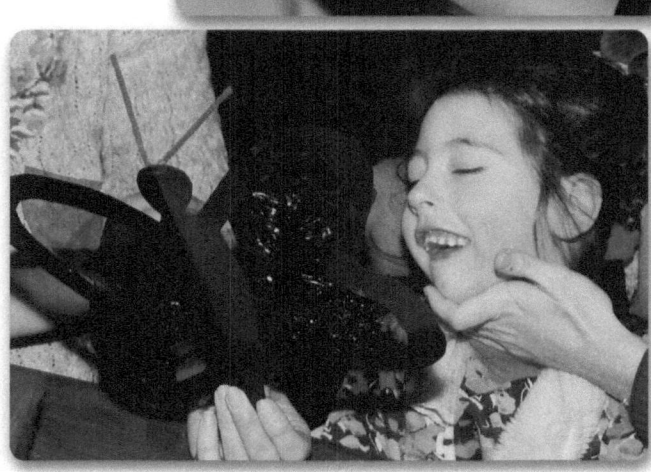

Making butterflies

Our last photo of Jacqui, a rare snowfall.
She told her Dad snow was cold!

My beautiful grown up children, Cassi, Angus & Frazer

Ian (Strack) my Man with Heart

My evolutionary friends Ronnie & Marguerite

Part 2

Finding the Feeling: Do You Remember How It Really Feels to Feel?

I began to feel a growing sense of dis-ease. There must be something better than this. I've got it all, right? I've worked freaking hard, so this life must be what I wanted, right?

The dis-ease started to fill every aspect of my life, and I was experiencing things that were forcing me to look at who I was, at what was important to me, at what I was prepared to put up with. For a long time, I resisted. Why was all this bad stuff happening? Hadn't I paid my dues? Wasn't I working as hard as I could? Wasn't I enough?

This restlessness is felt by so many people, women and men, as they transition from one decade to another. According to Marcia Reynolds, these days, women seem to be hitting these moments earlier and earlier—in their thirties, not just in their forties and fifties. Rather than a midlife crisis, we're having a quarter-life crisis, and we're being encouraged by the likes of Sheryl Sandberg and

Marissa Mayer to assess our values early in our careers.[1] I would certainly add a few more women of influence to the encouragement list, such as Brené Brown, Maureen Murdock, Oprah Winfrey, and Marianne Williamson.

Women often crash into the glass ceiling at work or find themselves looking for something else with all the children at school. Or they find themselves at the end of their career, alone but unfinished. Reynolds suggests you "embrace your restlessness as an opportunity for self-exploration and growth instead of letting it feel disruptive, confusing and scary".[2]

She recognises the uniqueness of individuals, but she outlines three life shifts that fit what I've seen and heard from women (and some men):

Age 30+: the questions focus on career choices to ensure long-term happiness.

Age 40+: the questions focus on life purpose to ensure the significance and value of your efforts.

Age 50+: the questions focus on legacy. To ensure age-defying relevance.[3]

Yep, feels about right; there must be something better than this.

Chapter 6

Is This as Good as It Gets?

Career wise, I continued to seek new intellectual challenges and test the limits of my skills and capabilities. I'd moved interstate, I began managing another statewide project, and I dragged the family with me. I'd come back to Victoria to work on a national project, got disheartened, moved out of health, and then moved into IT. I became general manager and then the CEO of a small IT advisory firm. We had a home, another house at the beach, an investment property, healthy children, and a happy family.

My restlessness searched for physical avenues to satisfy as fifty loomed on the horizon. I got fit, did my first triathlon (swim, bike, run), and then I trained some more and completed my first marathon. I had a great sense of satisfaction spending more than five hours running forty-two kilometres and finishing in the MCG (the spiritual home of sport in my state).

But there was still something missing. Mind tick, body tick … soul was next.

Awakening to Spiritual Aridity and Death

In *The Heroine's Journey*, this was my awakening to feelings of spiritual aridity and death. For me, the words associated with this are *closed, conflicted,* and *conscious*.

Murdock stated: "A woman loses her 'inner fire' when she is not being fed, when the soul's flame is no longer fuelled, when the promise of the dream held for so long dies. Old patterns no longer fit, the new way is not yet clear, there is darkness everywhere, and she cannot see or feel or taste or touch. Nothing means very much anymore, and she no longer knows who she really is".[1]

I started to realise my unaware, unadventurous, and powerless soul was holding back my curiosity and optimism. You might say, "Hang on a minute. You had it all: you took chances and built your career into something admiral." And you'd be right: I had all the external success I wanted. But what I forgot to take chances with was my internal self, my soul—the self that really matters. I wasn't connected to my dreams. I didn't even know what they were. They'd sat on the back burner for so long that they'd become a mouldy, congealed blob of *blah*.

I looked with envy at people who seemed to know what they wanted to do with their lives, who were purposeful, driven, and dedicated. In the world of business, I was surrounded by people who looked like they knew what they wanted. But now that I have a bit more insight into myself, I wonder if all of those people I envied were what I imagined them to be. Perhaps many of them felt the same as I did: lost, stuck, drowning.

I admired strong leaders, particularly women with powerful messages who followed their dreams, gathered followers, and spread the word.

As I got more experience in leadership and management, I often felt as though I was just cleaning up other people's messes. My frustration grew. I wanted to be my own boss, to do only what I wanted to do.

Tony Gaskin said, "If you don't build your dream someone will hire you to help build theirs." When I saw these words, they fit incredibly well with what I was feeling. The only trouble was that I had been building other people's dreams for so long that I'd forgotten what mine were about. Remember those dreams were mouldy, congealed blobs of *blah*. It had been a long time since I'd allowed myself to think about what I really wanted. I felt as if I had no opinions of my own—everything was a result of policy or management decisions and political or world views that were not mine. If you asked me what I thought, my opinion was always filtered by where I was working or the person with whom I was speaking. There were very few people I could be completely honest with without inviting retribution into my life ... or so I thought.

This desire to build my own dream took a long time to grow, but, eventually, it did grow. It needed a lot of nurturing because the soil was barren and dry, and I had quite a few false starts. But the change was that I became open, willing, searching—ready to hear and see and feel another way.

Murdock says that strong women can say *no* to the patriarchy, to the world that expects them to follow one path, but doing so comes at a price. She says, "There is a feeling of emptiness, of somehow not measuring up by following the obvious career path to advancement. There is a fear of disappointing others, letting them down, destroying their image of who they think you are. But there is also a strength in saying no, in being self-protective, in listening to one's authentic voice, in silencing the inner tyrant".[2]

I felt a great deal of pressure to continue down the obvious career path, even from myself. But I said *no* and, thinking this was different, I started my own business so I could pursue success in my own way and live and work doing things that I loved, the way I wanted to.

Murdock stated, "When the heroine says no to the next heroic task, there is extreme discomfort. The alternative to heroism is self-indulgence, passivity and lack of importance. That spells death and despair in this culture, our culture supports the path of acquisition of position: more, better, faster. Most people fear that the opposite of this hubris is invisibility, and they don't know what to do".[3]

I was already invisible in my own life, and the acquisition of more, better, faster for everyone else was draining the last remaining joy out of living. Saying *no* to what's expected of me did feel self-indulgent (and it still does from time to time), but it certainly didn't feel passive or lacking in importance. Many times, I had my heart in my mouth as I set up my business, and I was working harder than I ever had. (Of course, I wasn't getting paid for all the extra hours.) Even though it was my own business, it was still working—working in the same world, doing the same things. Even though I was happier working with great people and doing my kind of work, the dis-ease was still there. I didn't become less frustrated all of a sudden; rather, I slowly came to realise that the dis-ease was in me.

Murdock said, "When a woman stops doing she must learn how to simply be. Being is not a luxury it is a discipline. The heroine must listen carefully to her true inner voice. That means silencing the other voices anxious to tell her what to do. She must be willing to hold the tension until the new form emerges. Anything less than that aborts growth, denies change, and reverses transformation. Being takes courage and demands sacrifice".[4] I was doing, doing, doing, but I had to learn how to be. I had a lifetime of doing to let go of … or so I thought.

I'm very good at starting and terrible at finishing. Yet I finish some things, and I'm still doing, still practising. When I look at what they are, they tend to be short, succinct, and quick to implement. That's why I'm so good at project and change management, and why I get so restless with long-term operational management. Once I've done the same thing twice, I get edgy. There are so many more things to do than "waste my time" doing the same thing twice. This means that I follow the new and shiny things, restlessly searching for creative and joyful outlets.

So back to the procrastination and why I don't get around to finishing stuff. What stuff is it? Is it stuff outside my comfort zone (like talking to new people about what's important to me)? Could be.

What stops me? Which little voice says, *It's easier to stay small, to stay busy, to put your stuff last, to find an excuse—any excuse.* I need to silence the inner tyrant, the one that tells me I'm not enough, the one that tells me I'll never be enough.

I dreamed of being a writer, but I didn't know how or where to start. There was always one more bill to pay and one more job to do, but I *could* take time off and write. Nevertheless, I kept putting the dream off and, at times, that felt worse because the decision to procrastinate or put my stuff first was clearly mine.

I am going to be a writer; I am a writer. I am going to be a published author; I am a published author. I am going to write for my life; I am writing for my life.

I need to let myself and others know that it's okay to be imperfect, okay to be stupid, needy, angry, sad, and all other shadow emotions. This is good advice especially after trauma (big or small) or even after drama. My life belongs to me, and everything I think, feel, do, and believe matters, and that's what counts.

There are some points in your life when courage is the only choice. Brené Brown said, "Vulnerability sounds like truth and feels like courage. Truth and courage aren't always comfortable, but they're never weakness".[5]

I had a conversation with two women, two really good friends: Ronnie and Marguerite. I put my vulnerability out there, and admitted to them that despite what it looked like I had achieved in life, I was not content. In fact, I was restless as hell, frustrated, searching for something that would provide an escape from the misery. And then I heard the most marvellous response: "We're not content either." We admitted we were all members of the Discontented Women's Club.

Discovering I was not alone was a revelation to me. These were not just women I was reading about, these were real women—real living, breathing women. Realising that this persistent feeling of discontent and frustration and fear was shared provided me with a chink of light in the brick wall that surrounded my life. I could stop beating my hands on the wall until they were bloody. The wall had been there to keep all the bad guys out, but it also kept the good guys from getting in. And it kept me from looking at myself, from knowing myself. It's so much easier to push it all down, cover it up, and lock away the key.

The revelation came because I was finally courageous enough to share my vulnerability, to crack open the door to the truth about how I was feeling. Why did it take me so long? How brilliant are the two women who held the space with me?

These two amazing women became my evolutionary partners. We put ourselves on a path to a deep self-exploration, to find meaning, to being who we needed to be (and sometimes just being). Although the road ahead was all over the place, we made a commitment to each other to take the road, to stay honest and open, to remain willing to try. We were prepared to challenge the status quo of our existence.

At the time, I didn't realise we were in an evolutionary friendship. This understanding came later, when I discovered the Feminine Power Global Community work of Claire Zammit and Katherine Woodward Thomas. These women teach "a set of transformative principles – processes and practices by which women can awaken to their inherent co-creative feminine power".[6]

Zammit and Thomas say evolutionary partners bond inside of the futures they're creating. They help us reflect on things that are outside of our awareness. There has to be a mutual agreement of safety and an alignment. For Ronnie, Marguerite, and me, that was: "There must be something better out there; let's go find it and do it together."

When we slip into old patterns and behaviours, my partners are there to bring sympathy and empathy—but there is also a "willingness to embrace difficult conversations, turning into it rather than away".[7]

When I ring one of them and start ranting about the latest thing that someone did to me or start playing the victim or glaze over a hurt, they challenge me to think deeper, to feel deeper. They've seen me live through this before, and if I think about it, I may realise that too. They ask which lessons am I (my soul) here to learn. What could I do differently in this situation or the next to change the outcome? Sometimes this can be really frustrating, particularly if I'm lost in my head and playing the event on a never-ending loop of *poor me*. And sometimes they hold me when I cry. And sometimes they cry with me.

Evolutionary partners act from integrity. They're holding me accountable to becoming the woman I need to be to achieve my divine mission. These friends are threads of light to connect me to my brilliance, and each thread makes my light brighter. Women are the most abundant and underutilised resource. In the words of Zammit, "Never before have women been holding so much power to shape the future".[8]

We share our heroine's journey with our women friends, and they become our coaches, our crew, our companions.

I embrace my restlessness and begin to feel pregnant with so many ideas that make me feel like I'm going to burst. Previously, in response to a lack of support, I would have dimmed down my brilliance. I think I still do this to a certain extent. Ideas and inspiration are my gifts, and it's time to use them. I have my friends and family to support me—to do what, I'm still not sure … but to do and be something.

I'm a midwife to the unmanifested potential of my life. I am birthing my creative potential into the world.

The lessons I learned about myself and the world that I realised then—and that I realise now—mean a lot of different things.

We need to organise our lives around the potential of who we are. Not wishing, not hoping, not yearning.

Lesson: You can have it all if you take some action, if you give wishing some real power and make it your reality. Find out who you are, dig into your potential, and try things you've never done. Take it deeper, make it stronger. Don't be bound by the social mores or perceptions of who you "should" be. If anyone says you *should* do something, even if it's yourself—run a mile.

Trust your intuition and follow your gut.

Lesson: you're the only one who can become an expert at being you; you have the inside running if you believe in yourself and listen to the inner voice that encourages rather than disparages you. Let yourself feel what's right and do that. It won't always be easy, but it will always be rich, full, and amazing.

No one is coming to discover you and offer you the perfect job and life. It takes action from you to get traction on your dreams. Go all the way—don't hold anything back. After all, you only live once.

Be vulnerable, but know that it takes more courage. Still, you're not alone.

Lesson: there are a lot of other people who feel exactly as I do, who are searching for that same sense of purpose, who are suckered into those same illusory trappings of success. It's all pretty empty unless you know who you are and why you're here. Let yourself spend time acquiring that rather than things.

Part 3

Where Do You Find Healing?

Rosemary Maris, a gorgeous and intuitive woman I know, tells a story about a café called Mario's. There, souls meet between physical lifetimes. At Mario's, people chat over a drink, and as friends do, they decide to do something for each other. According to Mario's manifesto, Jacqui's soul and mine agreed to the arrangement of this incarnation. Jacqui agreed to a tough life—almost five years in a body that struggled to work, but with a spirit that was feisty and loving. I agreed to learn how to love and live a long lifetime with loss and letting go.

I used to think Jacqui got the raw end of that deal, but then I spent years thinking I was the one who was cheated. The word *bereave* originates from the Old English *berēafian,* meaning "to deprive of, take away, seize, rob".[1] For all those early years, I felt deprived, robbed.

Now I'm at a point where I can't wait to live every moment, to take the next breath. And, every day, I realise the importance and magnificence of the gifts she gave me.

I often wonder who I'd be if Jacqui had been born without a disability, and I wonder who I'd be if she was still alive with or without a disability. Each wondering is another path of maybes.

Who I am is who I am: the sum of all the choices I've made up to this point in my life. Who I am tomorrow is another story. The possibilities are endless.

Twenty years later, I can look at the gifts she gave me with love and gratitude. I'm awakening a consciousness about myself that's serving me very well, tapping into another me that has been asleep for two decades (or maybe my whole life!).

Consciousness is the state of being conscious; an awareness of one's own existence, sensations, thoughts, and surroundings; an apprehension of one's surroundings. Treading in the realm of consciousness was a little scary. But I've never lacked courage—fools rush in where angels fear to tread—and if courage is what it took, so be it. The search for my soul began in earnest and, as always, I was incurably curious and thorough.

Chapter 7

The Search Begins

A t first, I followed my usual pattern, where my skills and experience lay, and then I tried to intellectualise everything. Research it, find a solution to the problem, and read about what I could do. I was not living or working in the right circles to find what I needed. But then a chance conversation with my chiropractor sent me off to look into other avenues. Despite what I'd learned, working with Jacqui's IAHP Program, I hadn't really looked into alternative or complementary therapies that much—just enough to get by.

And when I mentioned I wasn't sleeping well, my chiropractor suggested I try Silva.[1] They had a method he'd used to get to sleep almost instantly. It sounded too good to be true but I looked them up anyway. And that's when the door to a different way of thinking opened. Silva had years of scientific evidence and credibility supporting the method. For me, it was as if they bridged the chasm of modern, Western medicine and alternative, Eastern philosophies. They gently introduced me to a more intuitive way of thinking and being.

In April of 2012, I made my first online purchase of a personal transformation product. This was a big milestone. The personal transformation sector can be a slippery slope if you're not careful—it's so easy to see what others offer as a silver bullet, a way to make everything okay again. This is not what happens for me. It took me a while to properly realise that everyone's journey is unique. Everyone's circumstances are unique; everyone has different needs and lessons to learn. I've made many purchases since—some good, some not so good. Different strokes for different folks. Some have left a lasting impression and changed me forever; some were flashes in the pan; some didn't even make a single plop; some I haven't even looked at since I bought them. I may get to those unopened boxes one day.

We take what we need and move on. And that's okay. I don't feel the need to finish something that is not good quality or is not giving me what I need. If I've found what works in the first part, all is well and good.

As I started using the Silva guided meditation and visualisation it turned me on to the possibilities of a different life. Almost immediately, I began to see positive synchronicities in my life and in myself. And most importantly, I was a lot happier. I was doing something, taking action, and directing how I would think and feel and live. Visualising and manifesting work is not as simple as thinking about what you want and waiting for it to happen. There's a lot more to it than that: taking action, working through fears, and learning from all experiences (positive and negative), for example. Each moment is an opportunity to learn … if you'll let it.

Energy flows where the focus goes. I had focused on grief and shame and guilt for a very long time. By changing my focus to growth and transformation and hope, I had a whole new world of possibilities.

Silva was a great start: I began to look after my inner health, and my outer world took on a different feel. A quote that I first saw around this time and that I've seen over and over in all shapes and sizes felt like a light bulb turning on. Marianne Williamson's words from *Return to Love* present the quote quite elegantly:

"Our deepest fear is not that we are inadequate. Our deepest fear is that we are powerful beyond measure. We ask ourselves, Who am I to be brilliant, gorgeous, talented, fabulous?".[2]

Breathing While Drowning

And there it was, shining a light on the real deal, giving me instructions for the next step. She also said, "Your playing small doesn't serve the world. There's nothing enlightened about shrinking so that other people won't feel insecure around you".[3]

Time to stop hiding, time to get my act together—whatever that is—and time to get on with making a difference in the world. Williamson said, "And as we let our own light shine, we unconsciously give other people permission to do the same. As we are liberated from our own fear, our presence automatically liberates others".[4]

Permission to shine, granted. My playing small doesn't serve the world (even though serving the world is what I wanted to do). Of course, it wasn't like turning on a switch. I had permission … but what was I supposed to do exactly?

For me, the best thing was to start my soul-searching with the mind; after all, the mind was what tortured me with images of failure, guilt, and shame. I began to journal more regularly again. I began to peer under some of those rocks and to shine a light on what I found. I began to question my values, my skills, my actions.

> I polarise and greatly invigorate.
>
> I choose joy, energy, happiness and wisdom.
>
> I live for myself, my family and friends. I am a giving, sharing part of the community.
>
> I choose to embrace the vicissitudes of life.
>
> I choose learning and understanding.
>
> I am in charge of my own reality.
>
> I do not take on another person's sadness
>
> I do not allow myself to dwell on things I cannot change.
>
> I choose positive energy both light and dark.

> I am surrounded by the light and love of my family, friends and community.
> I look forward to the future.
> I am in charge of my own reality.
> I am peaceful and happy.
> I am safe from harm.
> I am as healthy and as strong as I can be.
> I live with wellbeing.

A belief is a statement you say to yourself about something you hold to be true, and it guides your living experience. I was thinking about my beliefs, about what was important to me, and about what I wanted to believe about the future for me.

Even if I didn't believe it yet, I was convincing myself, focusing on the positive, keeping in mind that the energy flows where the focus goes. Sometimes this was still hard to believe in the face of how I was feeling and what I was doing.

> I am horrified at the amount of change required.
> I am overwhelmed by the road ahead and wary about how I will come out the other side.
> I need to speak the truth, I need to acknowledge my needs and address my dreams; give myself time to listen to my "self".
> I have time for myself, I have time for my family.
> I choose joy, energy, happiness and wisdom.
> I choose invigorating greatness.
> 'Take time to dream, it hitches the soul to the stars.'

Breathing While Drowning

How long since I dreamed a dream that took my soul to the stars? How long since my love and I took time to sit together and just be?

Where are the dreams of childhood, adolescent goals, a checklist of inconsequential things, or at least that's what they feel like to me now I'm old?

Too old to dream? Some may think so. Get stuffed, I've got far to go.

It's not too late to start again but maybe not from the beginning. Let go of all the rubbish, superfluous fluff and chunder.

Create my own reality ...

I choose joy, energy, happiness and wisdom.

I am at one with the universe and receive all I need in exchange for all I give.

Today I am brilliant, a compelling leader, assertive and positive, respectful. Today is something special.

Today I am brilliant, a compelling leader, assertive and positive, respectful. Today is something special.

Today I am brilliant, a compelling leader, assertive and positive, respectful. Today is something special.

Dwelling in a private universe every door an opportunity, every pause, a chance to look in a different direction.

Eyes open, eyes relaxed, mind open, mind relaxed.

> *I choose joy, energy, creativity, learning, expansion, love, courage and curiosity.*
>
> *Today I am indestructible, resilient, calm, thoughtful and thorough. I see further, I understand the connections. I find creative solutions. I am compellingly positive.*
>
> *Thank you.*

This was an amazing thing. Once I'd started down the personal transformation road, it was like a door opening to a new existence. I practiced my Silva method, and my mind and life responded, dragging my soul into the light. I created little oases of stillness that seemed to anchor the ocean of chaos. I felt a little control come back, and my hope rekindled; there was something more to life. I felt it wasn't too late to make my difference. I began to ask more important questions of myself.

These three questions came from Vishen Lakhiani, from *Mindvalley* to "help you see if you're truly aiming for the right goals in your life or if you're stuck in modern culture's 'Mean Goals' trap".[5]

3 most important questions.

1. *What do I want to experience?*
   Travel
   Share time with Ian
   See children happy
   See grandchildren
   See the world
   Spend time peacefully
   Run till I die

Breathing While Drowning

    Stay in love
    Keep marriage strong
    Be there for friends
    Listen to brilliant music
    See Europe
    Have house at beach
    Have house in mountains

2. How do I want to grow?
    Learn a language
    Write a book
    Publish a book
    Learn philosophy
    Lead inspirationally
    Grow intellectually
    Connect to intuitive nature
    Find calmness
    Be an inspiration
    Be creative
    Stay healthy
    Run ½ marathon
    Trek the Himalayas

3. What do I want to contribute to the planet?
    Be there for my children, husband
    Contribute to friends' support
    Create learning organisation
    Change the lives of people in health
    Make a difference to my world
    Help not for profits

Write inspiring books
Create space for peace
Be environmentally aware

A little over three years later, and I've ticked off many of the things on the list—some are still in progress, and some have yet to come. It's fabulous, exciting, and gratifying to look back a mere three years and see how far I've come, what I've achieved. The things that were on my list, my dreams, are now joyful memories.

Once I had a sense of the benefits of meditation from the Silva method—and believe me, it didn't take very long to see how finding a point of stillness several times a day helped me be calmer and more productive—it was full steam ahead. I know this sounds like a strange contradiction, but being still helped me be even more of a whirlwind of productivity. And I was loving my work and my life a whole lot more.

With years of training and experience in science, I love evidence. Even though it's now a balance of intuition and science for me, it's always great when science backs up why I'm feeling so good and good things are dropping into my life with startling synchronicity. For me, the Silva method was the perfect start. José Silva started life without formal education, and he worked in an electronics store before he began working with his children to see if he could raise their IQ to help them perform better at school. The things we do for love!

José discovered that achieving deep levels of the mind associated with alpha frequencies (a relaxed mind) could be learned, and at this level of mind, people's potential expanded immensely. He said that the main focus of the basic method "is to acquaint students with the potential of their whole person and how, by using more of their mind, they can slough off limiting ways of thinking and unproductive habits to become, as we are fond of saying, "the beautiful people that they are called to be".[6]

Breathing While Drowning

I wanted to be one of those beautiful people. I wanted everything. I occasionally find time to write. Journaling continues to help me hold it all together, to bring insight and to plan action. I try lots of different ways to reflect. Two steps forward, one step back. The habits of a lifetime can be hard to change.

Monday 11th June 2012

I remember.

From this life, this year, this day, this hour, this minute, this second.

Pursuing the dream, a published writer, visualising the moment, conscious that to make it happen requires action. Writing action.

This minute, a string of actions, thoughts, visualisations and imaginings, interspersed with memories of a past listening to the same music in a younger body, with a younger mind.

An hour ago, at the Beach House, a subdued lunch, conversation sparse, careful not to contribute to discomfort but rather to keep low key and relaxed. Experiencing a side not seen often.

A day ago trudging in the slipstream trying to find the right rhythm in my mind, legs are strong, I am strong, body is strong, I am strong, heart is strong, I am strong, head is strong, I am strong. I run a 2-hour half marathon. A little surprised at lack of stamina, where did that go? Focused on the negative, forgot to dwell on the good point, the buzz of adrenaline and achievement. Next time ...

A year ago, a long time, struggling through the negativity, felt like I was carrying the load of everyone's hopes and dreams.

Vacillating between highs and lows, why here, why now? What lesson did I seek, family, loyalty, personal gain, why did I say "yes" again?

Travelling the same lives again and again.

What about a lifetime ago? Who was I before this life? What days, hours, minutes and moments did I live, love and learn?

Perhaps humble, perhaps not ...

This lifetime trying to improve my lot, internally focused, so what does that mean in the last life, or the one before that? What moments intersect, seem familiar and yet; could not possibly be so, unless there is a shared soul.

It wasn't all smooth sailing; I had been in the ocean for a long time.

Monday 18th June 2012

Despite endeavouring to intervene and intercept the usual response, I really struggled to bring the pessimism under control. I will try the glass of water or something [Silva method] I am not so sure what the problem is. So it is difficult to ask for a solution.

I think I missed my run this morning. The yoga may be not enough.

> Is it that lack of control, is it a fear of not being up to scratch? Where does that come from?
>
> Maybe the lady was pregnant? She seemed graceless but I should have acted better, shouldn't I? Why the unrealistic response?
>
> Cancel, cancel
>
> Overwhelming, too much to do?
>
> So get organised, identify the priorities and get onto them, solve the problem.
>
> Start making phone calls today. Review all contacts.
>
> Help, help, help, stop me from drowning I need to get out. Let me write the things I want. Let me live the life of my own design.

Two steps forward, one step back. Years of living with negative thinking, of beating myself up mentally, of always making it my fault—those habits were hard to let go of. I still haven't let go completely, but I'm much more relaxed about life. Chance encounters don't make me want to curl up and die these days.

I was not working where I wanted to be, still working for someone else's dreams, and still yearning to write for a living … still yearning to write this book. And the call was getting stronger.

<u>Friday 22nd June 2012</u>

> A dream I had recently. Running, rhythm, routine, passed by a young woman who calls out, "c'mon Mum" and then a woman my own age passes

me with a wry smile and a "shared understanding" look. Got to keep running, trying to keep up — not so much.

Forging ahead maybe.

Body felt OK, air was neutral.

Weather non-existent.

"Pre-Copernican obscurest" Paul Keating describing Tony Abbott.

Sleepy, eyes closing mid-thought, mid-word. Need a big sleep tonight.

Been a busy week, ups and downs, swings and roundabouts.

Still lots to do, but having more fun doing it at the moment. Burden still there but the way forward is clearer.

Feet are hot and swollen, aching and stinging. Have to move weight from one to the other.

I was thinking that there may be a way out of the ocean. I began to write creatively again. It was sporadic, but it was a start: snippets of poetry, character outlines, plots, and plot devices. I began to let my imagination out to play.

Monday 2nd July 2012

To live a purpose driven life.

To live with worth and value

A talent and a gift which must be satisfied

Breathing While Drowning

> *Unique talents and qualities*
> *A purpose driven life*
> *Plato's ideal forms*
> *Silva "perfect blueprint" for disease is health*
> *Did you learn how to love?*

I'd come across the concept of intuitive healers when my older sister was diagnosed with breast cancer. My mum had died from breast cancer in 1991. *The Anatomy of the Spirit* by Caroline Myss suggested physical symptoms were a result of a deeper spiritual pain.[7] I read about the interconnectedness of mind, body, and spirit, and I learned how the physical symptoms are our own responses to our spiritual and emotional stressors. We're responsible for everything that happens in our lives; we choose this life. This changed the way I thought and felt about illness. I felt less helpless, less constrained by what Western medicine had to offer. There was a personal power that we could wield that might be able to change everything—maybe. It made so much more sense than believing Western medicine was the only answer. Often, we treated symptoms without addressing the cause of the primary disease. I could see how both of these could work together. My frustrating love/hate relationship with Western medicine took a different route.

My next purchase was Christie Marie Sheldon's *Love or Above*[8] in 2012. This was a really big step for me. If Silva could be said to be scientific and rigorous in its research, then *Love or Above* was a long stride away from that towards the spiritual end of the spectrum.

The Silva method was a part of the *Mindvalley* group[9], and when I read one of their e-mails about this small course by Christie Marie Sheldon, something clicked. Again, the rational and logical aspects attracted me first. Christie Marie Sheldon was an intuitive healer, and she had based her *Love or Above* work on the work of

Dr David Hawkins's *Power vs. Force: The Hidden Determinants of Human Behaviour*[10]. Hawkins wrote about the relationship between energy and emotion and how that could affect not only the person experiencing the emotion, but also the people around them too. I liked the subatomic nature of the explanation—this was surely science giving me something back.

Christie Marie Sheldon is an amazing and intriguing woman. With a background in finance, she is now an intuitive healer … how did that happen? She also has the most delightful giggle that peppers her conversations; it makes me smile when I hear it. *Love and Above* helped me discover a lot of the hidden stories that had been driving the direction in my life. I realised it was time for a change of driver, time to put a few of those slow pokes and detractors in the back seat.

And then, one day, I was on the train listening to one of Christie Marie's meditations, and I had the most amazing experience.

Friday 6th July 2012

I saw an Angel on the train. Good name for a book.

Actually it was yesterday or maybe the day before, doesn't matter, let go the control.

It was my higher self. I opened the doorway and I came through.

Bright, luminously blue/green white with wings, but translucent as well.

Felt overwhelmed but at peace, took lots of the hurt away. I had to have the hurt to toughen me up to help my resilience, the way ahead will not always be easy. There are more hurts to come. That frightens me a bit but I know it needs to happen.

Breathing While Drowning

It is a diva, both male and female. She stands behind me and sometimes places one or two hands on my shoulders to calm, comfort or strengthen me. Her wings spread over and around.

Now that she is here, there is no going back.

I respond to every prompt, every feeling, sometimes it's hard to wait my turn to speak, the ideas just bubble up, bursting to the surface.

Diamond core, grain of sand to begin
but fired in the suns of galaxies,
pressures of the universe become a jewel,
shining a light in dark places
Share the light, use it,
polish the unending facets,
smile at the twinkling, the joy
brought spontaneously through the beauty of the source.

I saw an angel on the train
and realised she was me
we'll go together she said, as
the road won't always be easy
and two are better than one.
Time to live a purpose driven life,
though time we have in plenty.

The power of the written word to explain is key, there will be 20.

Her hands on my shoulder, her wings spread wide, luminous, translucent, my breath caught in my throat.

Did I hesitate a heartbeat?

Perhaps, but forgiveness is there ...

some pain is hard to bear, and to know it again ...

Reunited, holding close, say I love you to her soul.

Without her I'd be closed, a cot case, no time for journey of the soul, shimmering the surface barely touching, wasted.

Bring it on, remember past lives first.

With this word I enclose the negativity and downers of the day. Thank you for the opportunity to experience this, I have learnt what I need, now it is time to give it back.

Desire, belief and expectancy all add up to faith. Have I lost my faith — in myself, in fate, in the universe?

What is the lesson from past lives? Is this the latest or am I mid-stream, should I go into the future?

What is my purpose? What lesson is there this time, what do I need to learn?

How do I go deeper and find the way? Do I need a guide?

Until I am on the right path? What happens?

Desire, belief and expectancy, a return to faith, but whose?

Restless, unfettered, polemic.

Words pour out like corruption, loosening tongues and ideas.

Resilience stirred and vomited.

Darkness deep and long.

Breathing While Drowning

> *Draw it out, give it back, Michael and me, please take it.*
>
> *Is this some of the pain along the way?*
>
> *I need space, time, green, water, earth, grounding.*
>
> *Resilience, patience, calm, peace. Leave the pain behind, the dissatisfaction needs action.*

Explore past lives? What? I kept getting this message when I meditated. I approached my friend Ronnie, and I asked her to help. She's also been heading down the road to get closer to her intuitive self for quite some time—longer than I have. We sit quietly, relaxing, and she guides me to recall a past life.

> *Firstly, south-east corner of Ireland I think. 1500–1600's maybe. Village in a valley with mountains, lots of green, emerald not eucalypt, but some rocks, cottage? Wattle and daub and partly into the rock, small doors and step down into the inside. She (Heather) is initially outside, long dark hair, slightly curly, some red glints, green eyes, pale face.*
>
> *Hair a little messy but loose.*
>
> *Gown feels coarse but clean, dark colour maybe navy or brown. Shoes hide/leather, woollen stocking.*
>
> *Hands small and efficient, nails short, skin rough but clean.*
>
> *Easy smile, comfortable in her own skin, calm, knowing, patient.*

Garden is all things, stones between "beds" colours and fragrances.

Its Spring and warm. Into the "herb" room which is on the right hand side of the house, windows important although there is a cool room not a cellar that is dug out of the hill.

There is a table, scrubbed but dark with stains and a high stool with 3 legs made by her Dad. Flowers carved into the underside?

One cupboard on the wall with 2 doors, pride of place because it has a lock, the key is on her belt, a leather belt, twisted of thin leather in an intricate pattern. Also has a small purse. Pots on window sill, a bit messy with lots of stuff here and there.

The cupboard is carved, also a gift from her father.

Her dress is blue, underskirt shirt is white, or an off-white, linen type.

Smell is warm and comfortable, earthy and rich with all the herbal fragrances.

She smells like lavender.

The house is a few generations old, a little saggy, small upstairs bedrooms.

Her daughter (Jacqui) has green eyes and dark hair, probs about the same as our Jacq.

Fine boned even as a youngster and remains slight when she is older. Full of enthusiasm as a child but very sure of herself and knows she is loved.

Breathing While Drowning

Dotes on her father, worries that he works too hard. Is in league with her mother to care for him. Likes to mess about in the dirt and herbs.

Follow her mother into the "business".

Calm and confident as a grown woman. Only saw her with 1 child, Frazer with slightly fairer hair and knowing green eyes.

Back to the story. Heather goes inside unlocks the cupboard and gets out a book, leather bound with thick pages, a diary and herb note book.

She sits at the table and opens to a half written entry. She re-read

'To my future self'. I know you will need to read this.

Ron asks me, "What does she want you to know?"

She wants to tell me that I can't take on everyone's burdens and pain. They have to carry it themselves. I carry it too deeply, it cuts me, I need to give it back so that they can learn from it and so can I.

Ron also asks me to ask her how she manages. She laughs and takes me outside to look at the garden. I bury them. I dig a little hole, mentally put the worries and pain in and plant a seed. Then I cover them and let the growing plant use the positive energy I leave with the worry.

I can do that.

She begins to show me around the village, grabbing a basket of flowers and produce.

We pass the smithy, and as she waves to the man, she tells me she is a midwife and delivered the smith's son.

We start up the street towards the rest of the village which is quite small but then I am leaving her. She turns and smiles and walks on.

Now I am old and I am still she. I am in a rocking chair, by the fire even though it is a sunny day.

Jacqui comes in with the young boy with Frazer's eyes. She tucks the blanket tighter around my legs, smooth back my hair and kissed my forehead.

She is a beautiful young woman, peace and calm shine out. She gathers up a basket and heads out the door, calling to Connor to say goodbye.

He is very solemn and comes over to the chair. He quietly pats my hand and says "It's OK Nan, it's nearly time." My heart is bursting with joy and Jacqui looks back as I pass on.

I am back with the diva, whose love and light surrounds me, comforting, healing. We are among the stars, particles in a crowded universe, drawing energy from the source.

We are zooming east towards the Americas; I want to say south but that brings the wrong memories.

I can see clearly now the rain is gone. I can see all obstacles in my way. Gone are the bad times, the past is gone. It's gonna be a bright, bright, bright, sun shiny day. (thank you Kenny Gamble and Leon Huff)

Breathing While Drowning

This was a truly wonderful experience, it helped me see things about myself that I couldn't see before. I asked for help, and I received it. The visit to Heather in a past life was a little scary, but it was comforting ultimately. Strangely, I had always liked the name *Heather,* and I almost called one of my girls by that name. The experience connected me to all the women who culminated in me: mothers and wives and daughters and sisters, centuries of life and experience and lessons learned to share with me. I thought about all my ancestors and the lines of DNA marching across centuries and continents. I could feel their love, their lives standing behind me, standing beside me. I thought I was alone, but if I had just looked beside me, I would have seen a woman ready to hold my hand. If I looked behind me, there was a woman ready to give me her strength. And now, when I open my eyes, there is a woman in front of me with whom I can share my experience. Also, there is a woman on my other side who needs comfort from me. *I wasn't alone.*

I meditated with stream of consciousness or channelled writing to ask my higher self what the plan was, what I should do, who I should become.

> What is your vision for your purpose in life?
>
> Write, I must write. Join the words translate the meaning share the ideas lead change NFPs WOB wisdom and learning. Strength in family.
>
> What do I have to become in order for this purpose to manifest?
>
> Independent, Silva Instructor, Writer
>
> What must I let go of or release in order to fulfil my purpose?
>
> Guilt, hurt, anger, loneliness, mistrust, power, money, status, sadness, order.

> What must I embrace?
> Trust, love, wisdom, family.
> Cassi, Frazer, Angus, Ian, MJ, Ron.
> Health, fitness, alternatives, openness, learning, technology and comms, global awareness, seek others. Start in past.
> Is there anything else I need to know?
> Past and future selves, you are a whole person, re-join the lives. Stop coffee, drink water. Relax and laugh more. Allow myself to be loved.

I encountered lots of exploration and lots of new ways of being curious. I was listening to my intuition very intently and working on my joy. And I stopped drinking coffee!

> Heaven help my heart. It would be good to wake up and my first thought <u>not</u> be about work. So here goes.
> I desire to get reconnected to my family, to know I'm loved and love them in return.
> The work thing will take care of itself because I have put all the foundations in place and I have others to help.
> I will be writing part time at the end of this year. Take a full day a week to write and the beginning of next year. I will start re-prioritising both work and home.

> *I will get myself fitter than before so my health and wellbeing are optimal.*
>
> *I believe in the power of the written word.*
>
> *The written word actualises the idea, the feeling, the action.*
>
> *I will start learning Japanese with Frazer in mind.*
>
> *I expect we will thrive and grow — burgeoning.*
>
> *Increase the vocabulary. The ICS feels good, is this the avenue?*
>
> *I have all the right skills to make a difference here. Silva instruction.*

The amazing thing that continues to delight me—though it no longer surprises me—is that that's how thinking and planning works. Whether you call it *manifesting* or *strategic planning*, it works. In *Wired for Life*, Martina Sheehan and Susan Pearce call it a tool for a lazy brain.[11] They say, "Once you have a plan in mind, your brain is designed to follow this path. The process of planning is like visualisation. By picturing the steps in your mind, you are wiring up the brain in the same way as if you were actually taking those steps".[12]

Lazy or not, my brain loves planning and loves learning, which makes it the perfect combination. I can still hear my mum saying "Practice makes perfect," and it does. "Your brain is learning the plan, and when the time comes to implement it, the steps come more naturally than if you had never considered the situation before".[13]

If you practice the visualisation or look at that plan, that list over and over, it's going to become more and more natural when you need to act. You'll begin to see the way forward more easily, your brain will recognise the patterns, and the opportunities will present themselves to you.

Time to write.

Research a storyline, characters, plot, find an environment and context with the lot!

Make them weep and laugh out loud.

Draw them in amongst the crowd of people and place they learn to love. Something, something, the wings of a dove!

Seriously,

Maybe the menopause turns off the firewall and the heat that begins to escape is an untapped energy source.

Flushes till 75 is a bit tragic.

Write about a joining of lives as chapters in the Book of a Life.

Research past lives and my future self, kundalini and the 7 chakras. Is it time to read "Sacred Contracts'?

Today I chose family over $. Instead of stopping for a Tattslotto ticket I managed to catch the earlier train.

Small steps.

Tonight it's time to remember my dreams and write them down.

'The several lives of Jessie Campbell'. Not sure who she is, perhaps we've yet to meet, perhaps she's me or a name to use in the book.

Breathing While Drowning

> As they are excluding fingerprints in the "missing family" scenario, the database reveals she has someone else's fingerprints, a much younger woman who appears to have no past, who appeared unexpectedly a couple of years ago.

When I reread this it seemed to echo my real life. At this point, I have had many lives, and I'm appearing unexpectedly in my own life as someone new—a much younger woman who left her dreams behind in a different life.

> What do I fear, why so tight and overwhelming?
> Is it loss of control, is it admission that I should have called it earlier? What is this lesson I need to learn? What choices, what decision? Can't save everyone or you have to try harder.
> What does this mirror? In me? What brings her to that point? Why so angry, I am just the most recent to hit the books, she was angry before I came. There are no controls, there needs to be.
> The choice I make is to try to interact with love and grace. It is not OK to take out your frustration on others, it is not OK to blame others for your mistakes. It's not OK to not own up to your errors.

As I become more conscious of my real *self*, it seems to spark opportunities for me to behave differently; people and experiences challenge me to stay true to my values, to live the ethical, joyful, learning, and loving life I want.

Monday 30th July 2012

>Place, room, landscape
>
>Forest of grey steel towers, hum of electricity conducting the lifeblood of the city. The extra sizzle of drizzle on hot wires, puddles pooled sporadically on grey concrete. Skies grey and leaden with clouds.
>
>Time of day, weather city/country, inside/outside, hot/cold, pleasant/not, what can be heard, seen or smelled? Now some person enters this scene: furtively, violently casually, accidently.
>
>Its early morning, whispers of light tickling across the soggy landscape. After days of rain the ground is saturated, the sunlight gently warms the puddles which softly mist in the chill morning air. The stillness and quiet is broken by the first warbling call of the magpie, greeting the new day.
>
>The echo falls softly, a pause, then the chorus begins, joyous, welcoming.
>
>Snug under the doona, she watches the awakening, the daylight stirring the tension in her gut, butterflies churning.

I'd been a long time, years, writing in the third person about business and health, and other worldly matters. I felt as if I would take just as long to learn to write "not" in the third person. Every snippet helps me to see the world or the world of my imagination a little clearer, a little brighter.

Friday 3rd August 2012

Halleluiah

> The possibilities are endless. Joy and learning, the release of tension, regret, guilt, negativity. Reach for abundance, learning, freedom to express and grow. Reach for the power of the written word, life, friends, family, country, fresh air.
>
> Sharp winter air frosting every breath. Deeply inhale the cleansing cold. In with the good out with the bad. The judging cold, the weak die, the strong live to fight another day.

And some days it all comes together. I can feel the joy brimming over. I remember Marguerite telling me around this time that it looked like I was fizzing over around the edges, that my energy was bright and bubbling.

Sunday 12th August 2012

> What is my purpose in life? This life?
> Writing, travel, outdoors, green, healing, quiet solitude, TEDx women, shooting stars.

> Sunrise silhouette light in a dark place, caduceus, heart, healing, Gaia.
> Loneliness, frustration, anger, heart, city.
> Vegetables, nature, land, grounded, water.
> Travel, snow
> Spiritual healing, raise vibration of chakras
> Look outside the game
> Resilience and strength
> 'A strong woman has faith that she is strong enough for the journey — but a woman of strength has faith that it is in the journey that she will become strong.'

That last quote is part of a longer poem, "Woman of Strength" by an anonymous author. Those words are the directions to my journey. I was changing from being a strong woman: one who could swallow grief and take a respected place in a man's business world. I was becoming more convinced that the journey was the thing, that the lessons will make me strong if I look and learn and change.

Tuesday 28th August 2012

> Grateful
> I am so grateful and thankful for the opportunity to be the boss, to put into practice all the things I've learned or seen over the years.
> I am so grateful and thankful for the gift of resilience, for the loyalty of family and friends.

> I am so grateful for the unconditional love of a good man, my best friend.
>
> I am so grateful and thankful for the gift of my children, Cassi, Jacqui, Angus and Frazer. Each brings love and joy and wonder.
>
> I am so grateful and thankful for good friends, good wine and good food.
>
> I am so grateful and thankful for this opportunity to change a young man's life.
>
> I am so grateful and thankful for individual thinkers.

Tuesday 25th September 2012

> I am so grateful and thankful to feel this sense of disappointment. This reinforces that I am in the wrong job, searching for the wrong balance. I do not want to be here and today I begin my exit strategy. Thanks!!!

Practicing gratitude makes an incredible difference in my life. I have so many things to be grateful for, and so many things that bring me joy. The negative is still there, but there is a greater sense of balance. It's much easier to remind myself of what I have and to step out of the ocean.

Both Silva and Christie Marie Sheldon introduced me to many more life-transforming concepts. I had plenty to occupy my mind, but the feeling was still missing.

My heart was very hard to crack. I'd kept it armoured in stone for a long time. I was pretty much closed for business from the neck down. I was thinking long and hard, but I was just beginning to feel joy. And I was a long way from working out what my purpose was, what the point of my existence was.

The Urgent Yearning to Connect to the Feminine

Murdock talks about this stage in *The Heroine's Journey*: "When a woman has made the descent and severed her identity as a spiritual daughter of the patriarchy, there is an urgent yearning to connect with the feminine […] there is a desire to develop those parts of herself that have gone underground while on the heroic quest: her body, her emotions, her spirit, her creative wisdom"[14].

For me, the search began in earnest. There's a whole other me in here screaming to get out … or maybe screaming to get help. I had almost no connection to the feminine, and I was way too emotional and out of control. I could not see any power at all in the feminine, and power was something I really needed—or so I thought. After all, that's how the world (of men and business) works. I had been taught (indoctrinated, really) that it's all about power.

Marianne Williamson stated, "Feminine power isn't something we go out and acquire; it's already within us. It's something we become willing to experience. Something to admit we have." And while searching for somewhere for myself and my friends to do some personal transformation research, I came across The Spirit of Women Retreat. The retreat offers a "great opening for releasing blockages and gaining personal strength and happiness […] a fantastic healing journey which will rebuild your self-esteem and empower you to take control of your own life".[15]

Hooley dooley! What a great opening! This was my first all-women retreat, and before I even got in the door, I wanted to leave. They all wanted to hug me! These strange (now I say open and friendly) women looked like they had never stepped foot in the corporate sector or done a multimillion dollar deal (so I immediately assumed they were not like me). Therefore, I assumed they wouldn't understand me—I was special: scarred and hurt. I felt like a fish out of water.

Although I'd looked forward to this time with my good friends, I had worked like crazy all the way up to the moment I left, and I was exhausted. Consequently, my tolerance was paper thin. As soon as they tried to touch me, I walled up, and shut down.

A fun few days of massage and good food was what I thought I was going for, but all these strange women trying to hug me before I had even got in the door threw me off completely. I had never been to a women's retreat before, and for the first few days, I thought I never would again.

What got me through? Curiosity got me there, and courage kept me there. It was time to take the lid off, to let myself feel again. Focusing on gratitude stilled my panic a bit.

The exploration was planned around four elements: air, earth, water, and fire, and all the exercises, discussions, food, and activities supported the element of the day. It became easy to get swept up in the flow, though I found it strange and overwhelming for the most part.

This was a big week for me. There were a lot of tears, lots of laughter, lots of great food, and some amazing walks in the beautiful Queensland hinterland.

I discovered this huge well of grief and emotion, and I began to understand how disconnected from myself I was, disconnected from the woman I am, from the world of feeling.

Wednesday 31st October 2012

I am so grateful and thankful that I am here. I don't know what it will bring but I am here.

What happened to that intelligent, articulate woman?

Tongue cloven to the roof of my mouth, discomfort in mind and heart, panic and pain.

Turn it up, what is this about? Why now, why this? What is there to learn? Learn by listening. Leave my stuff alone. Give me space, let me discover myself, myself!

Don't face me down the road to the journey you think I need to make.

This is not where I want to be either. Keep looking, keep listening, manifest happy, challenged not content, not comfortable, never that. Thanks, keep looking.

What kept me there was friendship, the love and courage of two evolutionary friends. Ronnie and Marguerite were right beside me, urging me on, supporting me, having their own epiphanies. These are two of the bravest people I know, prepared to go where no one has gone before—even into the unknown future as friends.

Sometimes, especially in the early days, they were mighty warriors, battling the incredibly high and deep and wide wall I had around my heart. They battled on and still do. I am so very, very grateful for their friendship and love.

Thursday 1st November 2012

Better day, time on my own. A run in my own space, feeling slightly less crowded. Had some short times to be on my own or with my buds.

Astrology reading was good, a reminder of what are the diverse parts of "me".

Crazy lady mud bath was little weird out OK.

So much sharing is killing me though. Sometimes it's OK to not share!

Spoke to everyone except Cassi tonight, Angus about to start his exams tomorrow. Frazer bored at school, Cassi and Ian busy.

Nice to hear their voices, nice to speak sensibly.

A couple of days in after a silent walking meditation and a big hug-a-thon I sensed the floodgates were about to open. This was one of those epiphanic moments, and I was panicking. I kept repeating this mantra to myself. "Shut the gate, keep me safe" over and over and over. But it wasn't working. Every time my mind relaxed I realised the "shut" the gate, keep me safe had changed to "open" the gate, keep me safe. I kept having to change it back. Then, there was the moment, I could hear my heart beating loud in my ears, I knew this was a turning point, and I allowed myself to hope, could I be safe with the gate open. Was I brave enough to breach this dam?

Then I experienced a kahuna massage, which changed my life forever. The kahuna energy worker messed with my carefully placed walls, and the gate burst open.

Once the dam was released, there was no holding it back. It poured out in a flood of emotion.

Friday 2nd November 2012

I should recognise panic and fear when it gets a hold of me. Shut the gate, keep me safe — what bullshit — open the gate, keep me safe golden goddess.

After the kahuna massage where my intention was to meet my higher self I did!

I am a dark and terrible goddess, stars on my brow. River of black hair, eyes of amethyst. Flowing robes of night struck with silver trails. I have a two handed sword to smite untruths and sever chains. I have a cup, a chalice with abundance that is mine to sip and to offer, which I do to all who come. My aura is purple. I need to do battle for those that can't. I exist in the stars and now I exist in me. My wings are large and black. I protect the earth and care for its mind.

I have another guide, an Aboriginal elder, not sure which mob but she is wise, her hair white, her eyes knowing. Raphael opened the tool box and gave me the key to the gate.

Without hesitation I went through. The other side of the gate is no different yet it is so different.

The pain was not worse on the other side.

Jacqui is Frazer, but Frazer is himself, he carries her soul and has become a new child to try that lesson again. I need to nurture the spiritual in all my children and my husband, put their feet on the path.

> Angus is a teacher, a healer, a light to the world. Cassi is a vision, a teacher, a radical, a channel. Ian is a healer, a homemaker.
>
> This dark and terrible goddess needs to brush her teeth.

During the kahuna massage, I sobbed and cried like a baby. I saw clear visions and felt twenty years of pain open up and threaten to drown me all over again. But I also saw myself as Rhiannon, a strong and terrible warrior with a sword, ready to smite the unjust and protect the innocent. I was held tenderly and safely, and I felt myself opening up to possibility. I didn't know what this meant, only that it was different from anything else I had ever experienced.

Kahuna is deep energy massage where the masseuse focuses on the emotional and spiritual effect of massage therapy and follows the Huna philosophy for healing and relaxation.

The retreat was one of a kind, and the leaders were so right when they quoted Sorensen and said, "Memories of this retreat will last a life-time and be a warm companion to you always".[16]

It was a defining moment for me, but rather than dipping one toe into the transformation water, I dove head first into the deep end. That's the story of my life: I go where angels fear to tread.

Saturday 3rd November 2012

> A much better day again. Water and lots of emotions. Spent time thinking about Mum and Dad and running through all the emotions around then. Still carried some anger about their deaths, more Mum than Dad I guess.

> *Let it go.*
>
> *Walked with Ron, drank liquid breaky and lunch.*
>
> *More massaging, this one a duo which was good but not as good as the Kahuna. More dancing and SWB. A small skit for our room of "love". We did a circle which was the Beatles "All you need is love". Let in the fire and let go of a stack of things. Time to get fired up, excited and expectant.*

I'd never had the chance to listen to other adult women express their dreams, dramas, hopes, and highs (as well as their pain, their disappointments, and their losses). I'd spent so long in the patriarchy where that sort of thing was not encouraged or tolerated. No time. Have to get things done. The discussion began to connect me to the rest of humanity—and more significantly, to the half of the world's population that were women. There were other people out there who'd suffered as much as I had, and some had lives that were just as messed up as mine. It was a revelation.

What still held me back a bit, however, was that there were very few women from the corporate sector. It was almost as if it was okay for them—they were kind of hippie-leaning folks who were more spiritually advanced. This is where I began to realise I believed the story that business women don't care and spiritual women don't wear suits. This story continued to dog my personal spiritual journey for a few more years, but it helped me find a direction and a purpose. To help others from the corporate sector find the feeling, allow the healing, and reconnect to their spirit.

It's not true, of course. What I've found is that the language is a little different, but when you get under the surface, we're all searching for meaning and love and a life that we dream of. Business women are spiritual, but sometimes they need permission to express themselves or ask for guidance.

Thursday 29th November 2012

> A breath of writing
> You know
> In your heart
> It will be
> Alright
> In the long run
> I only want
> If I could start
> Today again
> Please give me back today
>
> Disrespect
> One lousy hour
> Prayers in vain
> Start today again.
>
> Feels constrained, under pressure, racing to the finish line, thought and in the few seconds thinking of the line and then writing. Feels stilted and uncomfortable.

Not all days are good days. Sometimes all I can see is the ocean and the threat of drowning.

I bought Christie Marie Sheldon's *Unlimited Abundance*[17], in January of 2013. This seemed a bit on the edge in terms of evidence, but because it was about finances, it seemed like tangible stuff. It offered an energetic way to approach a rational and logical thing.

Sheldon has a great practice that I love and still use today to manifest in the moment. Ask yourself the following question: *What would it take?*

Wednesday 20th March 2013

What would it take for me to live authentically as my ideal future self?

My future self has an abundant life. I spend time with clever people, with people who are self-aware, people who think deeply and differently.

I want to write beautiful books, books that inspire and inform, books that delight and enquire.

I want to make a difference in lives.

I want to be loved by me more or properly, unconditionally.

I want to be a great mother, a great wife, a great lover, a great friend.

I want to be healthy, wealthy and wise.

I want to help women and men to be more authentically themselves. To think about themselves deeply and have a chance to vibrate at a higher rate.

I want to make connections. I want to give people peace, or help them find it.

I want to lead, I want to share knowledge and wisdom, I want to love, I want to relax, I want to make money, lots of it, easily.

Breathing While Drowning

> *I want to work in the garden, I want to work with words, I want to travel, I want to eat well. I want to help women who are tired like me.*
>
> *I'd like women to get inspiration, relaxation, renewal.*
>
> *I'd like parents to get revitalised.*
>
> *I'd like kids to feel the earth and the plants.*
>
> *I'd like to touch people, nourish them body, mind and soul.*

With Sheldon's *Unlimited Abundance* I discovered stories about my relationship with money that had been holding me back from free-flowing financial abundance. I found out about unconscious beliefs that sabotaged my effort to change my behaviour and my life. Busy, busy, busy; work hard; struggle; do everything for others. Rich people are mean, so don't get rich or you'll get mean. You don't deserve ease; you don't deserve abundance; you don't deserve your dreams.

I realised that, even though the dam was breached, I still had a long way to go.

The lessons I learned about myself and the world that I realised then—and that I realise now—mean a lot of different things.

Nobody judges us more harshly than ourselves, we are our own best critic but we are also the world, in fact, the universal expert on ourselves.

Lesson – let go of perfection and live now with every beautiful perfect imperfection that you are. I'm practicing self-compassion which is not so easy for me with years of beating myself up over every little transgression and failing. Most importantly, despite advice from others, I need to decide what to do, I need to decide who to be. And you know what? I'm pretty damn perfect, just the way I am.

Gratitude is a life changer.

Lesson – gratitude is surrendering to the joy of who and where and what you are, rejoicing in the every marvellous or mundane moment, every morsel, every magical memory. "Thank you" it is so worth doing and living. Gratitude raises those vibrations and opens you to the possibility of emotions of an even higher power like love. In the end, it's all about love.

It's never too late to start afresh

Lesson – No matter where you are in life, it's never too late to try again, to do or feel or think or be something different. We live with change in so many ways every day. We can look at the past but don't stare at it. Leave it there, look to the future and live in the now. You get a new chance every moment to make a different choice. Let go of regret and get on with it. It's your life to live, so live it.

It's amazing what you can do if you believe in yourself, your values, your purpose, and your dream.

Lesson: the first thing to do is get those dreams out, dust them off, and hang them on a wall where you can see them every day. Take a small step, focus on any small wins, and feel yourself getting closer. It really works. Our brains love repetition and patterns; make life the pattern you want.

Joseph Campbell said, "Follow your bliss and the universe will open doors where before there were walls."

Breathing While Drowning

Lesson: sounds like more of the same, but this is about realising that we are all connected to all things. Anita Moorjani had a great way of putting it: it's as though, for most of us, we only have a torch and are shining it into what we think is a dark room. We can only see a little way in front, behind, or around us. We imagine our world and our chances are small (what we can see). But the universe is a humungous warehouse. If we could only turn on all the lights for a moment, we could see acres of opportunities and how connected we are to all of them, how close they are. Let go of the walls, which are only there because we put them there, and our lives will become unlimited. In short, the warehouse goes on forever.[18]

Chapter 8

Coming Home

What else do I need to rediscover? What else is missing?

Healing the Mother–Daughter Split

Murdock said, "If a woman has spent many years fine-tuning her intellect and her command of the material world while ignoring the subtleties of her bodily knowings, she may now be reminded that the body and spirit are one. If she has ignored her emotions while serving the needs of her family or community, she may now slowly begin to reclaim how she feels as a woman".[1]

And so it was with me: over the next few years, I slowly began to reclaim how I felt as a woman.

If The Spirit of Woman Retreat opened the floodgates, then The Art of Feminine Presence blasted them out of existence. It was like I'd been in a very dark room, and then a floodlight came on so that every little corner and crevice was exposed. At first, as usual, I resisted, kept my eyes closed, and shouted that it wasn't for me. And then I began to realise I'd been almost dead below the neck for so long. Keeping all the grief inside, keeping myself from the really bad feelings—these things had kept me from the really good feelings as well, kept me from feeling like the woman I was.

Breathing While Drowning

When I read that last sentence silently, it made me pause. It feels almost like a betrayal. Is it really true, or is it a gross exaggeration? Do I have the literary licence to make such a claim? What about all the brilliant times I had with my family and friends over the last twenty years? Who was that laughing and loving and crying? It was me, and the times were brilliant, but I realise now it wasn't all of me. I had locked away the part that kept the grief at bay, the part that kept me going for the sake of Strack and my children. I had learned to live missing that part, that deep emotional connection to the woman I am.

It was as if life had been a pale watercolour up until that point. It was still beautiful, still colourful. But then I discovered oils, and the colours became vibrant and vivacious and vital, not just a representation—fully alive, out of the ocean and whole.

Rachael Jayne Groover is an Australian woman who created The Art of Feminine Presence. Overcoming stage fright and an enormous fear of rejection, she became an award-winning vocalist. She finished her full-time singing career performing to a live audience of forty thousand people before making the leap to live in the USA where she became an inspirational speaker and personal development trainer.

She began to realise it was presence that made the difference—not just being present in the moment (although that helps), but being aware and living as the powerful and feminine being that she was. Groover created a series of practices that help put us back in touch with the women we are, and she shared them through classes and through her book, *Powerful and Feminine: How to increase your magnetic presence and attract the attention you want.*[2] In that book, she stated, "When a woman embodies her feminine essence, her whole life is transformed. She becomes attractive, grounded and sensual. When she walks into a room, everyone appreciates the glow of her feminine radiance. She does not need to project a powerful persona to attract the respect she wants."[3]

Initially, it was the idea of power and respect that attracted me—the feminine bit was kind of "out there." I worked with powerful people all the time; they ran large organisations and commanded teams to change the world, and I thought that was what I wanted. But the respect seemed elusive. I was sick of being ignored because I was a woman. My opinion mattered, and I wanted recognition for my work, my over-and-above contribution. I'd begun to see younger men promoted to senior roles that they were not equipped or experienced enough to be in. In the meantime, more skilled women were passed over. Sometimes, the women didn't even apply for the jobs, meekly playing second fiddle because they felt they weren't good enough.

My introduction to Groover's work in December of 2012 turned out to be another weekend of just women. For me, being in a room with so many women for three days was really scary. So many of these women were expressing the need to reconnect to the feminine. *What the hell does that mean anyway?* Was it all goddesses, dreadlocks, cheesecloth, chanting about menstruation, and dancing naked under the moon? I wanted to run from the room whenever a new woman arrived. And that's when I realised that I was the odd one out *again*.

I have this thing I do where I jump without thinking. The emotion makes me say *yes* before I've properly looked at what I'm signing up for. And then, when logic takes over, I find myself in situations that make my skin crawl.

Is that the lesson I have to learn in this lifetime? But hey, listening to my intuition and throwing myself headlong into the next adventure has provided me with a whole lot of fun and learning … and some great stories. I wouldn't trade it for the world. Feel the fear and do it anyway.

So here I am at this weekend full of women, and here I stay, but I'm resisting it with all my energy. There were a lot of women who were splashing emotions and energy and revealing their innermost longings and secrets all over the place. It seemed to be a room filled with 90 per cent extroverts, which was not my cup of tea. It was a room full of women who had been on this personal transformation journey for quite a while. Some appeared to be professional workshop attendees. And they still didn't have their shit together. That's what I had come for, learning and answers—not more questions!

Breathing While Drowning

I'd also persuaded another good friend and business colleague, Lesley, to come because it seemed I could use whatever Groover was promoting in business. And although I was right—it was eminently suitable for business—we both wanted to go home after the first session. It's scary out there for women who have lived in their heads and survived by being tough and hard and closed off. That's what it takes in the world of work—or that's the way I'd learned to survive anyway. I didn't have the language to speak to these women, so I felt insufficient, not enough. I began to feel as if I had no place in the world. I didn't fit into the corporate jungle, and I didn't fit into the powerful feminine circle.

Take a breath. I can still feel some of the anger and frustration bubbling up years later.

I think the first afternoon of the three-day workshop started at 2:00 p.m., and by 4:00 p.m. I wanted to leave. Seriously, I was ready to go home. But two things stopped me: the first was that my good friends Ronnie and Marguerite knew this was what we all needed – are you seeing a pattern here? The second was the woman running the workshop, Rachael Jayne Groover. There was just something about her, something undefinable, a beautiful and loving energy that was hard to ignore. And her promise that she could teach this undefinable thing that she had to me was compelling. No cheesecloth, no dancing naked under the moon, just simple practices I could do myself to change my life. I believed her.

My main problem with staying was that the room had a few women who made me very, very uncomfortable. I had lived in the male yang world of business and management for so long that I had clamped down firmly on my female nature., I felt like I was in a foreign land, a land where people were really comfortable with their femininity. It took several glasses of red wine the first night (contrary to the workshop rules, I might add) to keep me there with help from my two evolutionary friends, Ronnie and Marguerite. Lesley and I were persuaded to give it another day.

I love men. I love their thinking; I love their strength; I love their ambition; I love their voices, I love their drive; I love their ability to lead, and I love their bodies—especially their butts.

It's taken me a while to learn that women also have depths and breadths that I could never have imagined. We are so complex and imperfect and complete. I love women. Writer Keele Burgin expressed what I love about women beautifully in a letter she wrote to a struggling women's circle: "I love women. I love big women, small women, women who refuse me (it is just temporary) and women who embrace me.

"I love the ones who are dressed up, dressed down and I love the ones that have found their perfect style and wear it with unconscious grace, whether they are at the grocery or at The Met.

"I love their fears, their accomplishments, their wit and their hiding.

"I love how women celebrate.

"Women have carried me, taught me, nursed me and pulled me through the world when I wanted out. They have held my hand when I was afraid of touch and taught me that I would die without it.

"I always look in their eyes, that is where I learn the most. Women can tell a story by saying hello in passing.

"I want the layers, the pain, the candor and the unknown".[4]

In reality, this was a gentle introduction to the world of energy. The problem was that I was so far away from it that it felt like I was on the yellow brick road going to Oz.

There were a few women who were completely over the top (in my view). They claimed to be having experiences I thought only possible on illicit drugs, it didn't feel authentic or real. I had no language to converse with them, and I often declined to offer a comment when they waxed lyrical and spiritual about what they saw and felt. I was sure they were making stuff up. I was feeling confused, closed, and determined to get out in one piece with my sanity and without giving in to the woowoo ideologies.

What I found, not immediately (because I fought like crazy for this not to happen), but gradually, was that there was a little trickle of awareness, a little glimpse of connection to something I never even realised was there.

What helped was that Rachael Jayne Groover was not what I expected in a spiritual transformation leader, she was stylish, confident, and could easily have passed as an executive in any corporate environment. It was not just the clothes; it was her sense of self-confidence that I was attracted to. This was something I wanted for myself. Chuck out all the insecurities and be the woman I wanted to be. Little did I know that this was just the door opener; in fact, the most valuable learning experience dealt with the feminine connection to the self.

Many of the practices could be done with little or no awareness of people around you. You could get in contact and stay in touch with your inner feminine. They explored the continuum of masculine and feminine, and I began to create some awareness. Groover spoke about the *womb space,* which she called the feminine energy centre and a way to *come home.*

The first image for *home* that popped into my head was a woman curled in the foetal position, tucked into a nut shell. It was me: totally focused inside, totally ignoring everything outside, totally protected from the world, impervious to all the bad and good things in the universe. I realised this was the young woman I had left behind in her innocence so many years ago. It was a younger me, shut off from a world of hurt and pain. This was not something I wanted to share with a group of women I hardly knew. I felt I would look like such a failure in this setting—after all, business women don't care!

After the initial weekend, I read Groover's book, began some of the practices, and started to notice changes in myself and in the world around me. Ronnie and Marguerite and I felt like we were really on to something, and we supported each other by discussing, reflecting on, and practicing Groover's ideas.

Most of all, I was happier. I was discovering joy and realising I had the power to change my life for the better, to change who I was, and to live how I wanted to live. I could do what I wanted to do and be who I wanted to be. I attended another weekend intensive twelve months later, and it was a completely different woman who walked into the room.

Having released my head to new possibilities and opened my energy through the kahuna, I began to work on my body, finding healing for the deep and wonderful feminine that I had shelved for so many years.

In my heroine's journey, this is the quest to heal the mother–daughter split, the split from your feminine nature. Murdock explained that she "developed the heroic qualities that society has defined as male [...] developed those skills of discrimination, logical thinking and follow through that serve me well in the outer world".[5]

Me too. The split is more than this, though. Her words were so clearly a narration of my own life: "We have separated from our feelings and our spiritual natures. We are lonely for deep connection. We yearn for affiliation and community, for the positive strong nurturing qualities of the feminine that have been missing from this culture".[6]

And here I am. I made the descent and have been scraped raw over and over, and begun returning through the feminine and trying to heal. Murdock stated, "When an individual or a society becomes too one-sided, too separated from the depth and truth of human experience, something in the psyche rises up and moves to restore authenticity. Breakdown momentarily sets life free from demands of ordinary reality and activates a profound spiritual process, an inner rite of passage with its own healing end".[7]

The Art of Feminine Presence work reconnected me to the power of the feminine. I realised that the feeling of being a second-class citizen worked only if I believed it and listened to the perceptions of others. So I worked on myself, I learned more about the practices, and I allowed myself to surrender to the powerful feminine woman I am:

sensual, warm-hearted, wise, wild, funny, creative, compassionate, courageous, and confident.

Other people started to notice the difference in how I was showing up in the world. They noticed I was changed—happier and fuller.

For me, this was touching the rainbow and finding that, even if it is painful, it's feeling, and that's better than not feeling. Wake up and smell the roses; you have children who love you and a man who is hurting and wanting to heal as much as you.

The words that kept resonating were those I heard from Christie Marie Sheldon when I began my exploration and transformation. Think about looking after yourself as if you were in an aeroplane emergency. You need to put your own oxygen mask on to help yourself before you can help anyone else with theirs. I need to find and be myself before I help others. What happens is that, as you begin to live the truth of who you are, you encourage others and give them permission to do the same.

I'm so grateful for Strack's support on the journey, for waving me off on each new adventure, for being there when I got back, for trying stuff and coping with loving me in all my evolutions.

I'm grateful for Cassi and Angus and Frazer for the same thing. As every onion layer came off and I shared where I was, they listened patiently, mostly while I unloaded and tried to inspire them to love me in all my glorious imperfection.

With each discovery, there would be pangs of guilt and shame. How could I let this go on for so long? How could I have avoided truly living? Each time I had to forgive myself, I had to remind myself that I was only human. Now there's the rub: only human, yes—but you're a woman, and you're trying to lead in a man's world. You're trying to play them at their own game. So you need to be better, bigger, faster, and smarter *in addition to being* a good mother, wife, daughter, and friend. I had wanted it all, but now I was not so sure. All those spiritual texts seemed to want me to leave the big, bad business world behind and that the only way to salvation was through following their way.

But I wanted to play in the game because I loved the game. Of course, I also hated the game. What I wanted was a different set of rules.

In early 2013, after several meetings and a very helpful marketing and planning session from my niece, Erin, Ronnie Z, Marguerite, and I founded The True Bliss Company.[8] Our vision is to be bold, fun, inspired, and authentic. We want to give people, especially women, the chance to try out personal transformation stuff without the trauma and drama that we'd experienced.

Although there's a place for major upheavals and insights in personal transformation, we'll leave that to others. We believe there's also a place for a gentler and more entertaining introduction to changing your life. We figured that we wanted to share what we had learned and to give others an opportunity in a safe and fun environment.

We had some help from Rosemary Maris, who challenged us to be practical and pragmatic as well as inspirational. She convinced us to put down our goals and plans on paper.

Friday 5th April 2013

What is it you see as the future of what we are doing now?

I am creating a place of healing, a beacon of light, a doorway. A retreat/resort where people can come to find a way to the divine within themselves.

Not everything will run from the retreat location. The "sense of self" and various courses, parts, elements can be mobile, available to travel. I will have sessions, workshops, weekends.

Breathing While Drowning

Every time we get together, it just feels right. It rarely feels like work; fun and unconventionality is in good supply. We spent a delightful couple of hours sitting in the sun at the Barwon Heads Airport creating our business vision and goals while Strack enjoyed a flight in a Tiger Moth.

We consciously worked to keep our friendship first, and so we planned and made our early gatherings as honest and simple as possible, which was a little challenging considering our different backgrounds. Meditation is a part of every business agenda; likewise, some celebrations are pencilled in, and we acknowledge where we all were and review our marketing and sales plans.

The feedback we get from women who attend our gatherings is brilliant, fun, positive, thought-provoking, and surprising. It's pretty much exactly what we try to provide: a little something for the body, mind, and soul.

With the help of family and friends, I'm finding my way home.

The lessons I learned about myself and the world that I realised then—and that I realise now—mean a lot of different things.

It's okay to care. In fact, it's more than okay, and it's also okay to be cared for.

Lesson: caring makes us human, caring makes us strong. Kindness and compassion are two of our strongest survival traits. There is nothing that fills my batteries more than caring for someone else. It's a start down the road to caring for yourself. Take the time; you are worth it.

Every adventure has its ups and downs. Go equipped, pack carefully, and get through it—you'll be successful, but perhaps not unscathed.

Lesson: when the adventure begins in earnest and you're ready, pack these into your kit: authenticity, boldness, fun, and inspiration. Of course, other essential equipment includes best friends, a sense of humour, curiosity, openness, courage, and a willingness to surrender (to allow what will be to be). How hard is surrendering? I can allow it in fits and starts, but it doesn't always come easily or naturally … not yet.

There is always hope, possibility, and love. It's okay to dream.

Lesson: even in the darkest hours, the greyest winters devoid of feeling, there is always hope, possibility, and love. It only takes a moment of acceptance for you to let it in, you don't have to reach out if you don't want to, but it's worth it if you do.

All that abundance stuff really works.

Lesson: if you can practice gratitude for what you have, imagine a more positive future and work on this moment (focusing on the good); after that, the magic will begin to happen. You'll start to be aware of how much you have already. You'll see synchronicities appear as the positive patterns begin to strengthen in your life and you recognise them first. And then you can run those stories rather than the old patterns of guilt and shame and grief.

Part 4

Searching for Connection

I'm choosing to be me—realising I have a choice—and that I'm the only one who matters. It's time to uncover my message, my purpose.

Some of the most emotionally difficult situations in my life have been the best learning experiences. I have a high IQ, but I didn't have a high EQ initially. This is what I came here to learn this time around: how to reconnect my emotions to my soul, how to allow myself to really feel; how to become emotionally intelligent; how to relate to myself and to others; how to learn and let go. And then I want to teach these things to other people, especially women who are closed off—closed for business from the neck down, like me. Get out of our freaking heads and into our hearts and homes.

Chapter 9

A Conscious, Purposeful Life

Over the next couple of years, I attended a myriad of courses discussing finding my purpose, soul-searching, goal setting, and action plans. Some were great, useful, and life-changing events. The first time I wrote a letter about my perfect day was brilliant and powerful. From the letter, I created some plans and began to work towards making the dreams come true. I often use this tool when I'm coaching people; it frees the imagination and creates possibilities. It gives you permission to dream, and it gives you a place to start.

Saturday 14th September 2013

My perfect day starts as I wake up next to Strack at Gisborne. We laugh and jump out of bed because my granddaughter is coming to visit, and we are planning our next holiday. Our room is clutter free, windows sparkling, bright curtains on the windows, my wardrobe is full of colourful, relaxed clothes and a few nice jackets for my speaking engagements.

Strack kisses me and heads off to his beautifully outfitted garage to work on his latest wooden masterpiece. He hugs me again, whispers how much he loves me and is so glad I took the leap and followed my bliss and passion.

I jump into some running gear, my body is fit, slender and toned. I head out of the house and smile at the well-tended garden.

I run towards the mountain, feeling the sun, feeling the rhythm of feet, pounding the earth, joyful striding, smiling, laughing at cows and sheep munching quietly in the sunshine.

I get back after about 10km, take a shower and change into comfy clothes. I'm not in a hurry and I make a cup of tea, healthy breakfast and go out the back door to sit in the courtyard. The garden is beautiful, tangles but tended.

After breaky I go across the garden to the Studio.

Breathing While Drowning

My smile is huge as I walk towards it, straw bale, round, lots of windows, beautiful garden, water trickling. I open the door and a sense of peace washes over me.

I sit on a rug on the floor, cross legged and calm, the doors open and sunlight on my face.

I meditate and thank the universe for all that I have. I am so grateful I began to ask for abundance, to seek my purpose, to use my passion.

The cats wander up to sit in the favourite sunny spots.

I make a cup of tea and turn on the computer.

First I open up my latest book and write, inspired for three hours.

I stop as Strack drops in to bring me a snack and we share some time relaxing and chatting about our next trip.

He tells me that so many people love his woodwork that he has no fear of starving or paying the bills. He laughs at how he used to worry secretly that our dreams would always be that — just dreams. He says he checked the bank account this morning and our savings, the account we can spend or invest as we wish has just hit $4.8 million!!!

I laugh and tell him that was just my first goal, next one is $48 million. We start to talk about Jacqui's foundation and helping more disabled kids get access to education and equipment. Ian kisses me, heads off to the foundation with some toys he has made.

I go back to the computer and check my schedule.

The week is pretty relaxed as always. I have a speaking engagement every 1-2 weeks, I have women's circle once a week.

True Bliss has a 3-day retreat planned for the Beach Sanctuary next week. It is already booked out.

Ron Z and Marguerite and I are meeting at the Studio tomorrow to plan the purchase of another property and to chat with someone who may be the perfect manager.

True Bliss is so well recognised now, I smile at how easy it was to follow my bliss and make a difference for good in the world.

I step out into the garden and spend some time meditating on how grateful I am for all that I have and asking for opportunity for more abundance. I go back to the computer, checking on the balance sheets for True Dialogue and True Bliss, both are in the black, with sales in the millions of dollars and quality products that help people find meaning and bring in great passive income.

I feel content, peaceful, happy and relaxed, I have learnt to let go.

Back at the computer, I gradually respond to emails, requests for help, conversations with friends, family, Facebook and the CEO of both companies.

Breathing While Drowning

I see a note that my Board Pack is on the way for the two Boards I give time to.

After an hour or so I turn the computer off and sit on the verandah.

My granddaughter and Cassi come running down the path. I pick her up and swing her onto my shoulders. Cassi is beautifully happy, fit and gorgeous.

We walk around the garden, the sun shining, chasing butterflies. We say hello to the gardener who has come to help with the pruning.

We go into the vegie palace, pick fresh stuff for tea and head into the kitchen to make it.

The kitchen and house are clean and uncluttered, the housekeeper smiles and says she is finished for the day, everything is clean and in order.

We chat for a while and she says she is so grateful to work with me as I have a way of putting words together that helps her make sense of her life.

We enjoy our dinner with all my children and their partners and my other grandchildren dropping in.

The dinner is full of love and laughter and I look around the table at the happy loving faces and wide open hearts.

The front door opens and Ron Z and Marguerite come in to pick me up.

I tell my family to stay as long as they want, to take a bed. Ian smiles and kisses me and wishes me luck, "even though I know you won't need it" he says.

We step outside and laugh about which car to take. I look at my sporty red car but opt for the larger jaguar as it is far more roomy.

We head off to the city and the TED event. All of us have been asked to speak. The event is about following your bliss and how we came to where we are, rich in money, love, wisdom and health.

We all look fit and fabulous, dressed in simple, elegant and expensive gowns, shoes and bling.

Arms linked we step onto the stage and inspire the crowd, the energy is alive with our story, of calm, courageous connection, of following our bliss.

We accept the gift for the event and donate it to one of our favourite charities.

We go to a restaurant nearby and laugh and tell stories about the journey, amazing and inspiring ourselves. We call it a director's meeting and make some plans for more fun and learning, more sharing of wisdom.

The driver arrives and takes us all home.

My house is quiet, all the bodies asleep in the extended bedrooms and Ian is quietly waiting for me.

He kisses me gently and asks how the event went.

Breathing While Drowning

> *I tell him how following my bliss, my passion to use words to help people learn, is so effortless now that it just feels like breathing.*
>
> *He smiles and leads me to the bedroom. We get ready for bed and gently and passionately make love, falling asleep in each other's arms.*

"So effortless now that it just feels like breathing." An unfettered imagination is a gift, and in the last few years, I've nurtured it more and more, seeking creativity in all sorts of ways, shapes, and forms.

Practicality and pragmatism are strong constants in my life too. Much of this, I'm sure, is from my childhood. Stretching scarce resources around eight children was my parents' relentless balancing act, and they did it very well. Everything had to have a purpose—or more than one—which meant there was little frivolous purchasing.

Even now, practicality is one of my filters, and one of the key values I make sure is in everything I offer. If it isn't useful, don't do it or put it out there. I suspect that holds me back a little from experiencing art and more sensate pursuits. Sometimes things just exist with no other purpose other than being. There you go: their practical purpose is to be.

I am capable, and I learn things easily. Curiosity gets me started, persistence and thoroughness keep me there until I know how it all works.

I had a sense of frustration follow quickly from a brief sense of accomplishment each time I achieved a career milestone. These were almost too easy, things seemed to always appear when I wanted them or even before I knew I needed them. Others would say, "That's okay for you, you're smart or lucky." I quickly dismissed my achievements because they were never enough; I was always striving for more, for the next thing to achieve.

But on reflection, I realise that my practice was to put it out to the universe in the form of a wish and, nine times out of ten, it would happen. I made it happen by intent, thoughts, and actions. Unconsciously, I followed the process: wish, want, and act. These days, they call it manifesting.

Jacqui's death tested my wishing and wanting to the limits. She was the one out of ten that didn't happen. I had no control; it was her life, not mine, to direct. Her death was not what I wanted, but maybe it's what I needed. I'm not sure I'm ready to commit to that concept entirely yet. I'd have her back in a heartbeat if something I could do would help. In the meantime, I'm living a conscious, purposeful life because her lessons are too important to waste, and because my life belongs to me. Everything I think, feel, do, and believe matters—and that's what counts.

I've seen and heard and felt the changes in myself, in my life, and in the lives of my beautiful family around me—all good. We laugh a lot, we enjoy each other's company, we're interested in each other's lives, we're confident going out into the world knowing there's love and support at home. Life is good, even if it's not.

I've always been restless, in search of the next something. I have an insatiable curiosity about what's around the corner; I love new things, and my natural inclination is to think of the idea, get something started, envision the whole thing, then move on. I don't worry about finishing it. I can see how it works now, and how all the pieces fit together—I don't need to actually do all of them. I almost never feel compelled to finish something if it's only for me.

Now you may think this is a handicap, and at times you'd be right. But for a strategist, this is an essential skill. To be able to see all the planes in the air and have them flying around without crashing is crucial. To also be able to see where and when each one will land safely, and who and what they'll bring with them, is what gives me the buzz. It's what makes me so useful and very good at facilitation and strategic planning. I love understanding where all the pieces fit. Criteria and constraints in, ideas and strategies out—pouring out, a creative waterfall.

Breathing While Drowning

Over the years, working as a consultant and a leader, I've had to teach myself to finish and to slow down and explain my thinking and my visions and plans. Rather than this being painful, I found I learned so many more things about myself, about other people, and about the work I was doing. Still, at times, I railed at dimming my light, hiding my brilliance. As is the way of this world, I often saw my ideas and effort taken by others and made their own with no acknowledgement sent my way. This was done as often by women as men.

And then the awakening: finding mindfulness, living in this moment. The biggest lesson is that I had to learn new ways of doing things, and I needed to do things consciously. I had to learn to recognise the patterns and to change the way I thought and felt and responded. I needed to develop new skills and capacities to help me respond differently. So the search begins in earnest, and I need to observe and consider my past—but not as a victim, as a clearly cherished case study, look at the past, but don't stare at it. Recognise the patterns, ask my good friends for help (and not just once). That is so hard for me. Choose a new future, choose a new way to respond. Try that. Consider the outcomes, review, and do it again (or do it differently: filter data, make a new choice).

There's always a choice. A choice to be involved, to be honest, to contribute. I asked my eldest son, Angus, why I was not content with a small life, a contained life. Why was I not content to settle for near enough or hiding?

Angus replied, "It doesn't really matter the why, it matters that you accept you have the need and just go with it. The why will come along as you pursue it." Wisdom from the mouths of babes, my babes.

I have this ferocious determination to live fully. Mediocrity is unfulfilling, boring, and exhausting—how can I play a larger game?

In May of 2013, I started my own business, True Dialogue. It's all about embracing good conversations, conversations that matter, working with people I love, and doing transformational work. And, of course, it was new, and that's why I wanted to give it a try. I wanted to see if I could do a great job for myself, my family, and my clients. I wanted to take out the middle man and be a small business of my own ... follow my own dreams.

I start with the things I'm good at and use the skills I've gathered over my thirty years of work and my fifty years of life (plus a few years on both accounts): coaching and leadership, strategy, facilitation, and project and change management. Helping people, teams, and organisations reflect, learn, and grow. Helping them find their confidence so they can do whatever they want to do and be whoever they want to be.

I keep learning and listening to people who have transformed their own lives and are living to help others do the same. People like Brendon Burchard. Now there's a man who is making a difference, someone who took the lessons from near tragedy, and turned them into his crusade with the mantra to "live fully, love openly and make your difference today".[1]

I became an active listener, and when I heard people, I learned things about them, about myself, and about the project or work. People fascinate me; they are amazing.

Early in my career, some people suggested that I was not a great listener. In fact, I was perceived as a bit of a cold fish, apparently more interested in the technical and process side of things and less connected to the human side.

I first got this piece of feedback when I moved down to Tasmania to do a critical care course. When I got there, I learned that they had dudded me. I was not in the course at all; rather, I was filling the roster on an ordinary surgical ward. They told me to apply for the next course entry three months later, which I did. And then I didn't get into that intake either. When I asked why, they said I didn't have enough experience (yet they let in two people with less experience than I had—but those people had trained at their hospital ... go figure). It all felt a bit unfair and dishonest, and I left pretty soon after, returning to Melbourne to work in the operating theatre and to do midwifery instead.

Breathing While Drowning

For the six months I was in Tasmania, I learned many things about being on my own without any family backstory. I had some good friends, but it was a fresh start to who I was ... or so I thought.

Some of the comments on my application, written by my charge nurse at the time, suggested that I was more interested in the technology than the people. I was quite shocked at this as I had thought of myself as pretty compassionate—I was a nurse, after all, and I worked hard and always made sure people were comfortable and settled before finishing my own tasks.

I often wondered whether this feedback was in part because I refused to continue the archaic practice of waking people up at 6:00 a.m. for a cup of tea regardless of whether they had slept or not and regardless of whether they needed to be awake. Anyone who's spent a night in a hospital will know how noisy they can be, and how hard it is to sleep. Mind you, I also had a tendency to question the medical consultants' "my word is law" pronouncements and some of the "we always do it like that here" practices, which probably didn't help. I was also from the mainland, not Tasmania, so I was starting from a disadvantage in some people's eyes. After feeling the discrimination at Uni, I pursued nursing, felt similar discrimination, and left.

I've always had a desire for the patient's needs to come first, preferring this over everyone having to play by the hospital's rules and be a numbered cog in the machine (both patients and staff).

But here's the thing: I've had time to think about some of the whys in relation to myself, time to consider matters, time to look for patterns. I've wondered: *What brings me joy? What doesn't?*

And this is the way I began to recognise how I operate, why I'm successful: it's the way I encourage you to live. Get conscious, become aware. Get curious, ask questions. If there is even 1 per cent of truth in the feedback, it's worth considering. Once you've considered it, you may find it changes your life. As Brendon Burchard said, "Don't develop a thick skin, develop consciousness."

I considered the words and began to listen more carefully, to look at how I interacted with people, to practice active listening. This practice bore fruit. People say to me now that I'm a great listener and they feel heard because I'm really present. Years of listening actively made me a great listener, and now I've become a great coach. It's not just listening—you have my full attention; I'm here and present, listening with compassion—I want to empower you to do whatever it is that brings you joy. I'm home when I listen, so I'm really hearing you.

Being a great listener has many benefits. For me, it's the beginning of a trusting relationship (or not). Within a couple of minutes of active listening, I can almost certainly decide whether I wish to continue the conversation and the relationship.

I began to learn that, even though I knew the answer to problems, sometimes other people didn't see it, or sometimes they saw different answers. And even more interestingly, sometimes they saw different problems. So listening not only gave me insights into humanity and people, it also gave me more data to throw into the mix of problem-solving.

How can you take listening to a whole new level? Learn to be present and mindful. And so I began to research this and more. Once I relax and am present with another person, one of two things happen. The other person either relaxes, notices a good listener is present, and moves into a more meaningful conversation to the benefit of both of us. Or, alternatively, they remain unaware of the opportunity and continue blathering on about themselves or something else with no point, no care, and no connection. With the latter type of people, I've learned to shut down the conversation quickly and politely.

Healing the Wounded Masculine

Anyway, back to Brendon Burchard. After I absorbed most of the Silva method, Christie Marie Sheldon, and Rachael Jayne Groover, I became aware that Burchard is the next one whose work had the most influence on my life, the one who initiated the most change. I found I'd gone over the spiritual borders into the land of woo-woo ideologies and got a bit off track. Essentially, the pendulum had swung too far.

Breathing While Drowning

The people in the transformation industry are fabulous, and they're just as fallible as people in any walk of life can be. I learned many things and made some wonderful friends, but I was still lost, still didn't know what my life purpose was. I often felt there was a patronising thought running through the minds of the other people: *Oh you're from the corporate sector, the evil empire.* Which is true, I wasn't from the world of sitting around and contemplating my navel. It was my perception for sure, but there was that itch of not quite belonging … again.

Because I had pursued a more spiritual path, it was as if I dismissed all that had gone on in my life before. I was trying to live their way, and I was repudiating all the great work and living I'd done over my thirty-year career, disavowing its validity. It's as easy to devolve all control of your life and choices in that world as it is in the corporate jungle. It's just another language if you're not careful. You can get so caught up in considering the way you are that, in fact, you're no way. You're interpreting your life at the whim of the latest fad, the popular guru or mindset. And there's always something to fix, something to heal, a different way to look at things, and a unique way to unpack and redo your life.

It got to be exhausting, and I only really dabbled at the edges. Nowadays, everyone wants to send you stuff via e-mail to get you into their funnel so you begin buying their message and their material. Ultimately, I didn't want to read the e-mails because I knew I would probably buy something from them—their messages were so compelling, and I felt really gullible. Often, I would buy something, begin it, and then not finish or practice or use it after the first time. Still, there were a few that worked really well for me.

Brendon was a lifesaver because, for me, he bridged the chasm between the two worlds. Here was a man obviously in touch with his own form of spirituality, making a difference in the main game, in the world of business. He had such a unique way of being and working, and he was totally comfortable making his own way.

One of the most powerful tools I learned about from Brendon Burchard was a clarity chart.[2] This set of nine words was a practical application of the concept that what we focus on and practice is what we become. You find your own set of nine words, add your big why, print it out, stick it up in front of you, and practice being those nine words. It really works.

My first words were:

Self: three words that now best define who I am that will be used to guide my personal life, including my thoughts and actions are creative, bold, and hilarious. I needed some fun in my life, and for months, I went around feeling hilarious and finding fun in lots of things. A few months later, I changed hilarious to mindful.

Interactions with Others: three words that now define and guide how I will engage and treat others I meet in life, including loved ones and strangers are caring, connected, and inspiring.

Success Markers: three words that now remind me of what it is that made me the most successful and will make me even more successful are curious, innovative, and thorough. I changed innovative to authentic because it kept coming up over and over.

My big why at that time, something that was driving me and is worth my struggle and journey, something that is bigger than just me, something I am willing to fight for (or love for) was

To give my family the greatest quality of life I can, to help myself and everyone I meet to be inspired to live the purpose and meaning in their lives and be the best they can be.

So now you use these words as mantras when you start your day, when you interact with people, and when you take action on your dreams.

I've recently updated my words again at the urging of my latest coach, the legendary Hafizah Ismail[3] to take them to the next level. Now I have the following words:

Self: creative, vibrant, and joyful; Others: present, inspiring, and compassionate; and Success: curious, adventurous and remarkable.

My big why is to live vibrantly and fully, and to create for myself and my family the greatest joy and quality of life I can. To help myself and everyone I meet to be inspired to live the purpose and meaning in their lives so that they can be the best they can be.

Wednesday 1st January 2014

New Year, New Book

This year I am going to be: happy, joyful, fun, bold, inspiring, authentic. I am going to draw massive abundance in all areas: wealth, health and wisdom.

I am going to finish a lot of projects and see them through to a beautiful completion.

I am going to be a great mother, wife, friend and person!

I am going to have lots of new things in my life.

I am going to be creative, bold and mindful.

With others I am going to be caring, connected and inspiring.

My success will be helped by my curiosity, authenticity, resilience and thoroughness.

I am going to create a fabulous future for my family.

I am going to. Lots of fabulous intent, but the other voices are strong too. As well as trudging along on my quest for healing, I found the urge to write Jacqui's story becoming more and more compelling. But I couldn't find the right place to start. I began over and over, struggling to sustain the writing and to get the book flowing. As I try to put pen to paper, Blackheart shouts into the void. As I recall the memories, the ocean swallows me, drowning me again.

Sunday 16th February 2014

Not good enough, inadequate as a mother. Went off to work and left Ian home with the children, including Jacqui Bree who needed so much of his time.

Feeling like a misery guts tonight. I was going to do so much more with my time but I didn't. I don't want to get holier than though, it just doesn't cut it. I certainly wouldn't bother reading it.

Perhaps I can start with some of the stories.

Western Medicine

Do no harm.

I think Western Medicine has taken a detour somewhere and gone further, do no harm, but don't bother healing either.

No, still too antsy and angry.

Why so tonight? Ian is away with Angus, driving the Kombi back from Perth. I always feel a bit bereft when he is away, particularly for this long. Frazer and Cassi just do their own thing. So basically I feel like a taxi housekeeper cook! But I'm frustrated 'cos I wanted my time Saturday reading a novel and watching television. What was I thinking? A day off, how decadent. But I shouldn't take my frustrations out on the kids. I should just freaking do it.

I remember holding her gangly body and gently kissing her nose, stroking her silky chestnut hair. Wondering what life would hold for her, for all of us.

Breathing While Drowning

> Jacqui was born with a severe brain injury. She chose to come into this life with the kind of life threatening disabilities that I had only ever read about or seen on the telly. Her first few weeks I think I knew there was something wrong, or at least not quite right. Cassi had been the ideal baby, achieving milestones in leaps and bounds, a delightful precocious first born.

I'm antsy and angry for sure. It was becoming okay to share some vulnerability with friends, but to shout out my grief and shame to the whole world required more courage, more … something.

Monday 17th February 2014

> This is a story of how I learnt to breathe while drowning, and make it look as if I was a brilliant swimmer.

I ploughed onwards, putting anything on paper that I could, snatching moments here and there between work and living.

Wednesday 19th February 2014

> What does drowning feel like?
> For me it was a slow death, every day the same pain, every night the same nightmare.

> Can't catch your breath, overwhelmed, out of control, at the mercy of, not the water, but the emotion, grief, despair, hopelessness.

> **Sunday 23rd February 2014**
>
> 'drowning'
> 'breathing'
> Two mutually exclusive activities you might think, not so fast.
> Add to the mix, one feisty brain-injured daughter, her tragic death at 4 years 10 months, the need to keep going for the others and suddenly you can do both — drown in grief and guilt and keep breathing, living a life half made. Joyous in lots of parts but always lacking something, a depth of feeling, an openness and expression of vulnerability.

Each time I started to write, it opened the wounds I thought were long closed and healed. But sometimes help came from unexpected sources.

I spent time travelling regional Victoria with my friend Dr Cathy Balding.[4] We had a seven-month change management coaching programme with a group of rural, aged care services. It was Cathy who introduced me to Brendon Burchard. All of Brendon Burchard's books are worth reading—I've read then all—and some are covered in highlighter with corners turned down on my favourite spots. Some I love more than others. I love his generosity and messages, and his practicality in terms of taking action. I adapted his one-page productivity planner that I first used 11 November 2013, and I still use it today to get stuff done.[5]

Cathy was good for my soul. In fact, she's good for anyone's soul. She has an uncanny and innate ability to cut through the crap and help you find the diamonds in the dross. I was full of ideas and possibilities and ways to go, full of ideas for my book—so full that I couldn't see the way forward or what I wanted to do. I'd peeled back a whole lot of layers, but I was still going around in circles.

One beautiful, balmy, moonlit night, while sitting outside the pub in Omeo, and before a workshop the next day, we had a great conversation about life, the universe, and everything. She interrogated me—there's no other word for it—and it made me cut through the waffle to the core. I had to start thinking about what was important to me and what I wanted to start building the rest of my life on.

Tuesday 3rd March 2014

I help women find their confidence so they can rediscover that they are more than enough to do exactly what they want to do.

I help women who are stuck find the courage to take the next step.

I help them by teaching them to be in the moment, how to make good decisions and get over the hump.

I help women to be great, to be confident, to be myself (themselves) not who they want me to be.

I give them skills and tools that build their confidence to do whatever they want to do and be what they want to be.

Breathing while drowning ...

I want to help people rediscover their confidence so they can be who they want to be and do what they want to do. It's all about confidence, so often that's what people tell me is the missing piece. "If I only had a little more confidence I could do … (insert whatever you want to do here)".

Everything I do, whether it's with an individual or a team, begins with building confidence to work, to lead, to innovate, to build, to love.

Sometimes, confidence can be found in a moment, and sometimes it takes a little while to dig it out from under the crap that we tell ourselves. I spent a lot of time thinking and learning, and then, in a creative mind dump, the words all came together. Most of us would like to have the confidence to "show up reliably and consistently as our best selves".[6] We'd like to feel confident enough to step into every chance life throws us, giving it our best shot every time, making the most of our opportunities.

Sometimes blossoming confidence is supported in unexpected ways.

Thursday 13th March 2014

Tonight on the way home in the bus, I felt Mum was with me really close, holding my hand.

I looked up at the stars and felt them calling me home. Don't struggle any more, don't strive, come home now, you've learnt enough. Mum so close, so much love, thank you.

I had tried writing the book on my own, done some short writing courses, got lots of help from books and made the plan.

Anne McIndoo's book, *So, you want to write! How to get your book out of your head and onto the paper in seven days*, was really helpful.[7]

Breathing While Drowning

Cathy Balding put me on to the book. She'd used McIndoo's book to help her in the early days of writing the first of her two books.

The planning was fine and fun, I'm great at planning, seeing where it all fits. But the early drafts were too raw, the hurts too close. So I wrote a fable, a fictional person confronted with a story, a heroine's quest to find something. It got stuck on Chapter 3 … again. I'm a great starter, lots of ideas, but the finishing part is harder. Taking something to a conclusion is quite the task for me.

Wednesday 2nd April 2014

What a beautiful expression of gratitude, is it calling me on my authenticity, challenging me to take my own medicine?

Let go of outcomes, burn a little fire down the line and send it with love and light.

There's something about women sitting in a circle.

Advertise the pamper, do the fem presence meditation.

Find the book, write the story.

Confidence

Creativity

Courage

free me   competence

free me   calamity

free me beautiful creative

free me help help

beautiful sensual,

Veronica Strachan

> *me fire*
> *help me free escape*
> *want need love sharing joyous*
> *Still a way to go.*

I used to believe people were born either with confidence or without confidence. I thought it was all tied together with being extroverted, something I most definitely was not. I used to feel as if I was a leaf blown this way and that by forces of nature, by the world of work, and by other people's agendas. I often felt as if I wasn't in control of my life, and that I was powerless to change. I figured I was an introvert and didn't have much confidence, so that was my lot in life: to forever look with envy at the confident people who had it all.

People with confidence seem to have this incredible belief in themselves and everything they do. Other people stop and listen to what confident people have to say. Confident people walk into a room and bring a bucket load of energy and fearless enthusiasm with them. It's as if the party starts when the confident people arrive. Confident people are leaders wherever they go—trusted, valued, and inspiring to others. Confident people effortlessly advance and leave their mark on the world.

But even though I didn't have a lot of confidence, I still had big dreams and a burning desire to leave the world a better place. I wanted to change lives, and I began to realise I would have to change mine first.

After all the years of reading, analysing, talking to people, attending workshops, conferences, exploring and investigating, I came to realise that we're not born with or without confidence. Rather, confidence is a belief. So, just as we can change our beliefs, we can learn to be confident. With practice, we can become more

Breathing While Drowning

confident until confidence becomes a skill we don't need to think about, we just have it—like driving a car or brushing our teeth.

I worked out that there were some concepts and practices that worked for me consistently. I'm a strategist, and I see and breathe patterns and connections. I distilled all the successful ideas and experiences and created my principles of conscious living—the ten Cs. I applied these to a number of areas that I was working in.

These principles work for anyone who is prepared to follow each step and commit to practicing. I use them myself and teach them to others in my coaching practice and leadership and business programmes.

Conscious living leads to confidence, and that confidence can be applied to any part of your life: work, relationships, and business, for example. And use the lesson I learned. Don't take these as your whole truth—they're my truth, so use and practice them, and then find your own style, your own group. Adapt and refine what I've shown you.

Feel the frustration and the fear and do it anyway. As one of my coachee's eloquently summed up how many people feel: "I don't want to be unhappy. I have no joy. I want more." So go out and get it, or go inside and find it!

Here's a taste of what I use:

1—Get conscious

First, *conscious*. Waking to the awareness of who you are. Realise the separation from the feminine.

You are the sum of all choices and experiences up to this point in your life. This first step toward "going confidently in the direction of your dreams" (thanks to Henry David Thoreau for that gem), is about getting conscious or aware that you're not content with the status quo, and that you're willing and committed to change. In this step, you grow your awareness of who you are now, and what you bring to the table.

Reflect on your strengths, your values, and the things that are important in your life—your big reasons why. Why do you want to change? Who do you want to become? What do you want to do? People who are conscious of who they are, and what their strengths and values are enjoy happier, healthier, more productive, and more purposeful lives.

There are a million ways you can get more conscious about what's important. Just by thinking and reading you become more aware. The best way I found to start was to journal. Start writing down what you're thinking, feeling, and doing. Do this every day at the same time. Make it easy to remember by leaving your journal and pen beside the bed, and write just before you go to sleep or first thing in the morning. If you're not used to journaling, give yourself a question or two to answer: When was my happiest moment today? What was I thinking, doing, and feeling today? What am I grateful for today?

And then go a little deeper. What are the things I value? Why? Am I being true to my values in how I work and play and live? Rediscover your strengths, the things that make you successful at what you do. Start practicing mindfulness and get back into your body and out of your head when you can.

2—Get curious

Curiosity is next, and it is always my friend—what could I do, where could I go, who could I be, what does it all mean? Identification with the masculine, the immersion in the world of leadership, management, profit, projects, and outcomes, can all connect to the powerful feminine.

Start thinking about the possibilities of becoming the person you want to be, and exploring and experiencing what you have to do to get there. Now is the time to dust off all those childhood dreams and give them another chance. Now that you're remembering and know what's important to you, who you want to be, and maybe even what you want to do, it's time to make a plan for getting there.

This step is also about getting organised and back on track, creating strategies that can give you step-by-step actions to get to where you want to go.

The practice of curiosity is to ask questions, and the easiest ones to ask are: Why? Who? What? How? Why do I feel like that? Why is that important? Why does that person seem to do things easily? Who could I be? Who could help me? What is it that I want? What is it that I could do in my life, at my workplace, or in my relationships to change how I am being? What is the best solution to the problem? How have other people changed their lives, started a business, or made a successful career? How have I done things successfully in the past? How can I use my strengths and what I value to live a life that expresses the very best of who I am?

Let yourself dream, it doesn't cost anything to dream. Put your dreams into the world—make a dream board, write them out, or talk to someone you trust. Subscribe to blogs by people who you admire or whose message feels like it has something to say to you. Check out Google and put your values or strengths or favourite things into the search box and see what comes up. Go to a workshop or three. Read a book or six. Get a coach or a mentor, someone who can be your confidential thinking partner, someone who'll be in your corner and ferociously focused on you.

Make a plan of action to get yourself moving towards your dream.

3—Get courageous

Third is *courage,* which I have in droves. Leap into the darkness, try stuff, think differently, think deeply. Bloody hell, I get myself into some ridiculous situations. This is the road of trials, and it might involve meeting ogres and dragons. Maybe it's not courage but lack of fear. Some would say acting without fear is reckless, impulsive, or impetuous. Maybe the word is *desperate.* Like the kids cutting themselves so they bleed and feel the pain—maybe that's what I've been doing all along, trying this and that to find out how to feel again. I just tarted it up in corporate shininess rather than black clothing. But no—*adventurous* is how I'm living my life, and it's my own, personal adventure!

Once you've thought about who you want to be and what you want to do, it's time for you to get courageous. This step is about taking action, small or large, to do something different. But it's not just any old action—although even that helps. It's action with a strategic intent "straction," perhaps. And action in the right direction is traction—remember the plan, the goal, the dream. Do something different, and do it now ... don't wait until it's perfect. Progress trumps perfection.

Brené Brown said, "Courage is contagious. Every time we choose courage, we make everyone around us a little better and the world a little braver."

If you keep in mind your values, your strengths, and your dreams, the actions just about line up and do themselves—just about. You still need to take that first step, and there are some days that it will be a grind. The only way out is through. And you will be amazed how coincidences and serendipity seem to ramp up as soon as you commit to action. Intent is good; action is better; doing both together is best.

So go back to your dream board or words, look at the big goal, and then pick one small action that could get you closer to the goal. And then pick another ... and then another. Write the list and do the first one. If the big goal feels too big, then pick one of the smaller ones and start with that. It doesn't matter if you make mistakes or change your mind, it's all experience, and it all builds your confidence to try again. Keep your friend or your coach close, ask them to keep you accountable, to keep you on track. If they don't want to, let that person go and find someone who will.

There's a quote attributed to Jim Rohn that reads, "You are the average of the five people you spend the most time with."

Look around you. Are the people you're spending the most time with helping you grow or holding you back? Do they want to come with you and grow, or are they frightened that your light will shine on their darkness? Maybe it's time to let some people go and open up to others.

Set up some behaviour triggers to support your new good habits. Brendon Burchard has a great prompt—he suggests asking yourself: "Who must I become and how can I immediately start living into that truth with daily practices?" I have this as a note in front of my computer screen and read it every day.

If you want to be fitter, put your exercise clothes out the night before so you can just fall out of bed and into your gear before you have to decide what to wear. Here's where that good friend can help: ask your friend to exercise with you. Or if you're creating a product or service, try a pilot first, test products and services with friends or small groups, ask for feedback, listen, and adapt. It's not so hard to be courageous in small steps. And those small steps start to add up and allow your dreams to get closer and closer.

4—*Get capable*

Fourth is finding competence, the illusory boon of success. And, yes, I found it: job, position, responsibility, homes, holidays, and so forth. I changed the word to *capable,* though, because *competent* is such a confining word. *Capable* feels so much more optimistic. Now I realise my capabilities, and I use them to be who I want to be, to work with people I love, and to create programmes that free people to be themselves.

This step is about realising you can do things differently and building your capability and agility. It's about finding your zone of genius. It's about checking your commitment. Being capable is being able to achieve (efficiently and effectively or kind of just getting there) regardless of what you want to do.

This step is also about practising, lots of practising and experiencing. As Robert Collier stated, "Success is the sum of small efforts, repeated day-in and day-out."

Think about driving a car. When you first learn, you have to concentrate on every little thing. After a few years, you do many of the things automatically and can talk and drive at the same time. It's important to remember that attraction works in the present, not the future—so take action now!

This step is not about judging in terms of good or bad, right or wrong; rather, it's about evaluating and analysing so you have evidence to make a decision. Analysing is examining methodically in order to explain or interpret. This is a good reason to keep journaling.

Think about the human body ... it's amazing. We don't need to remember how to breathe, it's handled automatically, but we can increase our lung capacity to get fitter or be a better speaker or singer by practising.

Think about the brain and its capacity to learn and do stuff. The soul can learn even more if you give it a chance to practise.

Go back to that friend and ask them to help you think about stuff you are capable of doing. What kind of skills do you use when you are successful at things? Just keep in mind that you are looking for support, not advice.

Just freaking do stuff. By taking action, you get experience, and every experience (no matter how it feels or how it ends up) gives you more information to help you make a decision about the next step you need to take.

And, of course, journal it. You can get great insights into how you work, your capabilities, and innate talents by recording your thoughts when you are in the zone of genius. And when things are a hard slog, you can choose to make different choices in the future. Because that's what it's all about: doing things differently. Remember Einstein's definition of stupidity: "Doing the same thing over and over again but expecting different results." Look for your zone of genius; what lights you up? Ask for feedback—it's scary, but it's worthwhile. Work out what's missing, and figure out what else you need to learn. And then go do that.

Breathing While Drowning

5—Be conflicted and confused (this is an easy one)

Living consciously, learning, and growing is not all roses. There are two other *C*s that can be going on at any stage, and *conflicted* is one.

Conflicted entails substantial uncertainty, it's fear that you're heading in the wrong direction, that you're going to fail, that you're going to succeed and garner unwanted attention, that you're going to end up alone. You've read in my story that I've had years and years of conflict in and with myself, with others, with my work, and with the world. All of this is okay. The confusion is okay. The awakening to feelings of spiritual aridity and death is okay. If that's what you feel and that's what you need, these can be beneficial results. The growing dissatisfaction, the frustration, the hollowness.

Take all the time you need to experience these, let them come, journal, remember, feel. If you need to, ask for help or ask for time alone. When you're ready, you'll reach the next step.

6—Be closed

Six is the initiation and descent to the goddess, death and darkness and silence closed, time to just be.

Closed is empty, waiting, lost, endless cycles of introspection, anger, sadness, diving deep into the darkness and staying there, being held, being whole. Days and weeks and months and years of closure are like strings of dark pearls holding you together, sometimes just barely. And then, even in the darkness, there is comfort and time to heal and think and feel. Slowly emerging, a trigger releases, realising there is something else, stepping into one of the other stages when you're ready. It entails taking off the cloak, opening to possibility, taking a breath, and living and loving again.

We can do this: be closed and drowning and still breathing, and still living.

7—Get creative

Seven is *creative*: the urgent yearning to connect with the feminine. Hallelujah for that. I find women who hold out their hands, their arms, and their love to welcome me despite all my faults, failings, and foibles. Get into a circle, let them nurture you and help you hold responsibility for growing.

There are a million ways to get creative. So use your curiosity muscle and get looking and thinking about how you want to be creative. Now it's time to start adding to your repertoire, putting your own mark on your life, trying more and more things, filling your life with moments of bliss and the zone of genius.

Einstein said, "Creativity is contagious, pass it on." Keeping some things and discarding others allows you to make your life your way. Take some time to relax; creativity generally doesn't like to be forced. It prefers to sneak in when you're not concentrating, when you're least expecting it, like in the shower! Keep a notebook handy!

Try something different; take a risk. Get out that bucket list and start on some of those crazy ideas. Nurture your innate talent, whether it's writing, speaking, drawing, paper folding, crochet, listening, golf, building, or something else. Set aside time. You've learned by now that if it isn't on the schedule, it generally doesn't get done. So schedule in some creative time. Julia Cameron suggests an artist date with yourself regularly.[8] Go to a museum or a library or a lake or a magnificent building or a dark laneway or a festival.

Find other people who are doing what you want to do and follow their every move on social media (in the nicest possible way—no stalking, please), and then ask them for a few minutes of their time in person. Ask them how they get creative, and look at lining up all the parts of your life.

Now might be the time to get a styling session and help your outside match your inside. This helps people see the real you. I had a wonderful session with Ivana Bau[9], one of the beautiful women I met through the Art of Feminine Presence work. It felt like a coming out, another layer peeled off (again!). Her intuition is flawless; she helps you find the words to express yourself on the outside. My wardrobe changed from drab black and grey and dark to bright reds and oranges, which restored me to the creative, stylish, and powerfully feminine woman I am. It felt as though Ivana helped unzip the cocoon and let the butterfly open her wings and fly.

8—Get connected

Eight, the infinity symbol sideways, is *connected*. You must heal the mother–daughter split. Finding some things that connect you, some things and ways of being that resonate. Connect to the light and darkness, reconnect all the lost parts of yourself, including the feminine. Connect with your spouse, partner and children, or connect with people who are also searching.

It's at this point that you begin to realise all your joy, all your success is intimately based on how you build and interact in relationships with yourself and others. This is healing the mother–daughter split, reconnecting to the feminine (or masculine), and celebrating who you are. It entails being vulnerable and showing up real, flawed, and wonderful.

At our most basic level, we're all energy. And there is attraction and repulsion going on all the time as we live and love. When I read Anita Moorjani's words about us being all one across time and space and dimensions it made so much sense.[10]

Life's not either or—it's everything. Let me explain a bit further. Relationships with yourself: think about what you value, what you love, and what you spend time doing. Are they the same, or are you disconnected from what you love and value? Getting connected is making the steps to be what you value, to live with your joys and strengths, to practise what you preach, if you like. You've got conscious (aware of what's important to you), curious (wondering how your life can look and feel), courageous (taking the first step and realising you're capable of this and so much more), creative (you've unleashed your gifts and imagination to make your own mark), compassion (you've awoken to a greater awareness of others and yourself), and now you're connecting (making all the dots line up to your specifications—for yourself, your purpose, your life). You coordinate, consolidate, and allow all the thinking and feeling so that you're showing up with certainty, confidence, and the willingness to act in the direction of your dreams.

It's taking a different and deeper connection to all the relationships you have; more compassion, more patience, more understanding, more creativity, and more love. This makes such a difference in all aspects of your life. It's knowing you're connected to another person whom you can influence via your connection. You must stay true to yourself, your values, your work in the world. You must shine your own light so that they can see their own light better.

9—Get compassionate

Nine is *compassion*, a strong desire to alleviate the suffering, finding the inner man with heart. Keltner stated, "Humans are tribal beings, we're motivated by a desire to help, in fact there's good evidence that it's part of our deep evolutionary purpose and vital to the survival of our species".[11]

As you start to get your own life in order, get engaged and go out of your way to help the physical, intellectual, spiritual, or emotional needs of others.

People who practice kindness and compassion are happier, and they also practice self-compassion. Here are some of the reasons to practice compassion: it makes us feel good, it activates pleasure circuits and that leads to lasting increases in self-reported happiness, it reduces the risk of heart disease, it makes our minds wander less, it makes us more optimistic and supportive, it allows us to make better friends with greater satisfaction and growth, and it makes us more positive and less vulnerable to stress and harm to the immune system.

Breathing While Drowning

The good news is that *yes*, you can practice compassion and get better at it.

Albert Einstein once said, "A human being is a part of the whole, called by us 'Universe,' a part limited in time and space.

"He experiences himself, his thoughts and feelings as something separated from the rest, a kind of optical delusion of his consciousness.

"This delusion is a kind of prison for us, restricting us to our personal desires and to affection for a few persons nearest to us.

"Our task must be to free ourselves from this prison by widening our circle of compassion to embrace all living creatures and the whole of nature in its beauty.

"Nobody is able to achieve this completely, but the striving for such achievement is in itself a part of the liberation and a foundation for inner security."

Here's a biggie: when we think we're capable of making a difference, we're less likely to curb our compassion [12] As you keep building your capability to live the life you choose, you become more capable of making a difference in other people's lives.

Compassion has a particular connection to emotion and action. Keltner stated, "While cynics may dismiss compassion as touchy-feely or irrational, scientists have started to map the biological basis of compassion, suggesting its deep evolutionary purpose".[13]

Research has shown that, when we feel compassion, our heart rate slows down, we secrete the bonding hormone oxytocin, and regions of the brain linked to empathy, caregiving, and feelings of pleasure light up, which often results in our wanting to approach and care for other people.[14]

There are lots of ways to practice compassion, and the best way to really feel it is to start with self-compassion: self-kindness, common humanity, and mindfulness.[15]

To achieve compassion for self, integrate the old and new, and don't forget all the beautiful lessons and skills. Who knew that I had so much in common with Charles Darwin? Seriously, I do. One of his daughters died young, and it helped him discover deep insights and write about the place of suffering and compassion in human experience.

Okay, so it took me a while—twenty years or so—and though my words are not in the same league or even genre as *The Descent of Man*, this book is me sharing some of the deep insights I've had from my life resulting from Jacqui's death—suffering and compassion among them.

10—Be concordant

Ten is *concordant,* a beautiful word that brings to mind resonance, agreement, and harmony.

In the end, the one you want is concordant, the state of harmony where all the parts of you are in agreement and your life is your own. From here, confidence that you're living your truth takes you to wherever you want to be.

It's very seductive to be asked into the group with the cool kids, especially when you've never been one of the cool kids. But I realised that the best group to be in is my own. In that case, you know all the boundaries, and you can push them if you want. You know all the rules, and you can ignore, change, or break them whenever you please. Because concordance is not static, it's always changing and growing, it's agreement and harmony with yourself, so if you're always growing and learning, staying aligned is a moving feast. It may take all of the steps to find harmony, find peace for the next round.

Life is seldom as organised as we would like it to be. Although I've presented the steps in sequence, we can take them in any order we like. We can find ourselves in many at the same time, which can be really confusing (you may ask yourself, *How can I be conflicted and creative at the same time?*). We can find ourselves oscillating between two or three over and over until we're ready to move on. Your heroine's journey is your own; you're the navigator and the driver. Take your time and go wherever you're going.

Breathing While Drowning

Around this time, I was finishing the formal study for my life and business coaching certificate. I realised how well the principles of conscious living, the ten Cs would work to help others realise their potential and develop the confidence to do what they wanted to do and be who they wanted to be—that best version of themselves. My C7 coaching model was born. The focus was on the steps most tangible and ready for action: conscious, curious, courageous, capable, creative, connected, and compassionate.

C7 works in so many different ways for so many different people and situations. Coaching helps individuals who want to change their lives or live remarkable lives. The definition of *remarkable* is worthy of attention, your attention. My Remarkable Life Programme helps you focus your attention on your life, clarifies what's important, and helps you find your way to the life that expresses the very best of who you are.

The C7 model began to manifest in all the areas I was working in, and the model resonated with all people I was working with. Lesley Thornton and I had wanted to work together to develop a leadership programme for the health, aged, and community care sector. When I mentioned the C7 model, we could see that it was a great structure for what we wanted to provide. We'd seen so many managers and leaders drown in the expectations and get overwhelmed by new leadership responsibilities that we were passionate about helping them. We knew there was a better way; it didn't have to be so painful.

And so Practical Leadership was born.[16] Our vision is to teach and inspire and support people across three domains with theory, action learning, and (always!) practical applications. The three domains are: personal—our individual strengths and leadership capabilities; professional—how we inspire, instruct, and involve our teams, peers, and clients; and organisational—where the personal and professional interact to deliver great care and services for our clients.

I was starting to see everything in my life come together in a harmonious blend, and I knew what was important to me and how I wanted to live and work and lead: consciously, creatively, and confidently.

Our intent with Practical Leadership is that the combination of C7, emotional intelligence, and the three domains helps develop leaders who are curious on a regular basis about how they could do better. They're able to step back from the daily treadmill and look at the client, the organisation, and their team to get better insight into what's needed. They're courageous enough to do the right thing and capable of doing it.

Practical leaders are self-aware, motivated, and confident. They learn from their mistakes as well as their successes; they're open to ideas, manage relationships responsibly, and are skilled and effective operators. Plus, they're aware of their organisational role and the value of what and how they contribute to delivering positive outcomes for clients. The programme has appealed to a whole range of sectors.

But I digress, back to my story!

As I started to get my own life in order, practising self-compassion first, my sense of compassion, my need to go out of my way to help the physical, intellectual, spiritual, or emotional needs of others got stronger too.

The Strachan Clan Seil Fund emerged from a series of conversations I had with my good friend Dr Cathy Balding. These chats were about how I could combine what I wanted to do with my life with my favourite things to do and still make a difference in the world.

I admit I was well over fifty when these chats took place—somewhat late, you may think, to be wondering what to do with your life. However, as I always say, it's never too late to start afresh or declare, "Out with the old, in with the new." Of course, I can hear Cathy saying, "Yes, but don't throw the baby out with the bath water!"

Breathing While Drowning

Cathy also had dreams of bringing together women from health, aged, and community care to share stories and support each other. The short story is that we founded Women Who Care. The longer story is a bit more hilarious, and it includes Cathy falling off her chair laughing at me and being wishy-washy, but that's for another day.

I had four main reasons for starting Women Who Care:

1. I want to help as many women as I can to realise they can be whoever they want to be and do whatever they want to do. I'm doing this through leadership, life, and business coaching, speaking, facilitating, and writing. I work with women leaders, mid-career professionals, entrepreneurs, and small businesses in a wide range of sectors. My favourites are women leading in the health, aged, and community care sectors. Thirty-five years in the health sector leaves a deep impression, so as an older (and wiser) woman in that area, I want my fellow crones and matriarchs to do two things: share their wisdom and change lives by creating great care everywhere.

2. My favourite thing to do is have a conversation with purpose; a real dialogue that's a vigorous exchange of ideas about stuff that matters. And I love to learn something new that I can try to do in my own life, personal or business. Often, such talks occur over a glass or two and a good dinner. Although, I must admit that, if the conversation is scintillating, I usually don't notice what I'm eating—I'm too busy soaking up the splendid philosophies or contributing to the flow of fabulous ideas. There is something magical that happens when just women show up and chat. Shoes off, elbows on the table, let your hair down, and away we go: laughter, wisdom, vulnerability, creativity, resilience, ideas, support.

3. And, of course, there is Jacqueline Bree, born with a severe brain injury. Pretty much dismissed by mainstream health, we responded as only parents of hurt children can: we ignored the box they put her in and found an exceptional programme that helped her achieve extraordinary results. The Programme was 24 hours a day, 7 days a per week, and 365 days a per year. Strangers from our community, family and friends helped us out, and were changed by meeting and working with Jacqui Bree and watching her come alive through the Programme. Although Jacqui Bree died just before she turned 5, we don't regret a single moment of the time we spent on the Programme with her.

4. The fourth reason is that, as a family, we were constantly supported by the generosity of strangers, friends, and family. We've all learned a great deal from the gift of having Jacqueline Bree in our lives, and we believe that we can give back by building an ongoing fund to provide grants for organisations who help hurt kids reach their potential. And along the way, we want to help women grow and reach their potentials as leaders in the world.

So, Women Who Care Confabs are women leaders from the health, aged, and community care sectors getting together for a couple of hours over dinner. They are there to be inspired, instructed, and involved in sharing their wisdom from research, hard-won experience; discussing important issues and learning new things; and personally taking action to create great care everywhere. Above all, we have fun. The energy in the room is amazing. It is inspiring just to be in the room with so many smart, caring, and compassionate women.

As I sat and listened to the buzz in the room on 22 April 2015, the night of the first WWC Confab, I felt Jacqui's presence behind me, holding the space safe, and a beautiful sense of peace and completion settled into my heart. I felt my breath catch in my throat, and had to take a moment before I could get back into the conversation with my group. This was a full circle for me, a milestone achieved that I had been dreaming of for so many years. Voluntary action taken to begin to give back what I'd been given so many years ago: the compassionate and practical support of a community. Not just a one-off or short-term support service either. With Cathy's help, I used my skills, experience, and passion to establish something that, hopefully, has a life of its own and will continue to help and support women and children for many years to come.

We have a first target of $20,000 in the fund with the Australian Communities Foundation, and in the first year we have raised $3,500. Once we reach $20,000, we can begin to give out grants. A portion the profits from each book sold will be donated to the Strachan Clan Seil Fund.

The Women Who Care Confabs are interactive and practical, of course. A speaker is charged to use stories that prompt group discussion and then to leave the audience with at least three so-called Care Points—actions they can and should take to make a difference to their current situation, no matter what the topic is. The talk can be based on either research, hard-won experience, or both—and, preferably, it will be based on how that person learned or applied that lesson.

The speaker addresses at least one of the WWC objectives to inspire, instruct, or involve to help create great care everywhere and to demonstrate how knowing and doing this will improve the system and care for consumers.

The Care Points are ideas, lessons, actions, or instructions that the audience can implement in their own work and/or personal lives the next day. You can see my need for inspiring and practical help here.

Soon, we'd like to involve younger women and emerging leaders in the confabs, and potentially run them for other sectors as well. Following the first one, there was a call to set up a regional group as well. We held four sold-out Confabs in our first year, 2015.

We also have plans to hold a Women Who Care day long leadership "Womenar" at the end of 2016. We're working positively as a group towards improving care everywhere.

All profits from the Confabs and the "Womenar" will build the fund and eventually be donated to two organisations who help children with disabilities and their families to achieve their potential for a beautiful life (and, sometimes, a good death). The Grow Foundation supports families who want to access the Programme we used for Jacqui Bree, and Very Special Kids cares for children with life-threatening conditions by providing a children's hospice and professional family support services.

I'm not suggesting you need to start a philanthropic fund as I have, but there are a million ways to flex that compassion muscle, and the first focus can be yourself.

I intuitively included compassion as one of my principles of conscious living. At first, when asked why, my answer was that it was around the fact that people in health want to help; they're caring and compassionate, so this helps them connect to the principles. That's still true, but even as I said it the first time, a little sceptical part of me wondered whether it was just the people I knew, whether I was being overly optimistic and naive. But my friend Lesley agreed. As I started to build the charitable organisation, Women Who Care, with Cathy, it struck home so strongly that we are a caring group, a caring gender, and a caring species, and our natural inclination is to help others wherever we can.

If we see or hear or read about someone else suffering, a part of our cortex lights up, the same part that lights up if we are experiencing the suffering ourselves. Keltner says we're "wired to empathise." As well as the cortex, the amygdala, the brain's threat detector, lights up—as does the periaqueductal grey, which is a very old part of "the mammalian nervous system way down in the centre of the brain. This region is associated with nurturing behaviour. We don't just see suffering as a threat. We also instinctively want to alleviate that suffering through nurturance".[17]

Breathing While Drowning

For me, the nurturing happens in lots of ways that satisfy my preferences (introversion, intimacy, integrity, inspiration, and my innate gifts). As well as WWC, I participate in coaching one-on-one, coaching small groups, delivering inspirational and instructional talks, writing to encourage people to change, and organising groups to share stories and wisdom and practice compassion.

Choose your own route to compassion and exercise that muscle—you'll feel better for it, and so will the world.

As I became conscious of how the Cs worked for me, I began to explore the power of intent more seriously and to look for ways to build on the concepts of following your purpose and finding your mission in the world. I was curious about what my life could look like if I really followed my dream, found my purpose, and pursued it with passion. I was still chasing success.

In August 2014, I enrolled in the Feminine Power course with Claire Zammit and Catherine Woodward-Thomas, and connected with a group of women searching for meaning and intending to change their lives and the lives of everyone around them.[18]

September 2014

My intention is to unleash my creative light and allow it to shine brilliantly through my writing so that I share my true voice with my family, my friends and the world in a way that expresses the very best of who I can be.

My intention is to show up in the world truthfully as the brilliant, loving, caring, inspiring, creative and mindful soul that I am, every moment.

I deserve to have dreams and to have those dreams come true. I deserve to be loved and seen and respected.

My true identity — I am part of all that is, deeply related to all, and profoundly necessary to the wellbeing of the whole. Everyone, everywhere belongs to me and I to them.

I am a unique and essential citizen of the world. My contribution and authentic self-expression is essential to the wellbeing of all.

I am deeply loved by all of life, and it is right and good for me to have the best life has to offer. Life grants me the power to generate profound levels of abundance and wellbeing everywhere I go.

I came here to be seen and to have a profound impact on the world, and it is my responsibility to presence my visibility wherever I go. I came here to be seen. It is my destiny to be visible and I now take my rightful place in the world by being willing to presence myself fully.

I see myself. I am deeply present to my own feelings, needs and desires. I intuitively know how to ask for my needs and desires in ways that inspire others to meet them.

Everything I am seeking in life comes via a gateway or relationships with other people.

I begin to develop an inner sense of myself and being that person in life — a writer, story teller and teacher.

My relationship with myself is becoming a source of power in my life. I have strengths, wisdom and wonder.

Breathing While Drowning

This is where I bumped up again and again with the word *surrender*. The whole feminine seemed based on surrendering, and I just couldn't feel right about it. But this is where I heard *surrender* described in the most beautiful way by one of the women in the group, Carol Munchoff. I will be forever grateful for her words and her permission to share them here. What she described was not either/or, but both/all. It began to make sense. I still have to consciously surrender; I'm not a natural yet, but I'm working on it.

"I consider surrender to be more of a releasing into the flow of life rather than struggling against it. It doesn't mean to me that I let people have power over me or that I am weak. In fact, I think those that can surrender their attachment to the outcome and 'go with the flow' are among the wisest, strongest I know. To surrender is to trust that all you have done to prepare for this moment is all that could be done, and now it's time to enjoy and fully experience whatever the result is—without judgement or self-criticism, but with joy and gratitude that you are here to fully experience it. May we all find joy and love in our surrendering to and embracing the balance of our masculine and feminine powers".[19]

I trust that I've done all I need to prepare for this moment, and I will enjoy and fully experience whatever the result is. Finding the feeling was a choice, a choice to be a generator of life despite the disappointments. I choose to have faith that I'm an integral co-creative partner in the evolution of the world. I choose to believe in the inherent goodness of life.

Life is for me, I am never alone, my universal self, the observer, is always there. Life always cares about me. During the course there was a brilliant explanation of the difference in definition between desire and want. The original sense of the word origin and history for "desire" is "await what the stars will bring" which comes from the phrase de sidere "from the stars".[20]

How freaking inspiring is that?

Whereas the origins of "want" are from a "state of destitution, deprived, to be lacking".[21]

I want to live with desire not want. I'm over the scarcity and the "I'm not enough". I am what I am. And this I more than enough. Not only that, but every moment I change and grow and transform towards my desires, brings me closer to concordance, to harmony.

I desire to live fully, to inspire others by who I am and how I am. I desire to connect deeply to my higher power, and be a force for good in this world. At the end of my life, I desire that it meant something that I was here.

Surrender … finally I admit I can't do it all on my own; I'd become increasingly frustrated trying to get the fable written. It was stuck on Chapter 3. I asked for help and began the search for a writing coach. After a few false starts, I almost signed up with a coach overseas, but the time difference and the energy felt all wrong. I asked Marguerite if she knew anyone in her creative circle. She put out the call and it was answered by Megan Dalla-Camina, the author of *Getting real about having it all: be your best, love your career and bring back your sparkle.*[22] I remembered seeing Megan host a women's conference a few years earlier, so I made the call.

With Megan's coaching, I begin to realise that this kind of writing is hard—it's soul writing. I'm on a soul journey, and it's not going to be easy, but it will be healing. She helps me create writing habits that keep me on track. I find the vision for the book, I articulate what I want the writer to feel, and I open up to possibilities. I find my writing voice: vulnerable, authentic, resilient, hopeful, and optimistic. Megan helps me burn through procrastination and doses me with compassion and support.

After a couple of sessions and a few false starts—and after finding the balance between publish and don't publish, memoir and self-help—I finally wrote the introduction to *Breathing While Drowning*. Megan's words to me on 25th February 2015, were:

"I think there's magic in there."

Magic! My heart beats crazily, and I feel that I can do this, I can write.

Breathing While Drowning

So I begin to write ... really write. I start getting up early and putting my writing first. I say to myself, *My writing matters.*

My early morning writing habit was helped by the "Book. Write. Now." closed Facebook group started by the fabulous Tamara Protassow Adams, who is a writer, editor, and coach.[23]

I shared in early morning write-ins because it was comforting knowing that someone else was hammering away at the keys at the same time. For at least an hour each morning—before I did anything else for anybody else—I wrote for myself. I just started and the words began to flow.

I relived all of the angst and pain and gain, and after a few months, I start to come out the other side.

Finding the Inner Man with Heart

All of this exploration into the feminine helped me heal the wounded masculine inside. I swung way into the feminine—too far—and I lost track of the beautiful masculine. Now, however, I'm back to my centre. I acknowledge all the good things the masculine has given me, all the skills and experience and understanding, I practised to reawaken the feminine to reconnect with the core of who I was as a woman and then I integrated the two.

This fits with Murdock's healing the wounded masculine, by "finding the inner man with heart".[24]

I tapped in more and more to myself, accepting all the parts of me, dark and light, masculine and feminine. I'm creative and I get stuff done; I'm compassionate and I'm a great strategist—none of these things are mutually exclusive. I'm strong, resilient, open to learning, a great listener, and an inspiring and caring coach.

At the end of 2014, Marguerite and I attended our level two teacher training programme for the Art of Feminine Presence work with Rachael Jayne Groover and a group of brilliant, beautiful women we've met over the last couple of years. The women come from all walks of life, all sorts of businesses but there was a tendency to come from the healing and spiritual arts and services. We love spending time with these women. There is so much positive energy. They're all entrepreneurs and gorgeous souls, and there is so much acceptance, support, and love that they share. And, of course, there is lots of beautiful hugging!

Towards the end of the couple of days, Marguerite and I were driving home, chatting about a subject that kept popping into our conversations. These women had their ideas, their products, their services, but they feel daunted by the business side often—the foundations and structures, the governance and strategy; the very stuff of life for Marguerite and me.

Together, we conceived of the Art of Women's Business.[25] We developed the alchemy of ideas, clarity, and action.

Initially, we convened a mastermind group as a way to keep in touch with these women, and to help our fabulous friends pull their big girl pants up and get on with sharing their message. We met online from all over Australia and New Zealand to share tips and tools, try out bits and pieces, and support each other through times of wedgies (difficult and not-so-good times) and bloomers (good times and fabulous achievements). All of this was done with a hefty dose of humour.

Following feedback and flow, we developed workshops to support women who wanted to align life and work and get stuff done.

Of course, the C7 model fits what we were trying to do like a glove. Though the expression and language that we use with our Big Girls Pants programme is a little different than what I used when coaching individuals or teams, the 7 principles of women's business resonated in all our work. There is almost a palpable sense of relief when women read the principles—they just work.

As I become more conscious of me, of what I want, of the abundance and beauty that I have around me, I'm also rediscovering the beautiful man I married more than thirty years ago. I can see his strong masculine and feminine, and I realise what a treasure he is, what a beautiful counterpoint to my own emerging blend of feminine and masculine he is.

For our thirtieth wedding anniversary in May of 2015, Strack and I attended the Making Love Retreat with Janet McGeever and Gene Thompson.[26] I met Janet through the Art of Feminine Presence work. Janet and Gene's workshop is based on the work of Diana Richardson.

The workshop felt like being filled up with a warm, golden glow right down to the cellular level. Going to the retreat with Strack was amazing. In short, it was taking the shell off another piece of me and reconnecting it to the whole. Waking up the sensual, loved woman that I am, and opening my eyes to the beautiful, strong, and loving man that I've spent thirty years with.

Janet asked two things of us at the beginning of the six days: to be open and willing. I came with no expectations other than that I trusted Janet and felt connected through our common experience in the Art of Feminine Presence work. More and more, I follow my intuition and surrender to my universal self who knows where she is taking me/us.

One of the best things I learned from Janet and Gene was about how women compromised when it came to lovemaking, even with the most caring partners. And, yes, I have compromised when it came to sex, knowing it would still be okay—not orgasmic (or, sometimes, as I've gotten older, not even very comfortable … but still okay). No more just okay! Sometimes great and sometimes not so great. In this way, I was not respecting or being honest with myself or with Ian. But I thought that was just the way it was.

I came clean about what I felt deeply, how I felt about myself, about our love and lovemaking, and about our life together. The work Janet and Gene do is so important. It gave Ian and I a language and a safe context to explore how we wanted to be with each other and ourselves. Taking our time to be present with each other, to spend hours being together, making love, talking, or quietly experiencing each other deeply.

We have generations of stories and behaviours that put women in a subservient and unequal position that makes them compromise their bodies, their minds, and their souls. Restitution starts with me. I'm prepared to make a stand for me, for my children, for my friends, for everyone that I come in contact with. I will not compromise any longer. I don't need the friction and heat; I choose to experiment and experience cool, slow, conscious love.

How hard is that to keep up when we're not on holidays or a retreat any longer? What will happen when children and money and life come charging back like a bull in a china shop? Perhaps they'll come crashing and smashing along, threatening to drown the embryonic vision.

But if there's one thing I've learned about myself, it's that I am resilient and stubborn. If I want something, I will go after it. It can't be forced; it flows best with spontaneity. Nurture gently, allow it to evolve, build slowly (that is so difficult for me), don't control it—it's part of everything, and everything is part of me. I am calm and full.

I experienced the long, slow, exquisite awakening in parts of me for the first time. Rediscovering our love and recognising the beautiful masculine being who loves me was incredible. Seeing the beautiful, amazing woman that I am in the mirror of the love in his eyes is remarkable. I let him know that the strength of his love is where I have always felt safe to be vulnerable, to be loved, to be silly, or funny, or sad, or hopeful, or flawed.

To feel the beat of his heart under my hand. To trace the outline of his arms and shoulders, to kiss the softness of his eyes. To feel him deep inside, home, connected, open and willing, filling me. To feel the exchange of energy and love and joy.

It's a testament to Strack's love and patience that he came and dived into his first personal transformation workshop, his first of any kind of workshop in his life at fifty-four. It was a big ask—conscious loving. Although we've talked about it a lot together, it would be unfair to try to tell this part of the story for him. Suffice to say he was open and willing. I love that man; he expects nothing, which means I can give him everything. He doesn't judge, he just loves.

The lessons I learned about myself and the world that I realised then—and that I realise now—mean a lot of different things.

Love and trust and respect.

Lesson: love the one you're with, that's you, by the way. After that, it's a whole lot easier to love everyone else because you realise you are so perfectly imperfect, amazingly flawed and fabulous. What's not to love? Every day you breathe in and out, you think, feel, do, believe, and live. Might as well love it and get on with enjoying it.

Imagine your dream life and go get it. The journey is everything.

Lesson: dust off your dream, feel the destination, whatever it is, and freaking go do it, be it, live it. But seriously, you need to honour the journey, take the time to think and feel and do every moment. Don't shy away from the hard stuff, it's all there for you to live and love and learn and grow. Be mindful, live consciously, work creatively, and lead confidently.

Listen to the voices—all of them.

Lesson: those internal voices are all part of you, including those voices that say you're pathetic, you're not enough. They can be really loud, and no personal transformation would be complete without the book of excuses, provided by the voices—seriously, I have the best excuses.

A good way to get over them is just that: get over them, use every sense and spend more time listening to the voices that say, *Go for it, of course you can, let's try again.* Find out whatever it takes—read a book, do some EFT (try Brad Yates, he's fabulous[27]), meditate, talk to someone, take a bath, take a walk, stop and smell the roses. Start with gratitude, be grateful for the moment and what it's offering you. Let yourself curse and wail and grieve and laugh and sing and dance. Let yourself feel it, and then let it go.

Chapter 10

And now?

Jacqui wants her story told. Her story is inextricably linked to mine, and for me the message is incredibly powerful. It's time to shape and share the stories. I won't burden myself, my family, or my friends with my unlived life any longer.

The messages are simple. Love your kids as they are; stop trying to mould them into something you wanted to be, or something you think they should be. Don't judge people by your standards; in fact, don't judge them at all. You have no idea what they're capable of. You've got no idea what you're capable of. Love and learn and live ... every moment.

Stop searching for the answer outside, you always have the answer within you. Get conscious, wake up and smell the roses. Wake up and live, learn, create, and love. Consciousness is not raised by coercion or control; rather, it is raised by example, collaboration, and care. So for goodness sake, leave a legacy that contributes to the world, to the conscious evolution of your community, the human community.

Live and grieve on your own time. Your life belongs to you, and everything you think, feel, do, and believe matters—that's what counts.

Don't get suckered by the excitement and hype of the hero's journey because women have their own unique and powerful adventures, and we go on quests in our own way. It's messy and chaotic, but that's okay.

My wish for you is to have a remarkable life, a life worthy of attention, your attention.

Let yourself be surprised by life and the potential of you and those around you to live consciously, creatively, confidently, and remarkably.

Beyond Duality

Life and choices are never black and white, there are always shades, but they're not grey for any longer. Instead, they're every colour under the sun and then some. I'm moving beyond thinking and being in a state of wanting either choice; I'm being wherever I am, feeling and thinking and doing with a belief that I've prepared as well as I can for this moment. And I'm allowing it to unfold.

Beyond duality, I'm trying to incorporate the following quote from Murdock into my daily life: "We are all one and co-exist along a continuum of life".[1] It's the concept that we're all interconnected, described as *inter-be* as Thich Nhat Hanh tells us. "You cannot just be by yourself. You have to inter-be with everything else".[2]

Beyond duality, not either/or, but all. This concept slides into the universality of us all, that we're all one, all made of energy and all connected. Relationships are at the heart of the matter. The exchange of energy back and forth as words or actions or thoughts; molecules spinning as feeling, ideas, and movement. That I am both feminine and masculine, that we're all somewhere along the continuum at a place just right for us to experience life as we wish.

I'm conscious now, aware, searching. It's like I've opened Pandora's box. Actually, the image that comes to me is opening the lid on a bucket of crickets. The thoughts, ideas and emotions leap about like crazy, going this way and that, trying to find the answer, the meaning, and the purpose.

Honour the learning journey. It's not where you get to, it's how you get there. Hold the bucket and watch the crickets: feel them jumping and laugh and love the moment.

I am going confidently in the direction of my dreams. Curiosity is my modus operandi. I have an insatiable curiosity, a search for knowledge and learning and, at the moment, I'm curiously searching for equanimity.

Equanimity is the path; it's a fundamental skill for self-exploration and emotional intelligence. It's a deep and subtle concept frequently misunderstood and easily confused via the suppression of feeling and the acceptance of apathy. Equanimity comes from the Latin word *aequus* meaning *balanced* and *animus* meaning *spirit* or *internal state*.[3]

For me, equanimity represents stability and composure. It's the point where I can be less disturbed by my experiences—emotional or otherwise. I can stay on an even keel.

I'm in search of the still point, that point where body, mind, and soul come together: mindful, past, present, future, being. For me, the still point is not the spot where there is a lack of movement; it's the eye of the storm of being. It's here that I want to be. It's the all-time, no time, connected me.

Of course, we're never wholly right or wholly on purpose; rather, we're mostly there, experiencing, learning, relearning, growing, and transforming. It's perfect imperfection.

It's the being that is so hard. How hard is it to surrender for someone who has relied on strength and no one else to stay alive, to breathe, to be resilient? There is no one to compete with in the game of being me. I am the world's expert on me.

And, yes, I'll say it again: my life belongs to me, everything I think, feel, do, and believe matters—and that's what counts.

I'd like to be an inspiring, wise, creative, compassionate leader. I'd like to be a door opener, a catalyst for change, someone who ignites the spark in everyone she meets.

How would you like to be known, what's your legacy?

I'm wise, funny, curious, nosy, authentic, creative, bold, mindful, flawed, scarred, respectful, thoughtful, lazy, considerate, driven, bold, caring, selfish, connected, inspiring, learning, writing, vulnerable, thorough, and so much more. I'm a woman, a mother, a lover, a wife, a friend, a sister, an aunt. I'm a writer, a coach, a speaker, a facilitator, a strategist, a knowledge broker. And I'm only just getting started.

Who do you want to be?

My dream as a child was to be a writer. This dream survived the dream to be a green grocer, an astronaut, and a biochemist. When did I let it slide? Was there a moment when I could have chosen to step into it? Was there a turning point when I turned away? Somewhere along the way, I absorbed the belief that writing wasn't a real job … and I had to get a real job. Science is smarter than arts. You're smart, so do science. It was never what I wanted, but it satisfied my curiosity to a great extent.

Well bugger that. It's never too late to start. If I can run a marathon at forty-nine, I can write a book at fifty-four. I've given myself a deadline, and I'm on it—this is the final chapter.

The best thing about being my age is that I have all this experience, these skills, these stories, and a host of memories from my life to free me to be who I want to be and to do what I want to do. I have the power to make myself visible and valued.

My feelings, needs and desires matter to me. My life matters, and it belongs to me. I'm deeply loved by all of life. I was designed to be deeply connected to others. I have the power to keep myself safe. I can access the support I need to flourish and thrive; the universe is organising around my success.

I'm learning how to let go if it isn't working.

Breathing While Drowning

At my biggest, boldest, and most creative, I bring people, especially women, together to find their way home to themselves.

The re-emergence of women as a force for positive change in this world is so important to me. Women hold the power to define the twenty-first century, bringing men with them to a more balanced existence.

I love that Murdock wrote the following words in 1990, and it is even truer today: "I believe that women are deeply affecting the critical mass. As each one of us heals our own feminine and masculine nature we change the consciousness of the planet from one of addiction to suffering, conflict and domination to a consciousness that recognises the need for affiliation, healing, balance, and inter-being. Women need to breathe more knowledge, more prajna, into the world to restore the imbalance. We are a pilgrim people, we are on a journey together to learn how to honour and preserve the dignity of all life forms seen and unseen, therein lies our heroic power"[4].

I am a great connector. I feel like I'm constantly creating communities, bringing people together into circles of learning. The circle is an incredibly powerful way to be, and it supports our move as a world full of people who can see each other. Being beyond dualism is a focus in my life right now, but we are all part of a much larger story, an evolution of consciousness in the world. Murdock said, "The structure of community is a circle. Movement within a circle takes place easily and not at the expense of others"[5].

I have to agree: there is magic in a circle, and it becomes transformative magic when that circle is made up of women. Listening happens in a circle, everyone is equal and exposed. You can see all and everyone is accountable for themselves and the others. There's something about sitting around together that invites exploration and reflection, shared stories and vulnerabilities. It takes time to trust, but with good friends, we slip into the comfort zone really quickly. And when they ask, "How are you?" we know they mean "How are you *really*?"

Nothing beats being there in real life, but the spirit of circles can be achieved on video, teleconference, or even around a rectangular table. It takes a little more imagination, but it can happen.

I use circles in many different ways. I always try to have circular tables or groups when I facilitate for the magic equality that they bring. They give opportunity to all, and align with my values and facilitation style.

I am a woman, feminine and masculine, my body is soft and made up from so many round shapes, breasts, belly, hips, and butt—okay, maybe not so round these days. I totally embrace the softness, the roundness, and the ability to receive. I'm a vessel for life and learning. From that vessel, I can give and restore and heal. For decades, I ignored and even scoffed at recognising this part of me. Beyond dualism for me is bringing all the parts of me together and reconnecting and loving them all—seeing them as a part of my whole. I am recognising that I am a part of everything, and everything is a part of me.

I am a great decision maker. The hardest decision I have ever had to make was to stop resuscitating my beautiful Jacqui Bree. To let her go, to look into her eyes and know she was already gone. To look at the hope in the eyes of my darling husband and to hear, "We have to let her go, she's gone." To see the light go out in his eyes is something I will never forget. Even now I feel my heart tightening and my tears welling up.

Once you've made a decision like that and lived with it for a while, no other decision seems like much trouble at all. It all more or less seems logical, even the emotional part.

I am resilient. I bounce back no matter what. I have things to do, places to go, me to be. I can always find a silver lining, the small kernel of stubbornness that won't give up. Sometimes it takes a little dive into the darkness, some confusion, conflict, and closure. But I can adapt, absorb, learn, and move on. Knowledge is my right as a conscious being. No matter how many times I get knocked down, I get back up, stronger and smarter and ready to go again.

Breathing While Drowning

I am an intuitive strategist and organiser. I can see where all the planes are up in the sky, and I know when and where the best place to land each one is. This is how my brain works, I see the patterns, and the longer I live and work and breathe, the easier it is to see the patterns. I can see order to the patterns. I can make all the big overwhelming steps into small achievable steps. And I can adapt. The plans can flex and change as new things come into view. With the end in sight, the journey is the thing.

I am a compassionate coach. I carry this unshakeable optimism and belief in the magnificence of people to live fully and creatively and confidently. I love to see the light turn on in their eyes and their hearts when they realise what's important and understand their strengths and capabilities to bring their dream within reach.

I am a writer. This book is my proof.

I am enough.

Despite thinking I would change the world when I was young, I mostly drifted through life taken by the currents of the world and family I was born into. I was very lucky with my family, third child of eight, second daughter of three. I was loved and safe and encouraged. Maybe time has softened the edges of memory or my current state of gratefulness filters the painful bits out.

I loved books and other worlds. I loved heroines like Heidi and Alice; they lived happily ever after despite trials and tribulations. They had courage and tenacity and resilience. Snug in my working-class family, it was all a little unreal, but I wished it were so: I wished I could be the heroine and inspire people to kindness and thoughtfulness, to reconnect them to love and loved ones. Be feted for saving the day.

But when the time came, I didn't have what it took. I didn't step up and lead, tell the truth regardless, and fight against injustice. I didn't triumph over tragedy. Instead, I let tragedy bury me. I pretended to be someone else, and I was really good at it—pretending, that is.

Many people think that I coped really well. After all, I went back to work within a couple of weeks after my daughter had died (back to work as a midwife). I have three beautiful children, one conceived after Jacqui Bree died. I was the primary breadwinner and had a great career. I worked all across Australia as a successful project and change manager, a CEO, a consultant, and a board member. The owner of my own business (okay, four businesses—two more with friends, and a not-for-profit with another friend).

What I did do really well was pretend; I did that really, really well. I pretended that I was okay, pretended that life was good, pretended that I was happy. I almost convinced myself. But my higher self finally got sick of the pretending, sick of me ignoring my opportunities to stand up and be the heroine and leader that I had dreamed of being when I was a child. I took that one brave step and admitted out loud that I wasn't content.

Jacqueline Bree changed my life. Where I thought I missed being a heroine is in not having the courage to acknowledge how devastated I was when she died, how the bottom fell out of my perfect world, how hard it was to hold on to life. How little I had realised the preciousness of perfectly well children, of Cassi Kate, and Angus Peter.

When I lifted Jacqui's small coffin on to my shoulders it was unexpectedly heavy; in life she had been so light. Along with Strack and my dad, we carried her out to the hearse and away from me forever. The heaviness of the wood settled like the weight of the world on my shoulders and into my heart.

From that moment the unreality of her passing hit me like a tidal wave. I reached for her coffin to touch her for the last time, suddenly realising that this was it. I'd been going through the motions up until that point. I felt like I was drowning and couldn't breathe.

The only way I could survive was to hold my breath, hold everything, I swallowed all the emotion, closed it off in a small portion of my heart and swore I would not feel that pain ever again. What I didn't realise is that the universe was listening and heard that internal shout that I didn't want to feel ever again.

What I wish I had done was to scream and cry and grieve, I wish I had been outwardly sad that my beautiful daughter was gone. I would never hold her gangly body and kiss her nose again; never brush her lovely, smooth, brown hair again; never feed her, bathe her, dress her, watch her sleep, watch her breathe again.

What I wish I had done was embrace my husband and tell him I was not okay, that I didn't want to go back to work, that I needed to be sad a while longer. That we both did.

What I wish I had done was show my other daughter and son that I was really sad, and that it was okay, that I still loved them.

What I wish I had done was use my energy to lead a movement to help children and parents who are managing a disability. I could have given them a voice, an ear, a shoulder, and helped them navigate the health system because I was an insider.

But, of course, my higher self had different ideas. And now that I've sat around for twenty years and played around the edges of my life, I have a whole new set of experiences and bits of expertise to share. I wasn't ready then, but I am now.

Instead of staying home, I went to work, and the world of work welcomed me with open arms. No emotion here, business women don't care and spiritual women don't wear suits. You can't care and run a company; you can't be emotional and expect to be seen as a leader.

Along the way, I had so much help and love from my beautiful family, including the addition of the delightful Frazer Douglas. They loved my restlessness, selfishness, and crazy ideas. They kept me grounded, kept me safe until I could learn to face my demons, look myself in the face, and love what I saw—warts and all. They helped me forgive myself and find myself.

I am a woman who has a lot to give, who still wants to make a difference, and who still believes it's not too late to follow your dreams. I am a woman who recognises her shadows and is still an optimist.

Now my dream is bigger: I want to help all women who have closed off the caring part of themselves, the feminine part, or shut down their dreams of making a difference for the weight of responsibility. I want to do this regardless of whether the death they've experienced is physical, mental, or emotional.

In fact, why just women? How about men having the opportunity to live life fully present, to feel and grow their emotional and spiritual selves, not just their physical and mental selves?

So how come I can breathe without drowning now? When did I give up holding on and begin to let go? What did it take? It took time being confused and conflicted and closed—years, in fact—and then it took consciousness, curiosity, creativity, and capability. And all the time it took courage to be compassionate to reconnect to find all the parts of myself and bring them back to concordance.

So I'm going to keep following my bliss; otherwise, the dream is always a dream. I am a great listener, but I would love people to listen to me sometimes—really listen to me, not just the words that come out of my mouth, but the desires that come out of my soul.

I want you, my reader, to experience inspiration, hope, compassion, permission to dream, will to action, and humour. I want to share how I kept going, how I dreamed and worked towards the dream, and somewhere in these pages are how you can too.

The lessons I learned about myself and the world that I realised then—and that I realise now—mean a lot of different things.

Give up pretending and give yourself a chance. It's your time right now, and it's never too late. My life belongs to me, every thought, feeling, action, and belief I have matters to me—and that's what counts.

Breathing While Drowning

Lesson: your life belongs to you. You can choose to let it slip through your fingers unconsciously, robotically going through the motions, or you can choose to live consciously. Live a life that expresses the very best of who you are. Work creatively at whatever job you choose to do. Lead confidently in your own life knowing it's of your own choosing, inspiring and instructing others through your example. Start by living a conscious life, get curious about what you want and who you are, be courageous and step into who you want to be, build your capability, and realise you are enough. You have the stuff; explore your creativity knowing your life belongs to you. And what you do matters, practice compassion, connect the world to kindness, and go confidently in the direction of your dreams.

And sometimes I still descend into the darkness, the weight on my shoulders is crippling; my hands are too small to hold all the strings.

I can't keep breathing and hold myself and everyone else up. I'm just not strong enough.

I feel paralysed with grief; I can't believe I can take another breath. How can I live with this, without her? It's hard now to revisit the pain and dark times. They still come in waves from time to time, but now I can see myself going down and can reach out for a life buoy, a branch.

And now? I feel strongly that I need to make the best life I can with what I've got, not making do or being mediocre. We need to raise the vibrations of ourselves and the planet. We have such an opportunity to go to the next level. I want to ascend, and I want everyone around me to do so too.

How can we imagine a life spent just observing and existing is enough? It's not. Life has to be jumped into with both feet. Step forward.

So here's my Womanifesto:
Hold life lightly.
Spend every minute as if it were your last.
Love ferociously.
Learn voraciously.
Live boldly.
Create passionately.
Practice curiosity.
Laugh and let go.
Leave people to their own stuff.
Remember fondly.
Look forward hopefully.
Try stuff.
Make mistakes.
Try more stuff.
Be the person you want to be.
Cajole, encourage, support, help, teach, mentor.
Share wisdom, wine, and wit.
Always have time for a hug.
Bring the joy and be the change you want to see in the world.
Be the leader you would like to follow.

Have I loved today?
Have I created today?
Have I lived boldly today?
Am I mindful?
Live it, love it, be it.
Dream, direction, doing it.
Go out and create lovingly, live boldly, and be mindfully.

Breathing While Drowning

Hold life lightly ...

Be ...

Be gracious ...

Be willing to yield ...

Be free of obligation ...

Meet my limitations, let them be ...

Paste them to the ground, stellar soil, universal unguent, quantum space ...

Peel them off gently and rearrange to open heart and mind.

Trust

Be held, trust, it's OK

Be ...

Hold life lightly ...

My life belongs to me, what I think, feel, do, and believe matters—and that's what counts.

Thanks for reading.

Have a remarkable life.

6 November 2015, 2:08pm
Veronica Strachan

Thank you

Thank you for reading *Breathing While Drowning*. If you enjoyed or felt moved by my story, please consider taking a moment to write a short review on your favourite platform. As an independent author, I rely on reviews and word of mouth to share my stories. Even a couple of sentences can make a real difference. Your support and feedback are greatly appreciated, and someone who needs to read this story may find it by reading your review.

Since I completed Breathing While Drowning, I've created a companion workbook and journal that guides you along your own of self-discovery quest. *The Wholeness Quest Workbook & Journal* is based on the exercises I used myself, as well as others I've found successful during my years of life and leadership coaching. You can purchase *The Wholeness Quest Workbook & Journal* from online book retailers or from your favourite bookstore.

About the Author

Veronica Strachan was born to working class parents in the northern suburbs of Melbourne, Australia. The birth of her second daughter who had a severe brain injury, changed the direction of Veronica's life forever. The lessons she learnt from Jacqueline Bree's life and death are now her touchstone for living a whole, vibrant and remarkable life.

From her early career as a nurse and midwife, through evolutions as a project and change manager, CEO and consultant, Veronica now divides her time between writing and coaching remarkable leaders who want to make a powerful and compassionate impact on the world.

All sale profits from this book are contributed to Very Special Kids, which operates a hospice for terminally-ill children in Victoria.

Veronica and her daughter Cassi have teamed up for a new picture book series, *The Adventures of Chickabella*. Book 1 is *Chickabella and the Rainbow Magic*, Book 2 is *Chickabella Counts to Ten*. Book 3 - *Chickabella Shapes up*, is due for release in late 2020.

You can find out more about Veronica's writing and get in touch via www.veronicastrachan.com or follow her on Twitter @truedialogue and Instagream @writer_ron.

Bibliography

Introduction

1. Brown, Brené. 2012. *Daring Greatly – How the Courage to Be Vulnerable Transforms the Way We Live, Love, Parent and Lead.* London: Penguin Group.
2. Steinem, Gloria. 1992. *Revolution from Within: A Book of Self-Esteem.*
3. Webster, Bethany. 2014. *The rupture of the mother line and the cost of becoming real.* Webster http://womboflight.com/2014/12/21/the-rupture-of-the-mother-line-and-the-cost-of-becoming-real/.
4. Mohr, Tara. 2015. *Tara Mohr.* February. http://www.taramohr.com/2015/02/change-perspective-helps/.
5. Edelman, Hope. 1995. *Letters from Motherless Daughters Words of courage, grief, and healing (Australian edition).* Rydalmere: Hodder & Stoughton.
6. Murdock, Maureen. 1990. *The Heroine's Journey – Woman's Quest for Wholeness.* Boston: Shambhala Publications, Inc.
7. Murdock, Maureen. 1990. *The Heroine's Journey – Woman's Quest for Wholeness.* Boston: Shambhala Publications, Inc.
8. Dalla-Camina, Megan. 2012. *Getting real about having it all: be your best, love your career and bring back your sparkle.* Hay House.

Part 1: Defining Moments

1. Murdock, Maureen. 1990. *The Heroine's Journey – Woman's Quest for Wholeness.* Boston: Shambhala Publications, Inc.

2   Popova, Maria. 2014. *Brainpickings: Famous Writers on the Creative Benefits of Keeping a Diary*. 4 September. https://www.brainpickings.org/2014/09/04/famous-writers-on-keeping-a-diary/.
3   Bradshaw, Joanna. 2015. *Blog: I read like a squirrel and I'm not sorry*. 2 July. http://www.joannabradshaw.com/squirrel.

Chapter 1: The Unremarkable Early Years

1   Murdock, Maureen. 1990. *The Heroine's Journey – Woman's Quest for Wholeness*. Boston: Shambhala Publications, Inc.
2   Murdock, Maureen. 1990. *The Heroine's Journey – Woman's Quest for Wholeness*. Boston: Shambhala Publications, Inc.
3   Murdock, Maureen. 1990. *The Heroine's Journey – Woman's Quest for Wholeness*. Boston: Shambhala Publications, Inc.
4   Murdock, Maureen. 1990. *The Heroine's Journey – Woman's Quest for Wholeness*. Boston: Shambhala Publications, Inc.
5   Murdock, Maureen. 1990. *The Heroine's Journey – Woman's Quest for Wholeness*. Boston: Shambhala Publications, Inc.
6   Murdock, Maureen. 1990. *The Heroine's Journey – Woman's Quest for Wholeness*. Boston: Shambhala Publications, Inc.
7   Fairchild, Alana, Rassouli and Cohen, Richard. 2014. "Journey of Love." Cosmic Butterfly.

Chapter 2: The Unaware Years

1   Murdock, Maureen. 1990. *The Heroine's Journey – Woman's Quest for Wholeness*. Boston: Shambhala Publications, Inc.
2   Murdock, Maureen. 1990. *The Heroine's Journey – Woman's Quest for Wholeness*. Boston: Shambhala Publications, Inc.
3   Morrison, Kristin. 2015. *Home*. http://www.growfoundationforkids.org.au/.
4   Brown, Brené. 2012. *Daring Greatly – How the Courage to Be Vulnerable Transforms the Way We Live, Love, Parent and Lead*. London: Penguin Group.

5   Strachan, Veronica and Balding, Cathy. 2015. Home. http:// http://www.womenwhocare.com.au/.
6   Burchard, Brendon. 2014. *The Motivation Manifesto: 9 Declarations to Claim Your Personal Power.* Hay House.

Chapter 3: The Programme Years

1   Morrison, Kristin. 2015. Home. http://www.growfoundationforkids.org.au/.
2   Doman, Janet. 2015. *IAHP: 60 Years of Search and Discovery.* 14 May. http://www.iahp.org/60-years-of-search-discovery/.
3   Heath, Chip Heath and Dan. 2010. *Sw!tch: How to change th!ngs when change !s hard.* New York: Random House Business Books.
4   McGeever, Janet and Thompson, Gene. 2003. Home. http://makingloveretreat.com.au/.
5   Dawson, Leonie. 2014. *Blog.* 24 July. http://leoniedawson.com/how-to-achieve/.
6   Sheldon, Christie Marie. 2015. *Unlimited Abundance with Christie Marie Sheldon/About.* 26 September. http://www.unlimitedabundance.com/.
7   Williamson, Marianne. 1992. *A Return to Love: Reflections on the Principles of "A Course in Miracles."* Harper Collins.
8   Sharkey, Clay. 2010. *How cognitive surplus will change the world.* http://www.ted.com/talks/clay_shirky_how_cognitive_surplus_will_change_the_world
9   Burchard, Brendon. 2015. Home. https://brendonburchard.com/.
10 Popova, Maria. 2014. *Brainpickings: Famous Writers on the Creative Benefits of Keeping a Diary.* 4 September. https://www.brainpickings.org/2014/09/04/famous-writers-on-keeping-a-diary/.
11 Edelman, Hope. 1995. *Letters from Motherless Daughters Words of courage, grief, and healing (Australian edition).* Rydalmere: Hodder & Stoughton.
12 Kübler-Ross, Elizabeth. 1969. *On Death and Dying.*

13. Keltner, Dacher. 2012. *Mind & Body: The Compassionate Species.* 31 July. http://greatergood.berkeley.edu/article/item/the_compassionate_species.
14. Keltner, Dacher. 2012. *Mind & Body: The Compassionate Species.* 31 July. http://greatergood.berkeley.edu/article/item/the_compassionate_species.
15. Hawkins, David R. 1995. *Power vs Force: The Hidden Determinant of Human Behaviour.* Veritas Publishing.

Chapter 4: The Closure and Descent

1. Brown, Brené. 2012. *Daring Greatly: How the Courage to Be Vulnerable Transforms the Way We Live, Love, Parent and Lead.* London: Penguin Group.
2. Brown, Brené. 2012. *Daring Greatly: How the Courage to Be Vulnerable Transforms the Way We Live, Love, Parent and Lead.* London: Penguin Group.
3. Murdock, Maureen. 1990. *The Heroine's Journey – Woman's Quest for Wholeness.* Boston: Shambhala Publications, Inc.
4. Murdock, Maureen. 1990. *The Heroine's Journey – Woman's Quest for Wholeness.* Boston: Shambhala Publications, Inc.
5. Murdock, Maureen. 1990. *The Heroine's Journey – Woman's Quest for Wholeness.* Boston: Shambhala Publications, Inc.
6. Murdock, Maureen. 1990. *The Heroine's Journey – Woman's Quest for Wholeness.* Boston: Shambhala Publications, Inc.
7. Bays, Jan Chozen. 2014. *Mindfulness on the go.* Boston: Shambhala Publications, Inc.
8. Sheehan, Martina and Pearse, Susan. 2012. *Wired for Life – Retrain your brain and thrive.* Hay House.
9. Sheehan, Martina and Pearse, Susan. 2012. *Wired for Life – Retrain your brain and thrive.* Hay House.
10. Sheehan, Martina and Pearse, Susan. 2012. *Wired for Life – Retrain your brain and thrive.* Hay House.
11. Dyer, Wayne 2015. *My Greatest Teacher.* Directed by Michael Goorjian.

12 Moorjani, Anita. 2012. *Dying to be me: my journey from cancer, to near death, to true healing.* Sydney: Hay House.

Chapter 5: The Years of Guilt, Shame, and Despair

1 Felder, Don, Glen Frey, and Don Henley. 1976 *Hotel California.* https://www.youtube.com/watch?v=mpAkMk0phOs.
2 Covey, Steven R. 1989. *The 7 Habits of Highly Effective People: Powerful Lessons in Personal Change.* New York: Simon and Schuster.
3 Dyer, Wayne. 2015. *My Greatest Teacher.* Directed by Michael Goorjian.
4 Moorjani, Anita. 2012 *Dying to be me: my journey from cancer, to near death, to true healing.* Sydney: Hay House.
5 Dowrick, Stephanie. 1997. *Forgiveness and Other Acts of Love.* Allen & Unwin.
6 Burchard, Brendon. 2012. *The Charge: Activating the 10 human drives that make you feel alive.* New York: Simon & Schuster.
7 Gaskins, Tony. 2015. *Home.* 11 August. http://tonygaskins.com/.
8 Bedingfield, Natasha. 2004. *These Words (I Love You, I Love You).* Comps. Natasha Bedingfield, Steve Kipner, Andrew Frampton and Wayne Wilkins. https://www.youtube.com/watch?v=e5RuGj0g1tk.
9 Brown, Brené. 2012. *Daring Greatly – How the Courage to Be Vulnerable Transforms the Way We Live, Love, Parent and Lead.* London: Penguin Group.
10 Brown, Brené 2012. *Daring Greatly – How the Courage to Be Vulnerable Transforms the Way We Live, Love, Parent and Lead.* London: Penguin Group.
11 Brown, Brené. 2012. *Daring Greatly – How the Courage to Be Vulnerable Transforms the Way We Live, Love, Parent and Lead.* London: Penguin Group.
12 Brown, Brené. 2012. *Daring Greatly – How the Courage to Be Vulnerable Transforms the Way We Live, Love, Parent and Lead.* London: Penguin Group.
13 Neil, Mel. 2015. *Home.* http://melneil.com.au/.

14 Neil, Mel. 2015. *Home*. http://melneil.com.au/.
15 Brown, Brené. 2012. *Daring Greatly – How the Courage to Be Vulnerable Transforms the Way We Live, Love, Parent and Lead*. London: Penguin Group.
16 Murdock, Maureen. 1990. *The Heroine's Journey – Woman's Quest for Wholeness*. Boston: Shambhala Publications, Inc
17 Blanford, Monty. 1950. *The Philosophers Notebook*.
18 Blanford, Monty. 1950. *The Philosophers Notebook*.
19 Blanford, Monty. 1950. *The Philosophers Notebook*.
20 Gibran, Kahlil. 1923. *The Prophet*. Alfred A Knopf.
21 School of Philosophy. 2009. *Home*. www.schoolofphilosophy.org.au.
22 School of Philosophy. 2009. *Home*. www.schoolofphilosophy.org.au.
23 Burchard, Brendon. 2012. *The Charge: Activating the 10 human drives that make you feel alive*. New York: Simon & Schuster.
24 Gaskins, Tony. 2015. *Home*. 11 August. http://tonygaskins.com/.

Part 2: Finding the Feeling: Do You Remember How It Really Feels to Feel?

1 Reynolds, Marcia. 2013. *The "Turning Age 30, 40 or 50 Life Crisis" for Women*. 8 March. https://www.psychologytoday.com/blog/wander-woman/201303/the-turning-age-30-40-or-50-life-crisis-women?#_=_.
2 Reynolds, Marcia. 2013. *The "Turning Age 30, 40 or 50 Life Crisis" for Women*. 8 March. https://www.psychologytoday.com/blog/wander-woman/201303/the-turning-age-30-40-or-50-life-crisis-women?#_=_.
3 Reynolds, Marcia. 2013. *The "Turning Age 30, 40 or 50 Life Crisis" for Women*. 8 March. https://www.psychologytoday.com/blog/wander-woman/201303/the-turning-age-30-40-or-50-life-crisis-women?#_=_.

Chapter 6: Is This as Good as It Gets?

1. Murdock, Maureen. 1990. *The Heroine's Journey – Woman's Quest for Wholeness.* Boston: Shambhala Publications, Inc.
2. Murdock, Maureen. 1990. *The Heroine's Journey – Woman's Quest for Wholeness.* Boston: Shambhala Publications, Inc.
3. Murdock, Maureen. 1990. *The Heroine's Journey – Woman's Quest for Wholeness.* Boston: Shambhala Publications, Inc.
4. Murdock, Maureen. 1990. *The Heroine's Journey – Woman's Quest for Wholeness.* Boston: Shambhala Publications, Inc.
5. Brown, Brené. 2012. *Daring Greatly – How the Courage to Be Vulnerable Transforms the Way We Live, Love, Parent and Lead.* London: Penguin Group.
6. Zammit, Claire and Thomas, Katherine Woodward. 2014. *Women's Spirituality and Empowerment.* 28 August. http://evolvingwisdom.com/programs/womens-spirituality-and-empowerment.php.
7. Zammit, Claire and Thomas, Katherine Woodward. 2014. *Women's Spirituality and Empowerment.* 28 August. http://evolvingwisdom.com/programs/womens-spirituality-and-empowerment.php.
8. Zammit, Claire and Thomas, Katherine Woodward. 2014. *Women's Spirituality and Empowerment.* 28 August. http://evolvingwisdom.com/programs/womens-spirituality-and-empowerment.php.

Part 3: Where Do You Find Healing?

1. Harper, Douglas. 2015. *bereave.* 20 10. http://dictionary.reference.com/browse/bereave.

Chapter 7: The Search Begins

1. Silva, Laura. 2015. *The Silva Method.* 26 September. https://www.silvamethod.com/.
2. Williamson, Marianne. 1992. *A Return to Love: Reflections on the Principles of "A Course in Miracles."* Harper Collins.

3. Williamson, Marianne. 1992. A Return to Love: Reflections on the Principles of "A Course in Miracles." Harper Collins.
4. Williamson, Marianne. 1992. *A Return to Love: Reflections on the Principles of "A Course in Miracles."* Harper Collins.
5. Lakhiani, Vishen. 2012. *Goal setting redefined.* May. http://www.mindvalley.com/goal-setting-redefined#sthash.CmECQHzU.dpbs.
6. Silva, José. 2015. *José Silva: the biography and research of the mind pioneer/home.* 18 May. http://www.jose-silva.net/.
7. Myss, Carolyn. 1996. *The Anatomy of the Spirit: The seven stages of power and healing.* New York: Crown Publishers.
8. Sheldon, Christie Marie. 2015. *Love or Above.* http://www.loveorabove.com/.
9. Mindvalley. 2013. *Mindvalley.* http://www.mindvalley.com/.
10. Hawkins, David R. 1995. *Power vs Force: The Hidden Determinant of Human Behaviour.* Veritas Publishing.
11. Sheehan, Martina and Pearse, Susan. 2012. *Wired for Life – Retrain your brain and thrive.* Hay House.
12. Sheehan, Martina and Pearse, Susan. 2012. *Wired for Life – Retrain your brain and thrive.* Hay House.
13. Sheehan, Martina and Pearse, Susan. 2012. *Wired for Life – Retrain your brain and thrive.* Hay House.
14. Murdock, Maureen. 1990. *The Heroine's Journey – Woman's Quest for Wholeness.* Boston: Shambhala Publications, Inc.
15. Sorensen, Mette. 2015. *Women's Retreat.* 14 October. www.highspiritsretreat.com.au.
16. Sorensen, Mette. 2015. *Women's Retreat.* 14 October. www.highspiritsretreat.com.au.
17. Sheldon, Christie Marie. 2015. *Unlimited Abundance with Christie Marie Sheldon/About.* 26 September. http://www.unlimitedabundance.com/.
18. Moorjani, Anita. 2012. *Dying to be me: my journey from cancer, to near death, to true healing.* Sydney: Hay House.

Chapter 8: Coming Home

1. Murdock, Maureen. 1990. *The Heroine's Journey – Woman's Quest for Wholeness*. Boston: Shambhala Publications, Inc.
2. Groover, Rachael Jayne. 2011. *Powerful and Feminine: How to increase your magnetic presence and attract the attention you want*. Fort Collins: Deep Pacific Press.
3. Groover, Rachael Jayne. 2011. *Powerful and Feminine: How to increase your magnetic presence and attract the attention you want*. Fort Collins: Deep Pacific Press.
4. Burgin, Keele. 2013. *Blog*. 02 November. http://keeleburgin.com/.
5. Murdock, Maureen. 1990. *The Heroine's Journey – Woman's Quest for Wholeness*. Boston: Shambhala Publications, Inc.
6. Murdock, Maureen. 1990. *The Heroine's Journey – Woman's Quest for Wholeness*. Boston: Shambhala Publications, Inc.
7. Murdock, Maureen. 1990. *The Heroine's Journey – Woman's Quest for Wholeness*. Boston: Shambhala Publications, Inc.
8. Strachan, Veronica, Marguerite Davie, and Veronica Zeinstra. 2013. *Welcome*. 13 September. http://www.trueblissco.com.au/

Part 4: Searching for Connection

Chapter 9: A Conscious, Purposeful Life

1. Burchard, Brendon. 2012. *The Charge: Activating the 10 human drives that make you feel alive*. New York: Simon & Schuster.
2. Burchard, Brendon. 2015. *Home*. https://brendonburchard.com/.
3. Ismail, Hafizah. 2016. Home. https://hafizahismail.com/.
4. Balding, Cathy. 2014. *Home*. http://www.cathybalding.com/.
5. Burchard, Brendon. 2015. *Videos*. https://brendonburchard.com/videos/.
6. Burchard, Brendon. 2014. *The Motivation Manifesto: 9 Declarations to Claim Your Personal Power*. Hay House.
7. McIndoo, Anne. 2006. *So, you want to write! How to get your book out of your head and onto the paper in 7 days*.

8. Cameron, Julia. 2002. *The Artist's Way: A spiritual path to higher creativity.* New York: Penguin Putnam.
9. Bau, Ivana. 2015. *Home.* http://goddessoflight.com.au/.
10. Moorjani, Anita. 2012. *Dying to be me: my journey from cancer, to near death, to true healing.* Sydney: Hay House.
11. Keltner, Dacher. 2012. *Mind & Body: The Compassionate Species.* 31 July. http://greatergood.berkeley.edu/article/item/the_compassionate_species.
12. Marsh, Jason. 2004. *Big Ideas: In search of the moral voice.* 1 March. http://greatergood.berkeley.edu/article/item/in_search_of_the_moral_voice.
13. Keltner, Dacher. 2012. *Mind & Body: The Compassionate Species.* 31 July. http://greatergood.berkeley.edu/article/item/the_compassionate_species.
14. University of California, Berkeley. 2015. *Compassion: What is compassion?* http://greatergood.berkeley.edu/topic/compassion/definition.
15. Neff, Kristin. 2011. *Self-Compassion.* William Morrow.
16. Strachan, Veronica. 2013. *Practical Leadership.* July. http://www.truedialogue.com.au/practical-leadership.html.
17. Keltner, Dacher. 2012. *Mind & Body: The Compassionate Species.* 31 July. http://greatergood.berkeley.edu/article/item/the_compassionate_species.
18. Zammit, Claire and Thomas, Katherine Woodward. 2014. *Women's Spirituality and Empowerment.* 28 August. http://evolvingwisdom.com/programs/womens-spirituality-and-empowerment.php.
19. Munchoff, Carol. 2014. Personal conversation.
20. Dictionary.com. 2015. *Dictionary.com.* 25 May. http://dictionary.reference.com/browse/.
21. Dictionary.com. 2015. *Dictionary.com.* 25 May. http://dictionary.reference.com/browse/.
22. Dalla-Camina, Megan. 2012. *Getting real about having it all: be your best, love your career and bring back your sparkle.* Hay House.
23. Protassow, Tamara. 2015. *Home.* February. http://tamaraprotassow.com/.

24. Murdock, Maureen. 1990. *The Heroine's Journey – Woman's Quest for Wholeness*. Boston: Shambhala Publications, Inc.
25. Davie, Marguerite, and Strachan, Veronica. 2015. *Work It*. January. http://www.artofwomensbusiness.com/.
26. McGeever, Janet and Thompson, Gene. 2008. *Home*. http://makingloveretreat.com.au/.
27. Yates, Brad. 2015. *Start here*. http://www.tapwithbrad.com/project/start-here/.

Chapter 10: And Now?

1. Murdock, Maureen. 1990. *The Heroine's Journey – Woman's Quest for Wholeness*. Boston: Shambhala Publications, Inc.
2. Hanh, Thich Nhat. 1988. *The Heart of Understanding: Commentaries on the Prajnaparamita Heat Sutra*. Berkeley: Parallax Press.
3. Dictionary.com. 2015. *Dictionary.com*. 25 May. http://dictionary.reference.com/browse/.
4. Murdock, Maureen. 1990. *The Heroine's Journey – Woman's Quest for Wholeness*. Boston: Shambhala Publications, Inc.
5. Murdock, Maureen. 1990. *The Heroine's Journey – Woman's Quest for Wholeness*. Boston: Shambhala Publications, Inc.

www.ingramcontent.com/pod-product-compliance
Lightning Source LLC
Chambersburg PA
CBHW031400290426
44110CB00011B/221